W9-CCX-938

On Nature's Terms

NUMBER THIRTEEN

The Louise Lindsey Merrick Natural Environment Series

On Nature's Terms

CONTEMPORARY VOICES

Edited by

THOMAS J. LYON *and* PETER STINE

Texas A&M University Press

COLLEGE STATION

First edition

Thirteen of the pieces in this book were originally published as a collection in a special issue, "New Nature Writing," of the journal *Witness,* vol. 3, no. 4 (Winter, 1989), edited by Peter Stine, with Thomas J. Lyon as guest editor of that issue. Use of the material from that issue is with the permission of Witness Publishers, Inc.

"Dust-blown Dreams and the Canadian River Gorge," from *Caprock Canyonlands,* by Dan Flores, © 1990 by the University of Texas Press, is reprinted by permission of the publisher. "A Year As It Turns," by Edward Hoagland, is reprinted by permission of the author. "Apologia," © 1990 by Barry Lopez, is reprinted by permission of the author. "Cryptic Cacti on the Borderline," by Gary Nabhan, originally published in *Orion* (Autumn, 1991), is reprinted by permission of the author and the publisher. "Animals as Brothers and Sisters," excerpted from *Living by Water,* © 1990 by Brenda Peterson, published by Alaska Northwest Books, is reprinted by permission of the publisher. "The Woman Who Married a Bear," excerpted from *The Practice of the Wild,* © by Gary Snyder, published by North Point Press, is reprinted by permission of the publisher. "Sing Me down the Mountain," by Stephen Trimble, from the forthcoming *Children, Wildness, and Landscape,* edited by Gary Nabhan and Stephen Trimble, © by Beacon Press, is reprinted by permission of the publisher.

The paper used in this book meets the minimum requirements of the American National Standard for Permanence of Paper for Printed Library Materials, Z39.48-1984. Binding materials have been chosen for durability.

Library of Congress Cataloging-in-Publication Data

On nature's terms : contemporary voices / edited by Thomas J. Lyon and Peter Stine. – 1st ed.
p. cm. – (The Louise Lindsey Merrick natural environment series ; no. 13)
ISBN 0-89096-511-0. – ISBN 0-89096-522-6 (pbk.)
1. Nature–Literary collections. 2. American literature–20th century. I. Lyon, Thomas J. (Thomas Jefferson), 1937– . II. Stine, Peter. III. Series
PS509.N305 1992
810.8′036–dc20 92-5239
CIP

Contents

On Nature's Terms

Introduction: Out from under the Dome

THOMAS J. LYON

Four darkly titled books of the last decade seem to characterize our time, and our state of health, with ominous precision: *The Death of Nature*, by Carolyn Merchant; *The Death of the Soul*, by William Barrett; *Extinction*, by Paul and Anne Ehrlich; and *The End of Nature*, by Bill McKibben. The sense of terminus, which appears to be widespread, is perhaps strengthened by our approach to the year 2000, a date that (as McKibben points out) has assumed a certain mythic potency; but there are obviously deeper things going on. For one, many people seem to have realized, almost in a rush of recent agreement, that the Western, power-over-nature philosophy described by Merchant and Barrett has reached the end of its usefulness. We go on living daily life by this philosophy, to be sure, but with growing uneasiness. Numbers of us seem to be discovering, now, an awful, solipsistic emptiness at the heart of our traditional style. Furthermore, actual elements of the world—for example, hundreds and thousands of species of plants and animals, very basic proportions of gases in the global atmosphere, and (most quietly of all) topsoil—are being eliminated wholesale, altered in probably irreversible ways, or simply poisoned and lost, and all of this is going on at rates completely unprecedented. It is becoming clearer that business-as-usual strategies of mitigation won't be big enough and don't go deep enough. What is happening is happening on too many fronts to be solved in the managerial way; to admit this, finally, is to realize that we face a genuine crisis in human history. I think it is not an overstatement, under the conditions, to hold that our most basic attitudes toward the world—our whole sense of "man and nature," as the phrase has it—need to be revolutionized.

Nature writing (to come down to the book in hand) reminds us of our essential, animal nature, the simple capacity of being here and experiencing. This reminding is revolutionary, because it opens up the wild again. It gives credit to basic aliveness and the natural givens–the lines of the hills against the sky, the towering up of summer cumulus, the interesting look of other animals. Traditional management strategy, by the evidence, ends up with another kind of list: plantation forests that produce warped, weak boards, monoculture farming that kills the soil, and bears with ear tags and radio collars. Stewardship doesn't work if there is nothing at the core of it, no outgoing, wild connection to the wild planet. Planning ahead, keeping every kind of record, mitigating our latest construction project's environmental effects, we just get farther away from the source. Most of us are so distractedly active, so thickly insulated with ourselves and our works, that we have to be hit over the head with a week in a *wilderness area* to come somewhat naturally alive again and know what world we're in.

However, we do then (perhaps amazingly, under the circumstances) seem to remember. "You walk a stranger in a vegetating world," Mary Austin wrote in 1924, "then with an inward click the shutter of some profounder level of consciousness uncloses. . . ." At this level the nature essay originates. Nature writing affirms humanity as essentially unneedy.

The significance of this reclamation may not be immediately apparent, but what it amounts to is a clearing-away of the entire mistaken strategy of progress. Our ruling myth has been growth: from humble beginnings, from rude life in caves, perhaps, or before that as members of chattering, savanna-roaming bands, we have ascended (one of our favorite terms, as in *The Ascent of Man*) to agriculture and settled, village life, to specialization of function for individuals, thus to leisure and opportunity for scientific discovery, to clever exploitations of the laws of nature through ever more ingenious technologies, to urban-industrial living, with its extraordinary powers –even flight–and its luxuriant goods and services, its confidence of further improvements ahead, world without end. This is the frontier mind, and we all have it. The last five hundred years of European success–call it success, for a moment–have ingrained it in us. We have gone out all over the world, and by one means or another converted it to our time sense and our myth.

The desperate quality of this style, and its rather pathetic neediness and self-assertion, don't come clear to us as long as we're under the dome, cottoned in the folklore of comfort and control. Under the protective cover, our reference is only other people, and they're all under that same roof, too. "We meet at meals three times a day," Thoreau wrote with some sadness, apparently, "and give each other a new taste of that old musty cheese that we are."

Our stories, under these conditions, have a certain limit. Our literary fictions, insofar as they occur indoors, so to speak, may only distract us from seeing that amongst all our little plots, our ups and downs, we lack something much more primary and elemental: the earth. We crave to come out from under the dome and have vivid seeing and experience. Nature writing, then, is a form of story confirming that we are still alive, still capable, and that fulfillment, after all our flailing around, might be in something as radically simple as a blue-sky day.

But the genre is far from formulaic, as the following assortment of essays suggests. A nature essay can be about anything–or the loss of anything–in what e. e. cummings called the "world of born," including of course human nature. The urge toward connectedness that drives this writing, though–a quality of attention paid, a simple delight in seeing what is naturally here–is whole-making. This attitude is an identifying imprint, a wild signature or watermark in the text, a warrant of human origins.

A Faire Bay

JOHN HAY

"A Faire Bay" was written for "Music of the Spheres," a group under the direction of flutist Katherine Hay and Frances Thompson McKay. It was read to music composed by Frances McKay entitled "Rites of Passage" and played at Saint Mark's Episcopal Church in Washington, D.C., in the fall of 1987.

It is, said Captain John Smith, ". . . a faire Bay compassed but for the mouth with fruitful and delightsome land. Within is a country that may have the prerogative over the most pleasant places of Europe, Asia, Africa or America, for large and pleasant navigable rivers. Heaven and earth never agreed better to frame a place for man's habitation."

Out of the waters of the Chesapeake came a wilderness store of food –oysters, crabs, and clams, unending schools of fish; and in the glistening marshes where waterfowl fed on smartweed, wild celery and widgeongrass, sea lettuce and eel grass, were river otter, muskrat, beaver, and mink. Gentle, shallow waters along a shoreline of four thousand miles seemed to invite the world in to share its riches. And the Susquehanna and its great estuary flowed with a primal energy founded in the vast, still unknown continent behind them.

It was a tidal world in motion, never the same, as we ourselves have been in motion ever since we found it, taking all we could to satisfy our needs. But can we take so much that we become strangers to the Bay? Will the fishing ruin the fishermen, and the harvest of the rivers die?

Can we subdue and conquer these great waters beyond their capacity to receive us?

Where the Chesapeake lies under the mists of dawn, or opened out to sunlight-shattered waters, its surface falls and rises, inhaling, exhaling, like the lungs of the living world.

The Bay is a state of being, a great heart pulsing with the tides, exchanging sea and river water in its veins.

Twice a day the sea mounds in and rolls its free length up the Bay. Twice a day great water masses mix and change, as river waters run toward the sea.

In this body is the earth's desire. The fishes and the plankton suspended in its depth respond to beauties of transformation, everlasting change. Storms pass over them and they abide.

Now the thunder rolls, and pounds the great tympanum of the
Bay. Low and heavy it rolls and rumbles. Lightning swells
and flashes over the long, low shores,
and flying sheets of rain fall in out of violent darkness
with a wind whose spirit strips the trees.

So the Chesapeake has felt the hurricanes
across its giant back, in their wild screaming–
boats scattered and sunk, trees uprooted,
islands washed away . . .
in that fury the outer seas unleash,
born of the world ocean and its invincible demands,
moving in with judgments past undoing.

The mighty Susquehanna, empowered by a hurricane,
rising on the flood,
once drove the sea back

farther than living memory;
but the sea returns for its unending
conflict and collusion with the river.

The storm is over. The clouds clear off
toward that everlasting blue
which is the testament of vision,
the breeding ground of hopes and dreams;
and everything on earth prays to the sun.

"Life is a pure flame, and we live by the invisible sun within us."
—Sir Thomas Browne

Every cove, inlet and marsh, each creek and river has its own distinction, known to every life that seeks it out. Here is the wildness we rejected, the food we still demand, the oysters and the clams, the crabs and fish that were also the food of the people who lived with this land, in intimate dependency, thousands of years before we came, and gave their now legendary names to the rivers of the Chesapeake: Wicomico, Rappahanock, Choptank, Potomac, Poconoke.

"We always had plenty; our children never cried from hunger, neither were our people in want. . . . The rapids of the River furnished us with an abundance of excellent fish, and the land being very fertile, never failed to produce good crops of corn, beans, pumpkins, and squashes. . . . Here our village stood for more than a hundred years, during all of which time we were the undisputed possessors of this region. . . . Our village was healthy and there was no place in the country possessing such advantages, nor hunting grounds better than those we had in possession. If a prophet had come to our village in those days and told us that the things were to take place which have since come to pass, none of our people would have believed him."*

River water streaming and coiling in its abundance, backtracking,
pausing, running to the sea—
Out on the great Bay the passion of rip tides pulling at the
boats, rifting human balance and releasing it—
This energy and fury, and innate calm, the bold dignity of

*Ma-ka-tai-me-she-kia-kiak, or Black Hawk, Chief of the Sauk and the Fox. From *Touch the Earth*, compiled by T. C. McLuhan.

waters running their own free way, while the life within them
holds under the distant magnets of earth and sky.
Do we not belong here? Can we return?

White fog settles in over the shining grasses,
and tired boats, tethered to pilings,
lie on their own shadows.
Tidewaters gulp, and unseen fishes splash.
There is a whisper in the wind
over a deeper silence, where we might remember
being born.

Oh Chesapeake, how can we forget your marshes with their tidal swirling in our ears, and their inclusion of the multitudinous facets of light? These are sacred channels, keeping the tidal rise and fall of birth and death in an eternal balance.

When showers pass and clouds blow by, the "Johnny Crane," holding its yellow spear in readiness, reflects sky blue upon its wings.

While in a warm hour the frogs are croaking with the voice of water, a slim egret, with pure white wings and body like a shell, lifts from tall grasses with a snoring cry.

In September, the young menhaden flip and turn their silver bodies in the shallow river winding through the marsh. How beautiful the fishes, every tribe with its precious distinction, white perch, yellow perch, shad, and alewives, the slim young catfish and the striped bass. They have tracings on their skin of water's varying light, delicate and unequaled markings. Fishes lift the human spirit out of isolation.

To fill and lay waste the marshlands, to deliver them unto degradation, is to lose our own protection. They shelter origins, and the earth requires them.

Out beyond the channeled grasses, across the spreading waters, the winds are chasing an immortal distance.

The colonists came in from everywhere, around the compass, around the clock, settling into these generous shores; and they shot the deer, treed coons, stewed squirrels or snapping turtles for dinner, trapped beaver and muskrat, fished the rivers and raised corn and tobacco. They warred with nature and enjoyed its fruits. Canoes, punts and piraguas, bateaux and barges, flats, pinnaces and shallops plied the rivers. Out over the Bay, skipjack, ketch and yawl, sloop and schooner, grew in number so as to rival whitecaps on the waves. They raced their thoroughbreds and quarterhorses; they hated and they loved; they argued, quarreled and sometimes moved away. The watermen dredged for oysters, tonged for clams, and the soft-shell crab was a regional triumph. Home-cured ham, pork and pone, turnips and salad greens, hog jowls and black-eyed peas grew from this abundant land. And in the evening, when the golden sunlight of autumn flushed salt meadows and a hundred thousand wings wheeled in the air and began to settle in, their appetites were whetted by the splendor of the geese.

America was settled by a world from overseas that cut down what it found, and then moved on. Fire and ax destroyed the primal trees. Tobacco robbed the soil of its fertility, and the exhausted fields were abandoned to the wind and rain.

Erosion sent the topsoil down the Susquehanna, the Rappahanock, the Potomac and the James. For every mile, each year, hundreds of tons of sediment went into the Bay, and the Chesapeake began to age before its time.

Far out, the sanderlings skim across the headlands and the beaches, and wheel above the crisscrossed, tumbling green waters, as the spokes of the sun's wheel strike through running clouds.

A yellowlegs, turning on itself, yanking through the shallows, whips out its piercing whistle, and the gulls with their shivering, silvery screams and laughter, cry out for water's magical locations.

Backed by the continent, fed by its rivers, entered by the majesty of the sea, the Bay still speaks a language of capacity, of endless patience, but it will never endure a race that only knows how to spend earth's substance on a world of waste and greed.

Water is birth and mystery,
water in our hearts and minds,
the engines of love and deliberation.
Water is our guide,
however far we turn away.

America meant "improvement." Rivers were channeled, dammed, bridged over, made useful for navigation. We did not want them to stand in our way, with their own rules. We did not like them to run free, leaving us at the mercy of their floods and periods of low water, refusing us passage. We improved them, and left them behind. We loaded their timeless journeys with the deadly passage of our wastes.

"The rivers of Virginia are the God-given sewers of the State."
Thus spoke the nineteenth century.
Long live convenience.
God save Virginia.

The germinative rivers, the bringers of life, began to carry more black oil and poisons to the Bay. The silver alewives and the shad, mounting the rivers in their spawning fire, were blocked by dams and started to disappear. The famous sturgeon was nowhere to be found. Marsh plants began to die; underwater vegetation died; numberless oysters never reached maturity. What has happened to the rockfish, the great striped bass that spawns in the prolific waters of the Chesapeake, the pride of all the states that border on the sea? Why is its progeny being cheated of existence?

The eye of the Chesapeake is clouded over. While the rivers send their foul discharge into its heart and lungs, our own senses fail. Water is light and vision. Without its clarity we soon go blind.

What lies under these pulsing, ribbony waves? Billions of gallons of industrial waste, a desolation of herbicides and pesticides, sulphates and nitrates, chlorine, gas, and oil. What lies there but a wasting of the heart?

Only man can destroy the Bay; only man can destroy himself.

We are the victims of our own ignorance and love of power. We do not know the limits of these waters, until we pass them; and we never gave ourselves the time.

Native Americans declared: "A frog does not drink up the pond in which it lives."

That suggests a frog's intelligence may be on a higher level than our own.

But there is time, within the earth, for recognition.

Still and always, the seabird lifts to the impenetrable
light that dances on the tides—
And the eyes of schooling fishes stare ahead into the
waterways of the future.

These are true inheritors, children of amplitude, as it was in the beginning. They live at home with mystery, the great design of life, in which all species are kindred. We cannot live outside them and survive.

Until we learn to recognize these waters in ourselves, they will age, sicken, and die. Violence will be returned for violence, dying for dying. The rivers will turn against us; the Chesapeake will have its vengeance; the continent will call us aliens, strangers to its spirit. When the great network of living veins and arteries begins to shrivel and dry, the spirit of the people dies. The seas within us die.

America is not the product of industry but of shared existence.

To give up on the Chesapeake is to give up on ourselves. Listen to it. Watch its cosmic, universal eye. Rediscover sanity. Return. Come home again. Come home.

Love among the Lion Killers

CHARLES BOWDEN

> The Wilderness *through which we are passing to the Promised Land is all filled with fiery flying serpents. But, blessed be God, none of them have hitherto so fastened upon us as to confound us utterly! All our way to Heaven lies by* Dens of Lions *and* Mounts of Leopards! *There are incredible Droves of Devils. . . .*
>
> —Cotton Mather
> *Wonders of the Invisible World,* 1693

> *I have never heard a mountain lion bawling over the fate of his soul.*
>
> —Edward Abbey, 1987

When Harley Shaw went to college, he wrote a paper in his freshman English class on Ben Lilly, a legendary hunter who died in 1936. Lilly started in Alabama and worked his way west slaughtering bears, coyotes, wolves, and lions. Once he guided for Theodore Roosevelt. He married twice, but these ventures did not work out. His first wife went insane, and his second wife, he abandoned. He was a solitary man, a religious man, who followed his hounds on foot six days a week subsisting on a little parched corn. At sundown on Saturday, he tied his dogs–Ben Lilly would not hunt on the Sabbath. If a dog failed to perform up to his standards, he beat it to death. He ended up in Arizona's Blue River country exterminating the last holdouts among the grizzlies and wolves. His name still conjures up tales in that region. For hunters, Ben Lilly is truly a legend–Texas folklorist J. Frank Dobie once wrote a book stating just that in the title, *The Ben Lilly Legend*. Shaw as a boy was fascinated by wildlife, and so Lilly, the premier killer, was a link to the natural world for a boy growing up in the valley east of Phoenix.

Now Shaw is older, and he is Arizona's expert on mountain lions. He remembers his fascination with Lilly, and a soft grin graces his face. Harley Shaw has spent eighteen years following the lions on foot, on horseback, behind dogs, from airplanes.

He has never killed one.

Like us, lions kill. In the Southwest, their house occupies about 150 square miles on the average, and they move patiently through its many rooms. They are 5.5 to 7.5 feet long, and their weight ranges from 75 to 190 pounds. We seldom see them, perhaps if lucky, once in a lifetime. But they always see us. They like to watch; they will follow us at that slow walk for hours. They almost never attack–in Arizona perhaps once a decade according to our records. They seem not to regard us as a suitable source of food. But the kill is the thing, and what they like is something around 100 pounds and alive. Studies in Arizona find about one out of every five kills is a calf. They eat what they kill, not what others have killed. We have studied this matter, and we have numbers to comfort us. Every 10.5 days, an adult will kill. Or if a mother, every 6.8 days. In certain regions, at certain times, under certain conditions. Because we really know very little about them, very, very little. Our major contact with them has always been on bloody ground, the kill.

I am standing in a patch of chaparral on the edge of Salt River north of Globe, and the rancher is angry in that slow, hard way that ranchers vent their emotions. The voice is flat, almost monotone, the face placid, more a mask than anything else. In one month he has lost thirty-four calves to them, with calves worth hundreds of dollars apiece. But it is more than the money. It is the kill, the neck punctured by those large teeth, the small animal ripped open like an envelope. It is logical to argue that he was going to merely raise the calves to a certain weight and then ship them off to eventual slaughter, and that would be true. But that does not abate a rancher's anger. The calves were under his care, *his care,* and he has been violated by a force he never sees but whose presence he constantly suspects. He calls in the expert hunters and has seven of them taken off his land. That was months ago, but still he is not at peace. The fury of finding those dead calves in the morning light will not leave his eyes. He reaches the conclusion that many others have who stumble into their country: they like the killing. And perhaps they do. We will never find out. We do not know how to ask.

It is just before Christmas in 1988, and the Third Mountain Lion Workshop clogs the lobby of Prescott's Hassayampa Inn with 150 biologists, guides, animal control folk (trackers, trappers, poisoners, and hunters), plus a handful of conservationists, all tossing down drinks during the get-acquainted cocktail hour. A rumor floats through the room, one brought here by a government hunter from California. A woman about fifty-one has been found. The skull said to be punctured by a large tooth mark. The other whispered signs offer unmistakable evidence of a kill. The autopsy, well that's the kicker, the autopsy, according to the rumor, suggests that the woman was alive while being eaten. The kill. I have come here with my simple question: What is it like to kill with your mouth? The biologists turn away when I ask. There are things about the wilds we are not supposed to say.

And this brings us down to perhaps the fundamental fault line between us and lions. Our basic contact with mountain lions is the kill, and yet what little we know suggests this is not the major portion of a mountain lion's life. Harley Shaw has studied lions in Arizona for eighteen years, and he is the host of the big workshop in Prescott. He is fifty-one now, the hair and trimmed beard silver, a bearlike man who is not tall, the eyes and voice very alert and deliberate. At times, he can be a bundle of statistics and graphs and scat samples and radio collared plottings of lions. But now he is sitting down and just talking.

"Lions," he says, "more than other animals have time for contemplation. They lay up, seek high places and vistas. So you wonder what goes through their minds."

You certainly do.

As soon as we knew they were around, we tried to kill them. When the Jesuit priests hit Baja at the end of the seventeenth century, they ran into a culture—one now vanished, which we recall as the Pericue—that refused to slay lions. Imagine it is three hundred years ago, and Father Ugarte, a large man and a strong man, wants the lion dead. The cat comes in the night, slaughters the mission stock at his outpost in southern Baja, then vanishes. The Indians will not kill the beast–if they do, they say they too will die. The priest is riding his mule on a narrow path, he sees a lion, throws the stone, the animal dies. He places the warm body across his mule, rides back to the mission, and shows off his trophy. The Indians watch, the priest does not die. See, he says, now you are free, now you can kill the lions.

We have not stopped since that moment. As a people, we've had a hard time abiding lions because they want what we want–meat, especially venison, lamb, and beef. Between 1918 and 1947, twenty-four hundred lions were killed in Arizona. Mainly, they were taken out for stock killing. Legendary men emerged like Uncle Jim Owens of the Grand Canyon country, who is said to have bagged eleven hundred cats in his lifetime. A man named Jack Butler is reported around 1929 to have killed fifty-eight in eighteen months in the Sowats and Kanab Wash area around the Canyon. Government animal control people tried poison, traps, dogs, bullets–everything in their arsenal. In 1947, the state legislature took a look at the situation and decided to offer a bounty, one that floated betweeen fifty and a hundred dollars for the next twenty-two years. They were moved to adding this incentive because decades of lion killing had not seemed to dent the lion population. When the bounty finally became dormant in 1969 (it is still technically on the books ready to come to life if desired), another fifty-four hundred lions had been knocked down.

All over the West (with the exception of Texas) attitudes about lions began to change in the sixties, and first one state and then another shifted them from varmints to game animals, started issuing hunting tags and generally trying to manage them just like deer, bighorn sheep, elk, and antelope. Arizona made this shift in 1970 when it allowed one lion per hunter per year, stopped funding the bounty system, and gave control of the beast to the Game and Fish Department. Stock-killing lions could still be taken out by ranchers if they contacted the government.

What is the net result? No one's really sure. There are somewhere between two thousand and three thousand lions in Arizona–nobody has any good way to count them. The hunt has now been limited to six months a year, and Game and Fish is busily studying their new charges. Each twelve months between two hundred and four hundred of the cats are killed (the state figures run around two hundred, some critics figuring in estimates of unreported rancher kills tend toward the high end). And after a century or more of slaughter they still are out there. In the American West there is no place where lions are endangered. They have survived without our help, they have survived in the face of our hatred, and now we may learn if they can survive our desire to manage and understand them.

Almost no one has ever seen a lion kill. There are millions of people living in the desert, they are crawling up every canyon, the families are picnicking under the willows by every mountain stream, the bulldozers claw at every roll of the bujadas, the satellites spin by day and night with giant glass eyes watching everything that moves. But still almost no one has ever seen a lion kill.

But we can guess some things from the kills we find. Harley Shaw has seen many kills, made his notes, puzzled out the action that is now dry blood, broken bones, empty eyes with flies buzzing in the air. He has written a book and then rewritten the book and then rewritten the rewritten book. He has drifted into an obsession. The thing floats around as a manuscript, the publishers look, consider, hesitate. It is not a normal book by a normal biologist. The facts are all there, the slender scraps of fact we have sifted from the world of the lion. But there is a feeling gnawing at Harley as he studies his field notes and tries to understand how the cats eat. He has gotten too close, and he knows it. "I have begun," he writes, "to dislike the ways humans view themselves." He has begun to see the world through a lion's eyes–he cannot see that world, he has learned too much, sensed too much to ever think he can see that world, but he has a feel for its presence, and that has changed how the things now look through his eyes. Now he is there, he is so close, it is all in his notes, in his mind, in his senses as he thinks about lions, and it is not nearly enough, barely a beginning. He has about studied himself out of a profession: biologist. As he notes dryly of his work, "You will be forced to reexamine your beliefs."

They are out there right now, looking down at us from the sierras, cruising silently across the desert floor, lying up on a cliff and watching, waiting for the glimpse of the right thing. They cannot run, cannot really run at all, and everything must be a brief sprint. The lion drops down, creeps, slides, it must get within fifty feet or less if it is to succeed. The lion is alone, in this act almost always alone, a single force that must always do its work alone. This colors the act. The object of desire should be around a hundred pounds or less. The lion weighs seventy, eighty, ninety, perhaps a hundred pounds–sometimes more, but not usually. The animal is not as large as the feeling the name *lion* conjures up in our minds and hearts. The lion does not seek a fight, a combat. This would be a dangerous choice. The broken rib, the torn muscle and that half step is lost, the microsecond of speed and grace vanishes, and then the hunger comes and weakness follows that and the thing spirals into death. So the fight must be avoided.

The object is close now, a deer, browsing, alert, but as yet unaware. The skin of the deer is a fur almost gray in this light. It drifts among the chaparral, a ghost that is alive. The sun is up and warm on the gray fur but still it eats, feeling safe in the cover of the brush. It begins to happen, the lion is close, belly to the ground, and now it surges, slithers forward and nears. The cat rises up on its hind feet and those big front paws with sharp claws sink into the deer's back and the animal goes to the ground instantly. The mouth opens–feel the warm breath?–and the jaws settle around the back of the neck and the teeth penetrate the muscles near the base of the skull.

There are nerve endings at the base of the big teeth, very sensitive endings, and as the fangs plunge and tear through the warm flesh these endings pick up that gap between the vertebrae, and the teeth slide in, the lion swings its jaws, the neck snaps. Death washes across the deer's face. Harley has seen many kills, and if the lion is an adult, an experienced killer, it is over very fast it seems–the sites show little if any signs of struggle. With younger cats–and it takes a lioness almost two years to train up her kittens to a good and proper kill–it may be messier. Attacks on humans usually involve cats under two years, those who have not mastered the feel of the kill and the risks of the kill. Sometimes when a doe is killed, the fawn lingers around and is killed later. There is speculation that such objects provide training for kittens.

What happens next the biologists can only guess, but this is the guess: the lion leaves the kill, goes off a short ways, and lies down for perhaps an hour. The stalk, the leap, the teeth probing for that gap between the vertebrae, the rush of hot blood against the tongue, all these things have stimulated the lion, and it is not a proper time to eat until calm returns to the well-muscled body.

Now it is ready and rises and walks slowly back to the deer. The lion drags it across the ground to some place that suggests safety, perhaps under a tree or a rock. It is time to feed. First, the cat clears the hair from the deer where it will be entered–typically just behind the ribs, Harley notes. The procedure here is thorough, much the way humans prep for surgery. The claws flash, the deer is opened up. First the heart, liver, and lungs are devoured, then, it seems, the back legs, with the meat on the interior of the legs taken first. The stomach and intestines are pulled out and ignored. Eight to ten pounds of flesh may be swallowed at this first feeding.

Then the animal is covered. The cat will toss up grass, brush, soil, rocks, something, to cover the kill. Why?—we can only speculate. To hide it from other animals? To keep the meat cool to delay spoiling? Harley once found a mule deer kill on solid rock. The cat had placed a single twig on the animal.

The lion retreats, perhaps a couple of hundred yards, and beds down. It will lay up where it can see and come back often to check the kill. What does it do while lying up there, the desert vista before it, or the oaks of the canyon a carpet unrolling in front of it? This is not a small matter. The kills come every three to ten days in the desert. It depends, in part, on how long the meat lasts before going bad. Or so we suspect. We really have no clear ideas why lions abandon kills. There are just little glimpses. One cat in Idaho stayed and fed off an elk kill for nineteen days. What goes through the brain for nineteen days as the meat is engorged and then come the quiet hours sprawled up high, the eyes staring out at the big empty?

Normally, the lions will not eat carrion. If they do not kill it, they do not eat it. This has made them hard to poison. The wolves, they are gone from the desert. The grizzlies are gone. The lion is not.

Of course, kills vary. If the animal is large, the lion cannot reach up and sink those claws in deeply. Then the teeth go to the throat—Harley has a photograph in color, everything very red and bloody, of an elk's windpipe with a big puncture in it, the hole a memory of the cat's tooth. Then the lion kills by suffocation. But this is to be avoided. Those who follow the cats, whether to study them or kill them, agree on one thing: a lion is not likely to leap from a ledge or drop down out of a tree onto the back of a large animal. Such a ride is dangerous, and for lions danger is not the drug it seems to be for human beings. They will kill anything: steers, horses, sheep, elk, desert sheep, deer, javelina, people. They must eat. But all things being equal, the object of desire will not be too large, it will not struggle, the claws will grip the shoulders, the mouth will open, the teeth—those wonderful teeth with sensitive nerves at the base—will probe and find that gap between the vertebrae, and the neck will snap. Death descends like a summer shower, the lion walks off and rests. Then an area will be cleaned of hair for the incision. . . .

The lobby is fine soft couches, lamps casting warm yellow light, good wood in the tables, a fireplace that swallows large logs. On the ceiling beams, delicate floral abstractions open and spin across the painted surface. The floor is tile and cool to the eye. A woman plays the grand piano and sings the songs that you hum in elevators but can never name. One hundred and fifty lion people mill about this lobby. They drink, form small knots of conversation, eye each other's name tags. They have come from all over the United States and Canada, wherever the lion still hunts. Harley Shaw is the host. He wears a dark sportcoat, the patches leather, and looks like a professor of Elizabethan poetry with his silver hair, trimmed silver beard. This is the world of the per diem people, those who work in state agencies, federal agencies, who plunder government for grants so that they can continue their research in universities. These are the lions' modern official keepers. Everyone standing here with a glass of wine or bottle of beer in hand cashes checks signed in blood by the big carnivore that courses the mountains and flats leaving carcasses in its wake. This is not part of the rumble of conversations.

The lobby is filled with people who know the killing, men dressed in tight Levi's, wearing cowboy boots, the faces weathered, the hair trimmed, that careful moustache, the deliberate hat with the brim exactly bent. These men speak little if at all; they are ranch people, sometimes descended from lion-killing families, and now as the West shrinks and business takes the land for esoteric tax purposes, they hang on as federal and state killers of the wild things that make up the West that has always held them in its thrall.

They traffic in stories, anecdotes, glimpses of the trail and the hunt. Harley moves easily with them: they know what he wants to know. Science here searches folklore like a hungry scavenger seeking a clue that will destroy the mysteries. There was this cat in the Big Bend area of Texas that took to attacking people in the park, so it was captured and shipped to Florida where a big state project seeks to salvage the last few panthers huddled in the Everglades under the glow of the hot, cocaine night skies. Now the problem lion lives in a cage in a research center. Most captive lions are very shy and try to crawl under things when they see people. This one stares the biologists straight in the eye, gets up and presses against the wire. So they do an X ray, find a dark mass in the brain, and speculate it may be a tumor or a viral blob. They consider killing the lion, cutting open its head and looking at the brain. There has to be some reason why it does not cower in our presence.

There are many things to be explained. Recently, a lion was killed on the road near Fresno, California, and others are seen often on the local golf course even though it is fifteen miles across the big agribusiness fields to the sierra.

Death, that is the only place in which we can get near. Why do we want to get near? Why do we crave to get so very, very near? That is not a question to be asked, it is forbidden. We have our excuses. I will tell them to you. There is this thing called depredation–that means the lion eats things we want to eat, kills things we wish to kill. The calf stares blankly up at the hot sky, neck broken, underbelly ripped open, body gnawed, bones crushed like small sticks. The sheep scattered willy-nilly, twenty, thirty sheep dead, so dead, and only one or two even eaten. The rest, just killed, wantonly we say, killed for sport we say. Killed for reasons we cannot comprehend. And if we do not act, act right now, the lion will be back at nightfall and kill again and again and again. Depredation, we say.

Besides depredation, we say science. We want to answer the mysteries of life, curious questions of gestation, digestion, population densities, nurture, movement, prey selection, social organization. Diet. We want to put radio collars on them, we want to dart them with drugs and take their vital signs, spend many hours sorting out the remains in their scat. Weigh them, measure them, consider blood type, disease vectors. Learn how to age them by putting calipers to their teeth. Science, an excellent screen for our desires.

Besides science, there is envy. That is the one we will not speak. Not at all, seldom if ever. Envy. We go where they are. We take a truckload of dogs, pull the horses in a trailer behind us. The hounds are released, we saddle up and ride. We carry guns. We carry our food, cover our body with fabrics in order to endure the weather. Sometimes we have radios so that the hunters can communicate constantly. It has taken us years to train the dogs, hundreds and hundreds of hours on the trail. And if we are lucky, we may tree a lion. The cats, they are out there alone, they carry their culture inside their bodies, they move anywhere, set up a universe wherever they decide to lie up. When hungry, they kill and dine day after day after day. They breed–meeting by some miracle of scent like two lonely ships in an endless sea–train up their young, push on.

That envy. And from that envy comes our love. It is not a normal love, or perhaps it is, but at any rate it is not the love we normally admit to. It is not a desire to share or nurture or protect. It is much stronger than that, more powerful in its effects. It is a desire to join them.

So of course, we must kill them, kill every damn one of them.

They see a thin line between us and the natural world. And they guard this line with guns, poison, and words. We are standing, beers in hand, and the talk flows with missionary ease. Darrel C. Juve works for the

Department of Agriculture in Arizona, but he does not farm. He kills. The term is Animal Damage Control, and what he does is patrol that thin line between us and them.

He's in his late forties now and his world is plain. "A lion," he says briskly, "is nothing but a big house cat. Curious."

It's not just the lions, no, no, there are coyotes out there, bears, and if you look up, my God, the birds. Juve speaks without a smile, his eyes scanning people to see if they understand, if they can handle his message. Ravens? They kill. They kill calves, they kill steers. Drop down from the sky and peck their eyes out, blind them, and then comes the hard death with this black bird's pecking, pecking, pecking.

We've made some progress. Take the wolf, he's gone. "There's a good reason," he almost snaps, "why they were wiped out in the West." And then he pauses to make sure his next words truly sink in: "They destroyed millions of dollars of livestock." His face has that tension in it, the tension flooding a man who knows, who really knows, and yet has learned that others will shun his knowing.

He's got eleven people under him, the calls come in each day, there is no way to keep up, no way at all. The lion complaints alone would bury his force if he dealt with all of them. People, he continues, have lost touch with reality. Only 4 percent of the population produces the food for the other 96 percent, and now you see people going into supermarkets and tossing a nice plastic-wrapped chunk of meat in their baskets, and they have no idea where or how that piece of flesh got there.

"People don't understand," he says with cold anger, "that for them to eat, something has to die. We try to attach sentimentality to animals without ever thinking about what is really going on out there. Humane is not a word spoken by Mother Nature. The mass media depicts wild animals in unrealistic terms."

He is struggling now, trying to rein in his feelings, to make the words seem like a reasonable position, one arrived at after much research, the product of cool detachment by a scholar sitting in his study before the fire and musing over a glass of fine sherry. But he cannot maintain the tone.

"They," he flames up again, "they think there is a balance of nature—that's bullshit. There is no balance out there."

Out there. The heart of darkness. The ground where we are not in control. Wait, twist the lens, see it zoom into focus? Yes, that ground, the world seen through a lion's eyes, the warm blood-soaked breath flowing out the cat's open mouth. We deny it, we abolish it with fine shots in calendars, with musings about the intricate relationships between all living things. We avert our eyes so that we can always see Eden. Juve, ah, he insists on the teeth at the throat, at those long beaks tearing at the eye of a terrified calf. He wears glasses, Levi's, an oval belt buckle inlaid with a coyote (made by a convict, he explains), the brown hair is trimmed. The face seldom smiles, the voice is almost always urgent, the words clipped. He is the man with the mission. He has been out there. An image rises up from the snap of his sentences: Nature is this teeming unruly bitch at the gates of our lives, ready at an instant to violate our humanity. She waits out there by the picket fence so white against the green lawn. You stroll out, open the gate, and suddenly she walks out of the desert, dressed smartly, the lips full and inviting, the eyes dangerous with desires. Her hair is black, the teeth very even, the cheekbones strong, the voice, well, you can hear no voice, you merely sense a kind of purring coming off her body. She moves toward you, seems almost to glide, you turn, smile, tip your head silently forward as to say hello. Her dress rustles, a soft silky kind of sound, the hair is long and stirs with the breeze. She is at your throat, the teeth tear, and warm blood cascades down your body. Out there.

That is one mountain lion. Harley Shaw thinks the lion exists through human eyes, and the different eyes see different lions: stock killer, hunter's trophy, curious biological machine for studies by scientists, noble beast of the sierra and bajada. It all depends on who you are. For Harley, the lion exists in a very strange place: he says he cannot conceive of them except in front of hounds. Dogs have shaped his lion world, they are the door or window or what-have-you that permits him to go to the lion world.

He does not think this view has any particular merit. It just is that way for him. Out there, that black place full of sun, is very hard to reach, in the case of the lion almost impossible, and we can only stay a very short while—idle moments standing under a tree while the dogs bay, the wait for the dart to drug the cat, the quick measurements and sampling, your hands running over the warm fur, then retreat, the groggy animal staggering off and vanishing. Flies are buzzing around a kill, you measure scratch marks, you are being watched, you can sense this fact, feel it, but you cannot see. The lion?—the lion is that excited sound in the dogs' throats, the lion is that long slash on the deer's shoulder. The lion is something you make up to fill a big emply spot inside you.

She is standing before an auditorium of lion people, the hair blond, the dress blue, the face smooth and open. The room is dark and the light at the lectern splashes up on her and she seems like a spirit, a clean-smelling angelic form, reading thoughts to the soiled and the human.

Slides flash on the screen as row after row of biologists and lion hunters slump in their seats. She is from Vermont, from some institute or foundation, and the slides express her feelings about the wilds. Big color images of the desert in a real estate ad, huge close-ups of lions with their big tawny faces seeming dignified and noble and innocent. The mouth on the cats in these slides is always closed, the teeth a secret kept from the camera. Of course, there are two kittens sitting on the snow. She reads a poem by D. H. Lawrence, "Elegy to a Mountain Lion." Out there vanishes.

Can we call this love? Juve, like many men who kill animals, has ready explanations for the killing. There is a need. The coyotes, they'll take your dog. The bear, he will eat your calf. The lion, she murders everything she meets. The ravens, they are at the eyes. They must be stopped.

But there is another level in their words. The talk will drift, the drinks will take hold, the pretense of positions will become too great a weight to carry day and night, and then the talk will change. For a century we have been cleaning up the desert, setting this house in order. We have the records, incredible records where everything is columns of bounties paid, wages paid, damages reported, poisons bought and spread, traps set and accounted for, skins piled up and assessed, skulls sent to natural history collections. We have a record. The wolf? Ah, the wolf was easy to take out, he was not that smart. He could not adapt, not at all. The wolf lost, and because he lost to us, he lost our respect. You can hear this behind the words, you can. He lost our respect. The grizzly, he was easy too. Big, stupid, and now gone, and never ever coming back to the desert. We will not permit it. He does not deserve it. We took him out. The coyote, my God, the coyotes, they cannot be beaten, we kill them with guns, traps, poisons. Still they keep coming, and coming. The coyote is our enemy, we must fight him if it takes forever. And then you can hear a kind of love come into the words. The coyote is worthy of our respect. And the lion, nothing seems to touch the lion. They are out there, walking slowly in their kingdoms, and we kill them, kill hundreds of them a year in the desert, and still they keep walking slowly across their kingdoms. The men slumped in their seats in the auditorium, the Levi's skin tight, the black cowboy hats hugging their heads, brims bent low in the front and the back, the large oval belt buckles recording that good day at the rodeo, these men who kill lions worship them. You can hear it in their words, in the horror with which they describe the sheepbeds after a bloody night, the rich language that flows from their mouths when they recount the long, deep rips in a calf's small soft body. The feeling is also there when they speak of the hunt. The cat is so hard to find—if it is hot and dry, the hounds can find no scent, if they find scent the ground is so broken and difficult, the cat sees so well, senses everything, moves so silently, broods without whimpering, slaughters without being seen, lives without our knowing. Except for the blood.

You can hear a kind of love in their words. Without the cats they would not know who they are, would not have a clue. For the lion is something that exceeds their grasp; they have tried everything and still he exceeds their grasp, and from this fact, the love comes. The lion has kept the world from getting too small. The men who kill lions are ever vigilant to maintain this reality. Some men hunt lions with trucks, the dogs riding on the hoods until a track is struck, the lead dog wearing a radio collar with a beeper, and when a cat is treed and the lead dog bays, the collar lets off a special beep, and then the hunters zero in thanks to the radio. This, the men who love to kill lions, this they want outlawed, this they want stopped. They also oppose the winter hunt in the crisp snow because it makes things too easy—"murder," one snaps with contempt. There are other abominations they oppose. Will-call hunts, where a guide trees a lion, leaves his hounds and a friend under the cat, and then calls that doctor or dentist in the next state who will pay two thousand or three thousand dollars for the trophy, and the client then hops a jet and within a day is under the tree, fires once, the cat falls dead, and the hunt is successful. There are also men who trap lions, then cage them, and when a rich man wants to hunt, release this captive just ahead of the hounds. All these things the men who love to kill lions hate. They will admit this fact, they will say it in their low monotones, their lips barely moving, the sentences very short, often merely fragments of sentences.

Love, that word cannot be said. You can feel it, but no one will say it. Who will admit to loving something that will not love you back? There is that rumor floating around the room as we stand and drink, a whispered thing where the men huddle and clutch the beer bottles in their hands. In another state, the whispers go, a woman has been found. She is dead, middle-aged; there are the marks, the right marks on her body. She has been killed by a cat. The autopsy, people almost whisper, suggests that while she was yet alive, the lion fed on her. This can be determined, the murmurs continue, determined from the hemorrhaging. Alive. The rumor floats around the room, an electric current reviving the tired air. Months later, the story will become a vapor, a thing that never happened, that does not check out. But of course, that does not really matter. For there will be new rumors, new tales.

They are necessary, the menace is essential to us for reasons we can barely state. The mountains would have a new frightening emptiness if we could not imagine the soft padding of those clawed feet, the unflinching eyes scanning our every move, the muscles rippling under the tawny fur. He is out there. Out there. Love.

But no one will say that word.

Harley Shaw sips his coffee in the saloon. He is very calm, very careful. There are things he thinks about but finds difficult to say, almost dangerous to say. Much of this is in the book that he toils over and that no one seems eager to print. He seems small now as he sits and sips his coffee out of a clear glass cup. The book contains his odyssey–the break that spun him out of turkey studies into lion studies, the early years training the hounds, learning from the lion men, collaring the cats, charting their wanderings. The bad time when he caught a mother and her kittens and a lion died. The sinking–that is what it feels like when he talks or when he writes–the sinking into the idea of lions and then the country of lions and then into some place we do not have a word for. He tries to find the word. He uses that German concept, *umwelt,* the idea that any species is the product of the entire universe and encapsulates the entire universe in its being. Yes, the *umwelt.*

He has worked himself out of what was going to make him Mr. Somebody. That is the problem. The hounds are gone now. He no longer follows them in the saddle, listening for the bay, riding hard over the ridges to see a treed cat. The darts are no longer fired, the chemicals slowly dribbling into the blood, the lion's eyes getting glazed. The radio collars are still. Harley no longer clamps them around the cats' necks. Here he becomes hesitant, careful in what he says. He utters circumspect sentences like, "I am not opposed to darting lions if we're gaining some new knowledge." He cannot turn his back on knowledge, that is his business, his job. Gaining that little kernel of fact, writing that journal article–"deep down you know you're doing it to gather knowledge, and if there is any immortality it is that you are leaving something that may change things."

But this time he is the thing changed. He has run out of reasons to bother lions. He has run out of the arrogance to think he can penetrate their world. He hates the bureaucracy he works for, he has turned against his own species. He thinks lions should be left alone. To kill.

"You follow them step by step," he softly explains, "and then you relate to them."

The saloon is richly oiled walnut, the barmaids wear fine black slacks, white ruffled shirts, black ties at their delicate throats. They stand by the back bar slowly polishing fine glasses. Their skin is very white, the hair perfect, the movements silent as a cat's. The word *lion* seems as alien as the word *love* in this room. We sit in a cell designed to seal out the air, the scent, the scat, the tracts, the warm blood coursing across the tongue, the tooth seeking ever so surely the gap, the twist. The neck breaks.

How many are there? We don't know. How are they organized? We can guess. How many types, how many subspecies? We still argue. How do they decide what to kill? We speculate. How long do they live? There is no counting. What do they matter? We have no idea.

Harley backs away from the questions. "We should go camping," he says. Maybe in the dark hours, the fire crackling, our tongues loosened by liquor, the blackness protecting our faces, our minds will be freed from our roles, maybe then we can talk.

You can love something that is not beautiful, that is not useful, that is not easy. That is not safe. But you cannot know it.

Harley is talking again, even more softly. He admires things that can be solitary, he says. There have been some bad marriages, hard nights; solitary is not a thing to be despised if it can be endured. He sees the lion clearly now in his mind, the beast floods the room with its scent, the big pads move silently across the saloon floor.

"Out there," he says suddenly, "out there alone without tools without shelter without food. Down deep I have an image of myself as being totally wild. And I know I never will."

Out there.

Love waits. With long teeth.

NOTE: Harley Shaw's manuscript, *Soul Among Lions: The Cougar as Perfect Adversary,* was published by Johnson Books, Boulder, Colorado, in 1989.

Hermit

SCOTT THYBONY

After a long winter it was time to walk the forest. I jumped in the truck and headed north toward the Grand Canyon. Just south of the rim, I turned onto a road, more rock than dirt, cutting a straight line through the trees.

Shifting from first to second gear and then back again, I crossed an opening in the piñon-juniper woods and noticed a blue haze filling the road ahead. The wind carried the sharp smell of burning trees. I stopped the truck at the next rise to check the situation. Several miles away, white smoke lifted high into a pale blue sky, but the fire didn't appear to be spreading quickly. I decided to keep driving.

A road up ahead, one-truck wide, forked toward the rim. Taking the turn, I threaded a corridor of trees. Sunlight filtered through the branches, flickering dark-light, dark-light in a hypnotic rhythm as the mood of the woodland slowly settled over me. The narrow road led to a trail built by the hermit Louis Boucher, an old prospector who could see stars in the middle of the day.

When I first heard this, I tried to imagine him standing in the deep Redwall narrows of Hermit Canyon, head bent back, staring at the ribbon of sky far above. I wondered if he really saw stars. As astronomer I asked said no, adding that people also claim to see stars during the day from the bottoms of wells. An old wives' tale, he said, impossible.

One winter I drove to the McDonald Observatory in West Texas and joined astronomer Mark Bridges in one of the smaller domes. As he readied the thirty-inch telescope, I told him about the hermit who claimed to see stars at noon. "He was seeing Venus," Bridges said. "Here, I'll show you." He checked the planetary tables a moment, swung the telescope into position, and pressed his cheek against the side of the scope to guide his naked eye. "There it is," he said. I looked where he pointed and sure enough, the planet was shining like a bright star in the blue sky.

The astronomer said that a narrow canyon or a well could duplicate the effect of the slot in the observatory's roof. "It reduces the ambient light," Bridges said, "and increases the contrast. It frames a small portion of the sky making it easier to notice." What Boucher saw was not a star, but the planet Venus. It's there for anyone to see; you just have to know where to look.

Approaching the rim of the Grand Canyon along the spur road, I passed fresh elk and deer tracks heading away from the fire. On both sides of the road the forest grew wild. The woods were thick with so many dead junipers that the few piñon snags stood out black and desolate.

The road ended at Boucher's old juniper pole corral. When the Santa Fe Railway began developing Hermit Canyon for tourists, it latched onto the hermit theme. The company began building the Hermit Trail to connect a way station on the rim called Hermit's Rest with an overnight stop in Hermit Canyon called Hermit Camp located next to Hermit Creek. But before the new trail was finished, the hermit himself left the canyon never to return.

Leaving the truck, I took my pack and walked through the thinning woods. Close to the rim, the trees grew more gnarled. I passed the twisted trunk of an old juniper whose roots looked as if they had held fast while the earth continued to spin. The spiraling grain gave the tree the strength of a many-stranded rope, letting it resist the pressure of high winds. At first glance, the tree looked dead. But among the bare limbs grew a few clumps of green. Looking closer I saw a ribbon of living bark winding down the trunk into a crack in the rock. In a strange paradox, the tree continued to live by letting most of itself die.

Between the piñon and juniper grew cliff rose, broadleaf yucca, and big-leaf sagebrush–an outlier from the open flats to the south where thick tangles of sage grow taller than a man. I moved slowly along the rim toward the head of Hermit Canyon, taking time to observe the individual trees. Each recorded a slightly different history of wind and weather. After long exposure to the elements, each tree had become hauntingly personal, recognizable.

At the rim of the Grand Canyon, the world dropped away. Looking into a chasm a mile deep is like looking into an endless night sky; you become a single point–rootless, floating. Shadows climbed the walls of Hermit Canyon below. Long ago, darkness filled the inner gorge.

With just enough light left to see, I kicked a few stones from a level spot, unfolded a bivouac sack and pad, and shook out a sleeping bag. An hour after dark I fell asleep.

Deep in the night I rolled over and caught a whiff of smoke. It brought me instantly awake. The wind had picked up, moving through the tops of the trees, but there was no glow in the sky, no crackle of fire. The wind had shifted, carrying the acrid scent of burning trees. I was not sure how close the fire had moved, but there didn't seem to be any immediate danger. I lay in the dark listening as the trees caught the night wind.

Each had a different voice. The moving air hummed through a bristling piñon and streamed through the stiff branches of a juniper snag. The wind combed through the trees in a voice as old as the forest. A gust began as a low murmur and then rose in pitch as it gained force. It came close, then backed away, and finally rushed in from every direction, surging through the forest, wave after wave washing overhead. And then there was nothing. It passed, leaving a night full of holes and hollows.

Toward morning, the sky lightened a few shades, drawing me out of a shallow sleep. On one side stood the darkness of the forest, on the other the blank emptiness of the canyon. The wind had not returned; the air stood still. There was no sign of fire, no smell of smoke. We spend our lives waiting for the fire to come, only to roll over at last into the light of day.

I took out the stove to make coffee, moving slowly after a restless night. I'd done this so often I went through the motions without thinking. It had become a ritual, each step lost in the act itself. First I cleared a level spot and filled the pot with water. Then I primed the stove and touched it with a match. Before the flame had died too low I opened the valve. After adjusting the burner I placed the pot on the stove and waited. That's when I noticed the flicker of a star between the limbs of a snag.

Walking to an opening, I looked across the smooth back of the plateau curving across the horizon–black-green with trees, thick with life. In the growing light of morning, each tree began to emerge from the forest as slowly as a person parts from sleep. Above, the stars had faded until only one remained. I stood in the clearing and watched Venus shine like a hermit's star.

Ghosts

WILLIAM KITTREDGE

Not so long ago the scattering of native people in southeastern Oregon believed you could slip into caves under the rimrocks and descend into an underworld in which there existed a heaven of creatures. Trout were thick in little streams and would rise like ghosts to a grasshopper in the soft aftermath of an afternoon thunderstorm; the green moss would be soft and rich underfoot and the ripe berries would fall into your hands.

Mule deer would look back at you without apprehension, ears twitching at the little flies. This was where game animals lived before they emerged to share the world with us.

It is not altogether a fantasy; it is also a fairly precise description of the tiny fishing streams that collect in the isolated Great Basin ranges of desert mountains and work down to the swamplands where waterbirds congregate in flocks beyond numbering. Maybe those stories about an underworld populated by that richness of animals were not dreams at all. No one knows what those people thought or what their dreams were like, but it's certain their descendants were neither unintelligent nor unimaginative.

Maybe their stories were simply ways to celebrate what they loved about the world in its actualities; maybe the part about fantasies and dreams is my invention. I should be careful about projecting sadness from my disconnected times onto them.

The Northern Paiutes who lived in that country can be thought of as a deeply primitive people. They did not have much in the way of what anthropologists call cultural items, which includes everything from spoons to ideas of magic. They lived sparse and traveled light. The country did not reward them for owning very much.

The clans who lived in Warner Valley were known as "The Groundhog Eaters," a name wonderful in its inelegance. But you have to wonder what it meant to them as they managed lives that likely did not seem either splendid or numbing or even simple.

Many of us like to imagine the people we understand as native as living in quietude with a world that is entirely holy. That is not altogether a sentimentalization; there are people who seem to regard existence as a series of communal ceremonies; many of them do in fact seem to think everything is alive and holy.

But what we know for sure is simpler, and brutal: such people are almost gone from the earth; in another generation their dreams will be extinct.

In the best book on the subject of pre-white narrative in eastern Oregon, *Coyote Was Going There: Indian Literature of the Oregon Country,* Jarold Ramsey writes:

> The white response, organized during the Civil War, was brutally simple: extermination. The unpublished "Field Journals" of Lt. William McKay (a medical doctor who was himself part Indian) make it vividly clear that Army detachments like McKay's, sided by Indian scouts from Warm Springs and elsewhere, went through the upper reaches of the Great Basin country hunting Paiutes and other Shoshoneans down like deer, killing for the sake of what in the Vietnam era became known as "body count."

As those people moved through the yearly cycle of their so-called hunting/gathering, their existences turned on few actual mileposts (birth, initiation, marriage, children, death), and the content of their days is hard for us to imagine with any accuracy (how would we know if it was accurate?). It is even more difficult for most of us to value.

They existed in an endless sway of time many of us find frightening; we like to think they lived in communality; we like to think they did not ever consider themselves alone, since the world around them was alive; we like to think they knew it was a useless idea to consider anyone exceptional, since everything was part of every other thing. We like to think such things, but we don't know if we want such lives. We are still infected by our urge to go conquer time, to go *out,* and be individual.

In Warner Valley there is a long curl of high ground along the eastern side of Crump Lake (known locally as the Bar), where native people camped in waterbird season, spring and fall, over millennia. Up until the early 1930s the Bar was thick with wild roses and native berry brush. Then, in the devastating series of dry seasons that accompanied the economic ruination of the Great Depression, a lot of that tule-ground floodplain country around Crump Lake got afire, and the thickets of dead chest-high brush burned away, leaving reefs of ashes across a litter of beautiful chipped obsidian artifacts that had been lost, accumulating over centuries.

Each fall at that latitude and elevation there are days when the sunlight lies like glory over the dying red-orange reeds of the tule beds and the muddy soft water of the lake. Think of afternoons out on that bar amid the rosebushes, the waterbirds clattering as they come and go.

You could voyage into that country and try the art of sitting still in the silences alongside a seep spring deep in the hidden backlands. You could study the singular beauty at the heart of a desert flower while long-legged insects walk the surface tension of the water, and you could find your concern with the passage of time easing out of you, and you could be inclined to attempt the slow day-to-day dance of creatures, and imagine you have gone somewhat native. And probably you would be kind of right; the native people were much like us; we are the same species; it's just that some of our people killed them like animals, drove them away, gave them our diseases, and taught them the arts of farming and rodeo; we live surrounded by ghosts. Some of us think we yearn to live like they do, but not enough, not yet.

Coming Home

MARCIA BONTA

> *The only explanation women have given me for not writing about natural history is that they fear being alone in the landscape. Over and over, they tell me that they feel vulnerable; they fear danger—not from the land, but from men. They fear violence and never quite forget about its most disturbing expression: rape.*
>
> —STEPHEN TRIMBLE, "Sing Me Down the Mountain"

Whenever he could, my father headed us "up home" for weekends and vacations. Home was Pennsylvania, where he had been raised, a poor boy of working class parents, bright and determined to get a college education and make something of himself. He graduated from the state university in 1936 with a degree in chemical engineering. It was not his true calling–landscape architecture was his true calling–but it was a way to earn a living in the depression years. Chemical engineers were being hired, although not in Pennsylvania. Only the string of oil refineries along the Delaware River on the New Jersey side needed engineers. And so my father crossed the river, and my mother followed. For forty years they were exiled from "home" to make a living and raise a family. But all the while they were exiled, my father told tales of his life as a boy in the woods of eastern Pennsylvania. I was the child who listened the hardest and who longed for the kind of free-ranging childhood my father had lived, roaming the hills and valleys near his hometown.

Even as a small child, the only time that counted for me was the time spent outdoors. We lived at what was then the edge of town, near a chain of small lakes set amid a substantial woodlands laced with narrow trails. Being female, I was not allowed to go by myself into the wild area, but I usually managed to round up enough siblings and neighbors' children to accompany me. I was, in fact, a kind of pied piper of the neighborhood who led the willing youngsters deeper and deeper into a maze of wooded wetlands and impenetrable thickets, cajoling the more timid ones through areas that might have appalled their parents if they had known. Despite the sameness of the flat, southern New Jersey countryside, in the woods I had an unerring sense of direction that never failed me no matter how unfamiliar the terrain was.

Those explorations, though, were second rate in comparison to our time in Pennsylvania. Pennsylvania had hills and even mountains, and I prefer vertical over horizontal terrain. I also favor rushing streams over placid lakes and upland forests over lowland swamps. The southern New Jersey landscape has its own special beauty, but to me it remained an alien landscape. I passed my first eighteen years in suspended animation, waiting expectantly for my life to really begin. It would begin, I resolved, with college, when I would leave New Jersey forever.

I first thought I would attend the same state university my father had, encircled by the ancient ridges of central Pennsylvania. Instead, I chose a smaller, private university near the island-studded Susquehanna River. The campus looks westward over a verdant valley to a series of softly mounded, green mountains to the west. I had no idea, nor did I particularly care, what courses the university offered. The view of the mountains was my sole criterion for choosing that university over the half dozen other places I visited in Pennsylvania.

It turned out to be an excellent school for a budding naturalist, nurturing not only my Pennsylvania passion but my passion for learning as well. Time spent in stimulating classrooms was treasured almost as much as time spent roaming the nearby mountains and valleys. Again, because of my gender, I looked for suitable woodland companions. During my first two years, they were female friends. But in my junior year I found my life partner, also the child of exiled Pennsylvanians, with the same feeling of home I had.

First we explored on foot–sometimes twenty miles at a time–and then on his motor scooter. Every suitable weekend, we were out traveling the network of gravel roads built throughout Pennsylvania's forested lands. Returning late one evening, we saw our first aurora borealis display flickering across the splendid silence of the night sky. On another trip we stopped to walk in the woods and were caught between a pair of screaming bobcats. For an hour we sat in the underbrush and listened, hopeful yet half afraid that we might see them. But gradually the sounds faded away, and we were left alone, our minds firmly imprinted with an image of wildness in the midst of a peopled land.

During a hike in what is called the Seven Mountains area, we encountered another symbol of wildness–a black bear–that turned tail and ran when we saw it, much to our relief. In those days we were uncertain about the intentions of what most people considered fierce and dangerous wild animals–novitiates, as we were, in the ways of nature. We had never seen many of the commonest birds, which is why I almost fell off a mountaintop when I spotted by first scarlet tanager perched on a tree below. As I explained to my life partner, I had never quite believed that such a vibrantly hued bird lived part time in temperate Pennsylvania, despite the assurances of my field guide. To this day no other birds, even those I have seen in the tropics, seem quite so beautiful as the scarlet-bodied, black-winged male scarlet tanagers.

By the time we graduated from college, we had covered a significant portion of central Pennsylvania on foot and on motor scooter, convinced of its inherent beauty and "homeness" to us. Someday, we dreamed, we would own a country place there. Sooner than most people, after our own few years of exile in Washington, D.C., we bought our first country home–in central Maine, however, not in Pennsylvania. And we had two sons with a third on the way. Our five years in Maine were wonderful, but Maine remained alien to me. It was not home. There were too many conifers and not enough hardwood trees. I noticed this lack particularly in the winter. The Maine woods are deep and silent, muffled in white snow and overhung by evergreen boughs, picture-postcard beautiful to be sure, but not home. Home woods are on-and-off white, continually freezing and thawing, brilliant with winter sunlight that pours down over the woods' floor, unimpeded by the naked silver and black limbs of hardwood trees. Such light and openness liberates my spirit. The Maine woods stifled me.

Only when we crossed into Connecticut, heading south at last into Pennsylvania, did the woods begin to resemble home. Our Volkswagen van and U-haul truck were jammed with the accumulation of nearly eight years of marriage, including our three sons, two of whom mourned the loss of the only home they knew. But we *were* going home, I told them, home to the mountains of central Pennsylvania and to the state university my father had graduated from, where their father had a new job.

Like a mantra, I sang out the names of the places we passed, weaving in tales of my childhood, my youth, our courtship, our collective memories of Pennsylvania. There, in northeastern Luzerne County, was where Daddy's people came from. The coal regions of Carbon County had nurtured my grandparents and my favorite great aunt. That road led to the university where Daddy and Mommy had met. Just off the interstate, which had not been built during our college years, were the remains of the green wilderness we had explored as students. Favored above all the places was Ricketts Glen State Park, with its twenty-eight waterfalls along an eight-mile trail and its tract of virgin hemlock forest, embodying the best of wild Pennsylvania. During our college days and our years of exile, we had returned to hike the trails in every season of the year, renewing with each visit our vow to return home as quickly as possible.

Deeper and deeper into the mountains we drove, sweeping past the largest road cut in the eastern United States. Except for one trip with the college choir, I was farther west in Pennsylvania than I had ever been. So I had the sense of coming home and yet of entering new territory. That dual sense of familiarity and discovery has remained the dynamic that has nurtured me and will continue to nurture me for the rest of my life. Despite a fascination with the wider world beyond these ancient hills and valleys (a fascination we occasionally feed by traveling), no matter how far I go and how wonderful the places I have been—places as far flung and exotic as Peru and Japan, Australia and Costa Rica—I soon find myself realizing, like Dorothy in the *Wizard of Oz,* that there's no place like home.

Having come home finally, at the age of twenty-nine, I was free to become what I had been working toward during all my years of exile—a writer of place, eager to sing the praises of my own special niche on earth. I had kept a nature journal spasmodically during our years in the city, recording only those parks and green spaces we fled to on the weekends. To nurture my spirit, I also read the works of naturalist-writers Edwin Way Teale and Hal Borland. Louis Halle's classic *Spring in Washington* kept me sane during my own springs in Washington, and Gladys Taber's Stillmeadow chronicles of her home in rural Connecticut stirred up an interest in gardening and country life.

My spasmodic nature journal became an almost daily one in Maine, naively filled with the wonder and discovery of a novice to country living and to parenthood. Although I continued to read the old masters, such as John Burroughs, Henry David Thoreau and John Muir, and to discover new ones—Sally Carrighar, Ann Zwinger and Rachel Carson—I never considered entering the ranks of nature writers myself. Not, that is, until I came home. The incredible place we found ourselves in Pennsylvania so overwhelmed me that I had to share my discoveries with others, just as Burroughs and Borland and Thoreau—all naturalists of place—had shared theirs.

We found our home on the Fourth of July. Following the vague directions of a local real estate dealer, we edged our van along a narrow, gravel road that led up a wooded mountainside. Ferns and wildflowers covered the bank to our right, while a small, rock-strewn stream tumbled below the road to our left. At last we emerged from the cool, summer-woods darkness into the sun-filled grounds and surrounding fields of what could only be described as a small estate, with its two houses, large barn, shed, springhouse, and garage, all of which possessed elegant lines and an air of faded grandeur. Well loved in the past as the summer home of a wealthy family, its owners had sold it to less provident people, and already the decay had begun. But the price was right, as well as the mountain land accompanying it. Perched near the top of the northernmost ridge in Pennsylvania's ridge-and-valley province, our home is accessible only by the gated, mile-and-a-half private dirt road we had followed. By western United States standards, the road is not particularly steep and the mountain is not high (1,600 ft.), but to most Easterners, raised on roads paved to everywhere and used to convenience at all costs, our home is daunting to reach by vehicle and impossible on foot. We might as well live on an island in the middle of the sea.

Such a place has allowed me the kind of freedom from fear that remains an impossible dream for most women. In the early years, little boys clung to my hands or dogged my steps during most of my walks, but once the last son was off to school, I roamed alone and unafraid, an experience I had never had before. I was finally able to live, in my adult years, the kind of life my father had lived as a child. Only determined hunters carrying their guns walk over the ridgetop for two and a half weeks every autumn. Because we do not post our land, they are pleased to swap stories with a non-hunting female who, except for the absence of a gun, seems to have as much understanding of the woods and wildlife as they do. Our own land holdings amount to about five hundred acres of mountain land—a veritable kingdom here in the crowded East—but our land is surrounded by other privately owned mountain land, most of which is posted by its hunting landowners living in the farm valley below. Since they see me as nonthreatening because my use of the land is nonconsumptive, the landowners have told me to ignore their signs. So, in essence, I have thousands of mountain acres to wander over and every season of the year in which to observe the life cycles of my fellow wild creatures.

This freedom to roam unafraid, gathering vignettes of natural happenings, harkens back to the sense of home our primitive forebears were thought to have had, and it makes me and my life-style a kind of throwback to a less complicated age. Whether such a halcyon period ever existed is still debated by those who believe that humanity is naturally aggressive. But many feminist writers postulate a time when females were in control of the world as gatherers and nurturers, before the rise of male-dominated, violent societies. Whatever the truth may be about the ancient, socializing tendencies of humanity, the sense of peace and fulfillment I feel, living here, surrounded by loving, nurturing males, is the kind of home spirit many females yearn for in these latter days of violence and hatred toward women.

Home should be a place of comfort, a womb in which we can float safely and warmly, buoyed by people we love and a landscape that nurtures our spirit. My childhood dreams of coming home to Pennsylvania have been fulfilled beyond my wildest expectations. As a female child, infused with a love of the outdoors I could not fully indulge in because of both gender and place, I am home at last on land that will nourish me the rest of my life. And when my life is over, in final payment for the peace and beauty I have found here in harmony with nature and with humanity, my bones will in turn nourish the land, so that my covenant with the natural world will not be broken.

January Journal

MARCIA BONTA

January 1, 1991

Seventeen degrees at dawn and crystal clear. The gloom of December has been cast off, at least momentarily. I can only hope that the new weather pattern of light and peace will symbolize the new year, which everyone is fearing with its looming threat of war in the Middle East. Now that we have celebrated the birth of a Man who symbolized light and peace with our usual mix of idealism and materialism, we have resumed business as usual in the real world.

I sat, at sunset, tucked among the Norway spruce trees while dark-eyed juncos zipped in over my head so closely that I felt the wind from their wings. They made their clicking, scolding sounds when they saw me. But eventually they settled in for the night in nearby spruces, one or two to a tree.

Suddenly a loud screaming rent the pre-dusk stillness somewhere below me in the vicinity of the Far Field Road. At first I stayed where I was, since usually my investigations of odd noises are fruitless. But the sounds continued unabated, and I finally stood up and walked to an area overlooking the road. Still I could see nothing, but the screaming went on and on. Then I sat down and scoped the area below with my binoculars. Almost at once I spotted a large bird, looking mostly dark in the dim light except for a white line above its eye, leaping around on the ground and screaming like an angry troll. As I started toward it, it took off fast and low to the ground and was gone in an instant. Fixing my sights on the place it had been, I climbed down to find one small, downy, gray feather. Had the bird been pummeling small prey, such as a junco, or did the feather belong to the bird? Although I searched the area, I found no other clues to the bird's identity or hints regarding the behavior I had observed.

I hurried home to check my field guides. The most likely bet, I decided after studying the pictures, was an immature northern goshawk, but the experts claimed that northern goshawks are silent birds except during the mating season. Next I listened to my bird call record and easily identified the screaming as that of a northern goshawk. No other bird of prey sounded even remotely like it. To cinch the matter, I called our local bird expert, and he told me he had seen a couple of northern goshawks in the valley below our property a couple of days earlier. Later, I talked to a graduate student who is studying northern goshawks and who has been a licensed falconer for many years. I had witnessed, he said, what biologists call "play behavior" in young northern goshawks.

What a wonderful beginning for the new year!

January 2, 1991

Twenty degrees and cloudless at dawn, warming up to forty-eight degrees in the sun by mid-afternoon with clouds rolling up from the South. I sat in the woods overlooking the Far Field thicket and listened to the earth sigh and mutter with every vagrant breeze. In the distance pileated woodpeckers called. Other birds cheeped occasionally, but mostly the woods were wrapped in winter silence. Walking back up the Far Field Trail, I heard a quiet tapping and looked up to see a female hairy woodpecker working over a red oak tree branch. She was the only creature I saw during my two-hour walk.

I wondered, as I moved along, why I feel compelled to be outside every day, and I finally decided that my job is to bear witness to the beauty of the earth. I am neither a scientist nor an environmental writer. To me, the outdoors means just that—being outdoors—not to hunt, fish, hike, canoe, bike, or bird, but to be, even in the winter—especially in the winter—when nature is stripped to its bare essentials and few people are abroad.

Sometimes I'm tempted to move somewhere else, to another country even, and to learn a whole new culture, a whole new concept of nature. But I cannot bring myself to say goodbye to these old hills forever, despite the fact that they have been degraded by humanity's misuse. So I remain, a stubborn naturalist of place, content to look for the unusual in what many see as a commonplace and unexciting area that lacks the glamor of the north woods, the seacoast, the Rocky Mountains, or the desert. But there is always more to discover here, as I learned yesterday.

Again I sat in the spruces after sunset, but instead of a northern goshawk I heard a pair of great horned owls calling back and forth while occasional dark-eyed juncos flicked into the grove to roost for the night.

January 5, 1991

Forty-five degrees at dawn, raining and foggy. But there was a swift clearing late in the morning. Despite fierce winds and warmth reminiscent of March, the light is still January, casting its long shadows in the woods, gleaming rosy on the fields and mountaintops, seen in brief snatches as the clouds race across the sky. I could almost feel the earth spinning beneath my feet.

I seemed to be alone with the wind and the light and the fantastic, cloud-studded sky, when I walked down First Field and paused to soak in the spectacle. Then a flock of dark-eyed juncos flashed across the field. As I stopped to watch the birds, I suddenly realized that I was being watched when the gray and white silhouette of a deer materialized at the edge of the woods. We stood looking at each other for several minutes until the deer stamped its right front hoof in alarm, flicked its tail and ran off, followed by two others that I had not seen until they moved. Amazing how well the gray winter coats of the white-tailed deer meld with the tree trunks and snow.

January 8, 1991

Twenty degrees at dawn and fair, with a fresh layer of snow on the ground. I love such January days. When else is the sky as blue, the air as clear, the light as bright?

I was out early in the morning to listen to the silence and to identify each bird as it called. A crew of woodpeckers–downies and hairies–worked the tree trunks accompanied by the yanking calls of the white-breasted nuthatches. Black-capped chickadees and tufted titmice gleaned insects from shrubs and tree branches. Crows cawed across the sky; evening grosbeaks quarreled over the shabby remains of fall webworm nests still hanging from the tops of black cherry trees. Then a pair of northern ravens croaked along Sapsucker Ridge, one in front of the other, their wedge-shaped tails a distinctive badge that separates them from their smaller crow brethren.

Deer trails wove through the woods and over the fields, and I glimpsed several deer watching me from a distant hillside. I moved over the fields and spied the rounded brown body of a meadow vole as it emerged from its tunnel and then popped back in again as soon as it saw me.

The fields are a good place to search for insect life. Goldenrod ball galls swelled on dried goldenrod stems, and I found the hardened foam of a praying mantis egg case firmly attached to a dried weed. Suspended from a sapling spruce at the top of First Field was a round, beige, papery ball that looked like a small oak apple gall.

I broke it open and discovered spider silk gently cradling hundreds of minuscule crab spiders. Even though it was cold, I could see them wriggling under my hand lens, and I apologized for dooming the whole lot because of my insatiable curiosity.

I continued on to the thicket. Hieroglyphic-like marks made by a dangling grapevine brushing over the snow with the slightest breeze were a sharp contrast to the precise, fresh tracks of ruffed grouse. Two erupted in front of me with an explosive noise, and I wondered how they could have been so close in that snowy landscape without my spotting them. The thicket also sheltered a couple of white-throated sparrows, a female northern cardinal, and a scattering of juncos.

I walked for miles, following no trails, weaving in and out between the trees, slogging up and down hillsides, ducking under grapevines, pushing through thickets of briers, savoring the incomparable beauty of a perfect winter day.

January 11, 1991

Twenty degrees with fine snowflakes sifting down at dawn. The snow picked up momentum and fell heavily off and on all day. The feeder was mobbed with house finches. One female and two male northern cardinals and eight tree sparrows joined the party, while a solitary female purple finch pushed herself in between the house finches on the feeder at mid-morning.

Winter does not fit into our society's plans. Even I grumbled when a day I had planned for library research and shopping was scuttled by the weather. Tomorrow, the statewide Audubon conference is supposed to be held in Harrisburg. It seems odd that even environmental and nature-related organizations blithely plan conferences with no contingency plans at the worst time of year for traveling. Will the conference be held, and, if so, will others, like us, struggle there because we own a four-wheel drive vehicle made to defy nature? At least the local schools are smart. They have canceled school for the day. Too bad our whole work- and conference-ridden society doesn't do the same thing. Then we could all relax and admit that where nature is concerned we should adjust instead of resist.

Later in the day the conference was canceled, but not only because of the weather. Our state's most environmentally minded congressman, who was to be our speaker, couldn't come because of the impending vote in Congress regarding the Iraqi situation. Will there or won't there be war with Iraq on the fifteenth?

Despite depressing world news, I took a walk in the snowy sleet of the afternoon. Woodpeckers, both hairy and pileated, were abroad, along with white-breasted nuthatches and tufted titmice. Best of all were the golden-crowned kinglets with their high-pitched calls that, like the voices of happy children, spread instant good cheer as they foraged close to the ground.

Maybe that's why I need to get out every day—to connect myself with the sane world of nature and forget the often insane world of humanity.

January 16, 1991

Thirty-six degrees. I awoke to hear it raining this morning, and all day I have been encased in fog up to my doorstep. A song sparrow flew into the feeder. So did a single American goldfinch in his winter garb. Both are new arrivals to the feeder for the year. In mid-afternoon I watched a male downy woodpecker examining the dead, bent-over stalks of pokeweed below our back porch, but he was not tempted by the suet on the feeder.

Near dusk I took a walk in the fog and had about fifty feet of visibility. Nothing stirred except the juncos in the spruce grove at the top of First Field. I sat there, wrapped in muffled silence, the usual sounds from the valley muted by the fog. Raindrops hung in solitary splendor from the tips of the spruce needles. Juncos chirped at me from their sheltered perches deep within the spruce boughs. They seem to come into their night roosts one by one and from different directions, not in a concentrated flock as some researchers have reported. The same is true of the juncos who use the juniper bush beside the house.

A good day to start a war—gloomy with rain and fog—and so the Gulf War began early this evening with bombing raids on Baghdad. Yet here on our mountain it is so peaceful and beautiful, even on a rainy, foggy day. I am grateful to be living in such a place during these troubled, tumultuous times. Yet when, in the history of civilized humanity, have the times *not* been troubled and tumultuous? To take solace from nature instead of humanity is the true balm of Gilead for the human spirit, distraught as some of us are with the warrior mentality of so many human beings. Where is the peace of God that passeth all understanding? Why does the Prince of Peace's message fall mostly on deaf ears, even among Christians? I believe it is because religion, to most people, is helpful only in times of trouble. Otherwise, it is highly impractical, and its basic tenets are easy to ignore if you look at humanity with clear-eyed vision. In fact, religion has served as a rallying war cry more than once and is now doing so again.

January 18, 1991

Twenty-six degrees at dawn with snow flurries, but later a wind swept in and cleared the skies. The squeaks, groans, and peeping noises of trees substitute for bird calls in winter, although I heard, for the first time this year, the spring-like, "fee-bee" calls of black-capped chickadees.

Fresh ruffed grouse tracks wound along Laurel Ridge Trail, but mine were the only human tracks on the trails. Here on my mountaintop I can enjoy a stunningly beautiful, peaceful winter day while lying against the Far Field Road bank. I can contemplate the blue sky and scudding clouds, soak in the sunshine, and breathe deeply the bracing winter air. But halfway around the world missiles have been launched at Israel by Iraq, and most of the rest of civilization watches the action live from Tel-Aviv on cable television. What a sorry world we have where the winter entertainment is watching people at war. In the words of poet Richard Shelton, "Wars occur because men want them and peace occurs when they are tired." I hope they are soon tired.

January 21, 1991

Thirty degrees at dawn with a light wet snow falling—a wedding cake snow that brought in large numbers of birds to the feeder this morning. The tree sparrows doubled to ten and fed among the sixty-five house finches mobbing the porch and feeder. Those feisty sparrows frequently threatened the finches and any other birds in defense of their turf. The tufted titmice, black-capped chickadees, and white-breasted nuthatches seemed more intimidated, so they waited until the finches were spooked off and then snatched their own food. Twenty dark-eyed juncos, too, held their places among the finches and were not intimidated. The northern cardinals were their usual royal but ultra-cautious selves. Taken one by one, the other birds will challenge a house finch and usually win. But the overwhelming finch numbers defeated the others. When fifteen to twenty house finches crowd the feeder, pushing, shoving, and yelling like a gang of bullies, no other species dares intrude except an occasional extra-bold tree sparrow or white-breasted nuthatch that slides in from the side. But when a red-bellied woodpecker sailed in, they all scattered as chaff before the wind.

Shortly after noon the snow stopped, and the sun shone in fits and starts as I walked along the snow-covered trails. A puffball of snow sat on every mountain laurel leaf. Tree limbs and shrub twigs, with their two-inch-high snow layers, created a lacework of white against a deep blue sky. The snow glistened with light, and I spent unforgettable hours of beauty wandering through snow showers spilled off the tree branches by the wind. Once I sat quietly on the Far Field Road watching three deer peacefully feeding on the bank not far away. Chickadees "fee-beed" despite the cold. It must be the increased light, and not the warmth, that triggers them to sing their spring song in the midst of a snowy day.

January 25, 1991

After a two-day trip to Pittsburgh I returned to the reality of the mountain. To most people this place would be relegated to the realm of unreality, but to me this is where my real life is. All other is illusion.

Thirteen degrees at dawn, clearing and beautiful. I found the top off our trash can this morning and a few plastic strips from the orange juice containers on the back step. Then, while following fox tracks from the old garden area up to the top of First Field, periodically losing them where the snow had melted, I spotted a jelly jar lid with puncture marks in it and its edge slightly bashed in as if an animal had carried it in its teeth. In all likelihood it was a fox.

I continued to follow multiple fox tracks over to our neighbor's property, up his logging road to the top of Sapsucker Ridge, and then back along the ridgetop on our land heading for the Far Field. In some places veritable animal highways wound through the woods, and I wondered if the highway-building mentality originated from our mammalian connections. Most animals, like people, follow the crowd. But occasionally tracks deviated from the norm as if the creature *were* marching to a different drummer. Some took the way most traveled by; others followed their own instincts. Who says that animals are different from people? To follow animal tracks in the snow is to wonder just how different animals are from us. Some took the path of least resistance; others seemed to delight in the exotic. Still others chose the more challenging trail. But all eventually went over the rock-strewn mountainside where I could not follow without fear of falling. So, in the end, I was defeated by the physical superiority of the creatures I was following, left to ponder what I had seen as I drowsed against my favorite Far Field log in the winter sunlight.

Walking back along the Far Field Road and down First Field, I saw so many fox tracks that I envisioned the long, white, winter nights filled with dancing foxes paying court in the moonlight.

January 27, 1991

Seventeen degrees at dawn with a fresh inch and a half of snow, clearing into a sparkling day with Dresden-blue skies. Nine deer fed on the Sapsucker Ridge powerline right-of-way. Others crossed the Far Field Road and grazed above and below it. The silence was broken by the brisk scolding of a Carolina wren and the cawing of a gang of crows. At the entrance to the Far Field I discovered a maze of fox tracks with a sprinkle of urine on a raised hillock. Near the thicket I found a scattering of ruffed grouse feathers surrounded by small fox tracks.

Today is Super Bowl day so no one is abroad, but since yesterday was positively the last legal hunting day (the end of the extended ruffed grouse season), and fur prices are low, what is there to bring people out into the woods? They will make no profit except for their souls. Consequently, the only human prints on the mountain are mine.

As I sat at the base of a tree, golden-crowned kinglets came swinging in overhead to call and feed in the tree branches above me–wonderful birds to share a peaceful Sunday morning with. They acted as if I was not there and foraged within ten feet of where I was sitting without showing any alarm. Golden-crowned kinglets are the best and most satisfying of winter birds–easy to see and identify, not dependent or even interested in bird feeders, and able to make a good living off the meager offerings of winter. This winter, unlike other years, I have been finding them in same-species flocks. Previously I would often discover a couple feeding with tufted titmice, black-capped chickadees, downy woodpeckers, or brown creepers. They, like Carolina wrens, have been increasing over the last several winters, welcome additions to the fauna of January.

January 28, 1991

Thirty-one degrees at dawn with a light frosting of new, wet snow. But the sky cleared quickly, tufted titmice "peter-petered" from every direction, and there was a steady "drip-drip" from melting snow.

I was sitting at the base of Sapsucker Ridge by 9:00 A.M., soaking in the sunlight, basking in the beauty, listening to the birds–tufted titmice, black-capped chickadees, American crows, Carolina wrens, white-breasted nuthatches, northern cardinals, and downy, hairy, and red-bellied woodpeckers. Jet trails disappeared almost as quickly as they were etched across the deep blue sky to the northwest, but they remained in the southeast a little longer where there were still light clouds. The barn roof steamed as if on fire from the evaporating snow. Individual droplets dangling from tree branches twinkled like stars and captured prisms of light to dazzle my eyes. Mostly they were translucent, but a few flashed yellow, orange, and red.

I walked over to our neighbor's land, now owned by a lumberman, and passed her old garden–lost dreams, lost hopes, a sagging fence, a broken-down shed, an abandoned car. I remembered the happy days when her brother was alive, when a friend cultivated her garden and helped with her beehives, when she had at last found some peace of mind after a troubled life. But now she is gone, her brother is dead, and her friend has left his wife to live with another woman hundreds of miles away. There are no more human footprints. The back acres have been reclaimed by the foxes, and the birds sing with joyous abandon. In the end, all flesh is grass. Nature's peace settled like a mantle over the reclaimed land. Rivers of deer tracks flowed through the snow, and the squirrels proclaimed their rights to the trees.

January 29, 1991

Twenty-four degrees at dawn with Sapsucker Ridge lit scarlet from the rising sun. Jet trails remained like long white fingers in the southeast while the rest of the sky was blue. The machines at the limestone quarry in the valley were so loud that their noise penetrated the walls of the house this morning, and later, when I sat above the Far Field Road, I could still hear them. Other valley sounds also funneled up distinctly, so the illusion of winter's peace was shattered.

Several days ago the war took on an even more horrifying aspect as Iraq began flooding the Persian Gulf with Kuwaiti oil, creating the largest oil slick in history. Experts on cleaning up oil spills were rushed to the Gulf, and a bombing raid was launched to destroy the pumps emitting the oil. But what madness! Destroying an entire ecosystem from which all the Gulf area residents prosper. Birds and fish are dead or dying, and the slick is moving inexorably toward Saudi Arabia, where desalination plants process saltwater into drinking water. And there lies the explanation for what seemed at first like unreasoning madness. Destroy a civilization's water source and you destroy a civilization, especially a desert people's. But such a deed demonstrates how sick humanity is–always putting the petty ambitions of people above the nurturing of the natural world. The planet seems too small to support so many rapacious humans bent on victory at all costs. Of course, we did the same thing in the Vietnam War with defoliants, and we tried to talk Peru into using them to wipe out the drug trade. Why must nature pay for humanity's deeds? Or, more to the point, when will we discover that everything *is* connected to everything else and that when we fiddle with it we imperil our own survival?

An incident from William Warner's *Beautiful Swimmers* says it all regarding humanity's relationship with nature. A Maryland biologist tried to explain new conservation measures to the Tangier Sound Watermen's Union on Smith Island and asked for discussion. According to Warner, one islander finally rose to his feet and said, in answer, "Mr. Manning, there is something you don't understand. These here communities on the Shore, our little towns here on the island and over to mainland, was all founded on the right of free plunder. If you follow the water, that's how it was and and that's how it's got to be." The right of free plunder has beggared us and will continue to do so.

I sat quietly in the corner of First Field listening to the tapping of an unseen woodpecker. After a time I found it—a female pileated quietly tapping and then lifting her head as if she were listening for the sound of carpenter ants in the bark. She repeated that several times before flying off. Next, a pair of foraging golden-crowned kinglets flew into the area, followed by a white-breasted nuthatch, several black-capped chickadees, and a female downy woodpecker. The downy landed in a tree next to me and made more noise than the pileated. All ignored my presence as they went about their business, so I had the rare pleasure of feeling as if I were an integral part of the scene and not an unwanted interloper.

Continuing my exploration of Sapsucker Ridge, I discovered a new fox hole at the base of an old stump near the Sapsucker Ridge powerline right-of-way. I also disturbed two deer basking in the sunshine of the Sapsucker Ridge thicket. One bounded quickly up the hill, while the other leaped slowly along. The bottom half of its right front leg was missing, probably shot off during hunting season. Several years ago we watched a doe that had lost most of her left hind leg not only learn to run nearly as fast as the other deer she associated with, but give birth to twins and raise them to maturity.

In the warm sun of mid-afternoon the thermometer registered fifty degrees on the veranda. I heard a raven croaking through the walls of the house and went out to watch as it flew from its perch in the woods.

January 30, 1991

Forty-eight degrees by mid-morning and absolutely clear. I sunbathed against the Far Field Road bank in utter peace. Winter silence on top of a worn-down, ancient Pennsylvania mountaintop, with only the cries of occasional birds to keep me company, can be as purifying an experience as forty days in the desert. Life is stripped to its barest essentials to survive the winter, and the sun pours from the sky unimpeded by tree leaves. I can see far in any direction, so I tend to spot the shyer creatures, such as porcupines, foxes, even a bobcat once, in the winter. But my companions today were more commonplace–a pileated woodpecker flying silently past, a golden-crowned kinglet calling and fluttering in front of me, a tree sparrow flying up from the brush to shake its feathers at me, four deer filing up Sapsucker Ridge.

Later, I sat at the crest of First Field surveying the landscape and thinking, I hold all the joys of life in two hands–a loving, encouraging husband who has nurtured my growth and unselfishly lived here for my pleasure, three sons who were my close companions in their childhood and youth and who still share most of their lives with me, a home that is warm and simply furnished with minimal fancy furniture and maximum books, a handful of friends who share my concerns and interests, and a stable life-style dependent more on spiritual than material things.

January 31, 1991

Thirty-three degrees at dawn. An absolutely radiant day, not a cloud in the sky, and I was out at eight in the morning to walk down Laurel Ridge toward the Tyrone Gap. As I reached the end of the ridge, I had a graphic view of the limestone quarry. Layer after layer of gouged-out hillside with all the noisy, earth-eating machines sitting at rest in the bottom of the desolation. Without that sight and the sound of vehicles from the valley, the view of blue-misted hills and rolling farm fields would have been timeless. But people seem to adjust to the gradual degradation of their environment. Anything to further the technological success of our civilization. What? Question the folly of removing whole mountainsides as quickly as possible to fix up and build more roads? You can't hold back progress.

Winter is the time to see visions. I seem to hear prophetic voices, railing at humanity's failings, prophesying the end of the world. Light pours from the sky, bathing my thoughts with the heat of conviction. They are voices crying in the wilderness, preparing the way for doom that no one believes and no one heeds. The earth withers away as I watch, and I am stunned by the rapidity with which it destructs once it begins to unravel from too much use and too little love.

Sing Me down the Mountain

STEPHEN TRIMBLE

1

How alone do you feel in the wilderness?

The answer depends on what, and who, you take with you. Hiking alone, you experience the landscape in ways more intimate than any other, but the reality of what you perceive seems delicate, with no witnesses to the epiphanies. For five years after college I hiked alone, making pilgrimages to southern Utah canyons and traverses of Colorado mountain ranges. I worked through my fears (scorpions in the desert, bears in the mountains), grew comfortable with solitude, and took photographs to show friends, to verify I had indeed seen such places. I yearned for a companion. I wanted to see beauty, but I wanted even more to share it.

Perhaps that is why I began to write—to share these times of solitude.

I now see these lone walks as meditative, nonverbal, full of growth. I did not keep a journal; I wandered with my camera, looking to capture what I saw with my senses. I hoped for a clear, clean, direct line from the earth through my emotions to the film. I waded naked in streams, whooped when I clambered up a dry waterfall that gave me access to one more curving bend of sandstone cliffs and a new series of fern-festooned potholes in the upper reaches of a side canyon.

When a friend from those days asked me if I ever felt a part of the great flow of life, I thought for only a moment of my days prowling alone in the canyons before I answered, "Yes."

In 1977, I married a woman and adopted a dog. The marriage did not last, but the dog lived with me for more than eleven years. The card on his cage at the Tucson Humane Society read, "Name: Jack. Breed: wolf/shepherd." I always believed the shepherd was Australian shepherd but never knew for sure about the wolf. This gentle, intelligent being had too much personality to be called Jack. Since we lived in the Hispanic Southwest, we named him Carlos.

At home, Carlos slept on the floor. Camping, he had the luxury of nestling close to my sleeping bag. Carlos learned to be a photographer's dog, curling up by my camera bag or digging himself a cool patch of fresh dirt to lie on while he waited for me to exhaust my ideas with a photo subject.

Carlos was good company. I teased him and talked to him–when I needed to talk but might have felt too self-conscious to talk to myself. I could amble along, watching for the telling details that would become journal notes, and Carlos would not distract me from my reveries. He added another life to my experience and connected me to the wild world in a way only a nonhuman life can.

I came close to taking him for granted. Twice, when I forgot he was out of the truck and drove off without him, I realized how much I would miss him.

The first time, I had pulled over to sleep for a couple of hours one moonlit night near the mouth of Tsegi Canyon on the Navajo Indian Reservation. I let Carlos out to empty his bladder, went to sleep, and woke up to a few spitting snowflakes. Nervous about the weather, I cranked the truck to life and drove off.

Some fifty miles later, in the middle of Monument Valley, I addressed something to the back of the truck, and realized no one was listening (you could sense Carlos listening even when he didn't answer). Frantic–picturing Carlos dead on the highway–I spun around, raced back, got a speeding ticket in Kayenta, and at 2:00 A.M. reached near where I had left him. I began to stop every quarter mile and call into the darkness. Many Navajo dogs answered me from their owners' hogans. Finally, Carlos came trotting out of the night, back from his adventures, grinning.

The second time, I had been talking with Hualapai Indian people one summer evening, telling Coyote stories–or rather, talking around the edges of Coyote stories, since, in summer, one avoids telling stories that arouse the ire of what one Hualapai elder carefully referred to as "crawling long things." I left George Rocha's house in Peach Springs, Arizona, and drove a set of branching dirt roads headed for Madwita Canyon overlook, above the sacred place where the Hualapai lived with their gods in the Grand Canyon before emerging into this world. I stopped at a junction to hop out and peer at a fading sign, returned to the truck, and took the dimmer of the two forks. A few minutes later, Coyote trotted across the track through my headlight beams.

Some miles later, I reached the overlook, stepped out, and called Carlos. He was not there, and I realized he had jumped out when I checked the sign. I sensed Coyote laughing at me from somewhere off in the piñons. I drove back to find Carlos panting along the road trying to catch up, reminding me to pay more attention to him, to animals, to life.

Carlos's best time came in the early 1980s, when I spent several months hiking with him in the Great Basin Desert, researching a book. Few human companions joined me on these trips. When I think of these places, I do not think of being alone, though some observers would say that I was. I think of being there with Carlos.

Carlos and I climbed peaks in isolated Nevada and Utah mountain ranges and walked frosted sand dunes on winter mornings. He curled into the roots of a four-thousand year old bristlecone pine while I photographed its branches. I watched him sniff at the view—as I looked at it—when we stopped at the end of a long switchback climbing into the Jarbidge Wilderness.

Carlos was known to chase squirrels, bark at deer, and keep pikas and marmots at a distance. He also provided counterpoint to my solitary perspective. His concreteness, his vitality, his simple affection, made the abstractions of the universe less ponderous. When I lay down in my sleeping bag on the enormous expanse of cracked mud polygons that forms the level floor of the Black Rock Desert playa and looked into a bowl of sky filled with stars, his warm back pushing against mine and his paws trembling in dreams of chasing jackrabbits helped me to comprehend my relationship with the Milky Way. He was another life, in a land so vast that I needed such grounding.

Tumult in other parts of my life seemed very far away at these times. Now, when I read the ramblings in my journals, the miles of walking come back, vivid, the sunsets flare again, watched between sips of scotch from an enameled metal cup. Though each way of traveling in a landscape has its advantages, the companionship of this dog always cheers my memories.

II

The peace and satisfaction of those times away from other people soothe me even in recollection. But how wild must the country be to nurture natural history essayists? Does a nature writer need wilderness, or will a backyard do?

John Muir blithely sauntered off into the Sierra with a bit of bread and a notebook tied to his belt, to ride out thunderstorms at the tops of great evergreen trees. Thoreau, on the other hand, strolled the half hour over to Concord from Walden Pond virtually every day; he was admittedly more fond of Mrs. Emerson's cooking than his own. His famous dictum–"in wildness is the preservation of the world"–is frequently misquoted as "in wilderness . . ."

Thoreau was definite–wildness need not be searched for in wilderness–and as Thomas Lyon points out in *This Incomperable Lande,* Thoreau was the first American to state so clearly what we can learn from wildness when we find it: enlightenment, awakened consciousness, "the key to the opened self."

Natural history writers, and their readers, agree with Thoreau. They see the earth as a crucial key to understanding who they–and we–are. And they can turn that key anywhere: Loren Eiseley found wildness with an orb-weaving spider in suburbia and with pigeons in Manhattan.

While writing and journal-keeping require a certain amount of solitude, the nature writer's "out-of-doors" clearly does not have to be wilderness. The bent of personality that makes for a natural history writer comes from a need to write, a love of landscape, insatiable curiosity about the details of life in that landscape, devotion to language and image rooted in imagination rather than science, and a desire to ponder one's relationship to the earth–qualities that could come together in anyone.

That is why I have been so startled by a series of conversations I have had with women over the past several years. I have wanted to know why so few women write natural history. Men certainly have no corner on curiosity or devotion to language and landscape. I would wager that women more consistently keep journals than men. Fine female novelists and poets seem to have no more trouble than men seeing their books into print.

The only explanation women have given me for not writing about natural history is that they fear being alone in the landscape. Over and over, they tell me that they feel vulnerable; they fear danger–not from the land, but from men. They fear violence and never quite forget about its most disturbing expression: rape.

Not every woman feels this, of course. There are women mountaineers and Outward Bound instructors, naturalists and field scientists. One unsettling thing, however, about the latter category: of the five women field researchers who first occur to me (Dian Fossey, Jane Goodall, Cynthia Moss, Hope Ryden, Joy Adamson), two were murdered in their African camps.

Only a handful of contemporary women writers have focused on the genre of natural history. A few others have written single books chronicling a season on the land, but they have moved on. Of those who have stayed, there is Annie Dillard living at Tinker Creek, pondering solar eclipses, traveling to the Galapagos; Ann Zwinger running Southwestern rivers and hiking the deserts; Sue Hubbell beekeeping on an Ozark farm; Gretel Ehrlich cowboying in Wyoming; Terry Tempest Williams exploring the shores of the Great Salt Lake; Diane Ackerman journeying into the mechanics and poetry of our senses; and Ann LaBastille building herself a cabin in the Adirondacks.

One female friend suggests that women have depended on men for protection for so many thousands of years that there is a real evolutionary thread to the uneasiness solitude brings to women. She suspects a built-in physiological assumption that security can mean only that male warriors stand nearby with spears, keeping their women and babies safe from intruding tribes or predators.

More recently, many women may have had to sneak in writing around the edges of their other obligations. They could more easily find solitude after the kids were asleep, sitting at the kitchen table, than on an afternoon ramble through the woods. Such a difference would generate more pieces of fiction than nature essays.

And so I am left without clear answers, troubled by the fear women express to me. They avoid situations where they feel at risk. The vulnerability that comes from being a woman seems a constant, a given. I feel safer on a rocky ledge halfway up a mountain in the middle of nowhere than I do parking on a dark street in San Francisco to dine in a fine restaurant. But I am a man, and I am not sure men can understand this difference successfully.

III

In 1987, I married again. This one will last.

My wife, Joanne, cares deeply for the land. We walk and run rivers and camp together in the great spaces of the West. With her, another way of relating to the land becomes real. I am only beginning to understand it.

She both enhances and distracts from what I see alone. In solitude, working with my journal, sensory impressions turn directly into writing, a more formal response to experience.

Joanne asks questions and enthuses; we talk. In striving to articulate what we feel, how each of us reacts to the land, we use language earlier than I would alone to recreate the feel of light on sandstone or the smell of cliffrose. In some ways, I use up the words by sharing the experience; alone, I hoard them for my journal. Talking with the woman I love about the places we pass through makes the experiences warmer, simpler. The landscape becomes a part of everyday life, and I have trouble separating from it sufficiently to describe it as a writer.

At the same time, Joanne sees what I do not. She points out details I would miss. She questions things I take for granted; interested though untrained in natural history, she asks about birds and behavior and ecological patterns in an observant way that demands clarity and understanding in order to answer. She makes me think beyond where I might have stopped.

On the Black Rock Desert, we took turns leaving each other. One of us would step out of the vehicle with no gear—no pack, no camera, no water bottle—and simply stand there in T-shirt, shorts, and thongs, with the silence ringing in our ears, while the other drove out of sight. Each of us had a few minutes alone, turning in circles, trying to orient ourselves in the endless miles of barren clay—a near-impossible task. The disorientation was stunning; it was delightful.

When Joanne drove back, the distinction between aloneness and sharing overwhelmed me. The difference was palpable, though both can bring joy.

And now we have a daughter, just over a year old as I write this. When we hike with Dory, she rides in my backpack with her gurgles and small, singing sounds of delight only a few inches from my ears. She tugs at my hat, grabs for my glasses, trickles graham cracker crumbs into the neck of my shirt, and cranes her head around to look when I stop.

My relationship to the land was elemental when I was alone; walking with Carlos connected me to other animals in an embracing way. With Joanne, a powerful human connection goes with us up the trail. And with Dory, I return to an old and elemental connection again, but a different one. I walk up the mountain, and she sleeps on my back. I carry through the landscape the feeling of *family* that I would have carried while migrating into North America along the ice sheets or crossing desert land in Africa, looking for new country.

Having this daughter on my back gives me a sense of fragility and mortality I never had in the days when I always hiked alone. I walk more carefully, both when I carry her and when by myself, for there is so much to lose to a misstep. I feel vulnerable in a new way. My sense of time changed forever when Dory was born. People on the trail ask, "How old is she?" Up to about ten weeks, I changed my answer every few days. Once the answer could be calculated in months, I could let two weeks go by without marking the passage. But, oh, how different the passage of these weeks and months has felt with this living clock in our lives. Wilderness time—the kind that slows when you hike for several days, the past and the future fading, until you live exclusively in the present—will never slow quite as much again.

Her birth transformed my parents and Joanne's mother from parents to grandparents in the moment she slipped from Joanne into my hands. Our only surviving grandparent, Joanne's Grandma Rose, died just four months after Dory's birth. The generations all bumped up a notch. We all moved a little closer toward death.

When Dory was about six months old—and I was more aware of life and death than ever before—Carlos began to fail. Organ after organ slowed until his liver gave out, and he stopped eating. I talked with the vet, who gave him only a couple of days on his own. Carlos maintained his dignity throughout his life, and I felt he should die with dignity. I made an appointment; the vet's secretary entered in her book, "Carlos: euthanasia." I took Carlos home for one last night curled at the foot of our bed.

The next morning I looked into the brown eyes of my dog, said good-bye, and carried him in from the truck to the vet, to his death. He was weak and old, barely able to walk out the back door that morning to turn the snow yellow one last time. As rickety as he was, in my arms he still felt like Carlos, still my familiar friend of so many years.

The doctor injected him with the jolt of barbiturates that relaxed him so fast neither Carlos nor I had much time to think about it. One moment he lay on the table, alive. The next moment he sprawled on the table, dead. We wrapped him in a green plastic garbage bag, and I carried him back out to my truck. He felt warm and limp inside the plastic. He was not the same dog; I understood the meaning of dead weight.

I sobbed as I began the drive out to the desert to find a place to bury him. I was taking him to the Great Basin, the place where we had shared those fine days of solitude. It was the only place I considered. I would not mind being taken out there myself some faraway day.

I drove seventy miles. On the tape deck I played the first Bach cello suite and Beethoven's Ninth Symphony, music that suited Carlos—the first deceptively simple, the second intense but joyful. As I climbed between the Stansbury and Onaqui mountains, I pulled into a turnout near a line of hills overlooking Rush Valley, its sloping basin full of rough, aromatic sagebrush. The East Tintic Mountains, another small grey-blue range, rolled along the southeastern horizon under a high overcast. A front was headed in from the Pacific. I curled Carlos in his garbage bag into the main compartment of my backpack, shouldered it, and walked off into the piñon and juniper trees through calf-deep snow.

Carlos inside my pack? What an odd thought. I climbed a ridge, using my shovel as a walking stick, found an anonymous clearing between the little conifers, lay the royal blue pack on the white snow, and began digging a hole. The soil was rocky, full of cobbles eroded from the mountains in winter, washed down in summer flash floods to skirt the Stansburys with alluvium. I moved rocks, cut through roots, but did not dig deep.

At the bottom of the hole I put a small photo of Carlos with me and our old truck, a Zuni bear fetish carved with a heartline, and a chocolate chip cookie my mother had sent us at Christmas—Carlos's favorite treat. Then I opened the pack and poured Carlos in a limp curl from his garbage bag. He was still warm. I tucked his teeth under his lips and moved his paws to a comfortable position. I stood back from the grave and leaned on the shovel.

I looked up at the horizon. I had done my crying. Carlos had had a good life. This was the end of a time in my own life that had included more time alone, more time shared just with my dog, than I would ever have again. Family had ended my solitude; Dory was growing; time was ticking away.

I covered Carlos with stones, then shoveled earth back over his grave. It was deep enough to cover him but not deep enough to keep Coyote away. That seemed appropriate.

My pack felt unnaturally light when I walked back to the truck. I was drained. I drove home. Joanne was out of town. I picked Dory up from the babysitter; I could feel my life ceaselessly pushing ahead, curving into the future.

That night, the front blew through and left a foot of fresh snow in northern Utah, softening the mountains, the silent basins, and Carlos's grave with a clean, crystalline shroud.

Carlos's burial was something he and I shared with the desert, and with no one else, just as we shared those years of hiking together. His death ended a time in my life when "we" meant me and my dog, a simple time that I will not have again.

The new "we" in my life includes my wife and my daughter. My life with Joanne and Dory has the land in it, and our sharing of that is brand-new; I am still learning what it means.

Now, I make choices about what, and who, to take with me to the land. When I need to fill my journal with what I call "events," the raw material I mine for natural history essays, I go alone. I never again will go alone in the way I once did, however; I now take with me more than ever before, a sense of family and generational connection.

"How alone do you feel in the wilderness?" Not alone at all, no matter how alone I am. "How old is your daughter?" Let's see, this week she is fourteen months. Next week she will pass fourteen and a half months, so I must change my answer to fifteen months. And each time I work on this piece of writing, I must decide whether or not to change those numbers to keep them current.

It is the end of summer—almost the equinox. The seasons cycle, the earth spins, time wheels by. I walk down from a glacial basin high in the Wasatch Range, through aspen forest, warm sun, cool air. Joanne is ahead, with friends. I walk along alone—except for a small, banana-smeared hand on my shoulder giving me a pat. And a coo in my ear, singing me down the mountain.

The Afterlife

RICK BASS

In the summer, our friends from the city come to visit. They stay in the guest cabin, which is decorated with the heads of African animals, African relics—tribal masks, grass skirts, peace pipes. The man who owns the ranch lives in Florida, far away—the tail end of Florida, as far from northwestern Montana as you can get and still be in this country. He lives at the bottom of Florida, and this ranch is his playtoy. He wants us to take care of it while he is gone. He is an old man and has had to leave the ranch. He may never be back. It is for sale for half a million dollars, but there is no electricity—only generators, and kerosene lamps at night, for reading.

Night comes late, in the summer—around 11:30. The northern lights shimmer. We sleep with the windows open, and without a sheet. We're up early—it gets light again around 4:30 or 5:00 in the morning.

It's cold downstairs, in the morning. Elizabeth makes coffee on the wood stove. Elizabeth is a good cook and likes to cook, and by the time our friends are stirring–smoke beginning to drift from their chimney, or maybe one of them walking around with a camera, taking pictures of the old barn or the meadow, which is full of deer in the mornings, or of the mountains beyond (still with snow on them, always, up high) –7:30, 8:00–Elizabeth will have the full breakfast ready: grits made with half-and-half, hash browns, fried eggs, sausage, orange juice, huckleberry pancakes.

We eat at the picnic table in the backyard, and spread huckleberry jam over the endpiece from the loaf of bread Elizabeth has just pulled from the stove and slide butter over it, mixing it in with the purple jam. We split the crunchy endpiece four ways–Tim, and Lorraine, and Elizabeth, and me.

The dogs skulk around the corners of the table, underneath, snapping at crumbs. The sun is up over the trees by 8:00, and fierce in our eyes, but only just beginning to grow warm. The old man lived up here for thirty years. He is probably not coming back.

"I want to see the moose," says Lorraine. She's expecting a child in January. I wonder if the sun feels good on her stomach. I imagine that it does.

The orange juice is cold, and makes a good sound when Elizabeth pours it into our glasses, filling them back up. I used to eat this much all the time when I was younger.

Tim looks at the woods behind the house: at the trail leading in. The woods look dark, from where we are sitting, but once you are into them, you'd be surprised at the light. It's all vertical light, all coming straight down through the tops of the trees, but it's light nonetheless, such as you might find in a cathedral, coming in through the high stained-glass windows.

"Are there bears in those woods?" Tim asks.

"They say that there are," I tell him, which is the truth, though I have seen only one.

"Good," says Tim, my agent, staring at the woods. When he calls me on the shortwave from New York, I can hear the sound of taxicabs, horns honking, coming over the radio. His office is four stories above the street, above Fifth Avenue, but it sounds as if he is standing waist-deep in traffic, standing out in the middle of an intersection.

There's no sound as we eat our breakfast. There's no traffic on the gravel road that goes past the ranch, nor will there be all day. It's summer, and dry, too dry for logging, too dry for anything. The air is as still as it always is in this valley. We haven't cut the yard since we moved up here (the old man is still in Florida); there are daisies all around us. Lorraine slips her sandals off, wriggles her toes in the grass, picks a daisy with her toe and lifts it up to Tim.

"I can't eat any more," she says, getting up and gathering plates. "I'll get the dishes."

"Like fun you will," says Elizabeth. "Go on. Walk. Shoo." Tim and I do the dishes. I ask him if he wants a boy or a girl. "It doesn't matter to me," he says.

They're here for a week, maybe longer. There's nothing to do, there's everything to do. Tim puts on running shoes and later in the morning takes off down the road, disappearing around the bend. Lorraine sits out on the front porch with her feet up on the railing and reads, pausing between pages sometimes to look out at the meadow. Elizabeth is painting silk scarves, which she has stretched out on frames in the backyard—cobalt blues, lightning-strike yellows, and pinks, and underwater sea greens—and after she paints them, she tacks them to the barn to dry, the way settlers did with animal hides a hundred years ago.

The valley has changed, but only a little. You could not find this valley. Even if you could spot it on the map, you would not be able to find it. You have to get lost, to find this valley. Radio stations can't even make it to this valley.

"What's the weather going to do?" Tim asks when he gets back, sweating, glistening, puffing. He's been gone a long time.

"I don't know," I tell him, looking at the sky. It's all we can do: guess. "It'll probably pretty much stay the same," I tell him.

Lorraine has a movie camera, and she is bored with her paperback. The moose has come down out of the woods and into the backyard, to the salt lick, and is watching Elizabeth paint, as he always does, and he is eyeing the strange new car in the driveway, Tim's and Lorraine's old yellow Volvo: and he's eyeing Lorraine, too, as she takes small steps in his direction, filming him, watching him through the viewfinder. Lorraine's watching him watch her.

Lorraine is wearing her navy sweatpants and big baggy white T-shirt and trying to sneak up on the moose, a bull with huge velvet antlers, and she's walking like the Pink Panther, slinking—one foot in front of the other, taking long, slow steps. The moose is just watching her. There is a point where Lorraine could get so close that the moose would become disturbed, thinking she is after his salt lick, but that point is very close to him—five, six yards— and I do not think Lorraine will get that close.

The moose is quite shy, and almost always runs away from us, rather than at us, when we get too close with our still cameras. He's used to us, and hardly every charges any more.

"Careful, Lorraine," says Elizabeth.

The moose is as large as a small elephant, weighing maybe two thousand pounds. Huge patches of fur are falling out of his hide from where he's been rubbing against trees. There is a mist-cloud of gnats around his head, which is not the best thing in the world for his temper. Tim watches nervously, wanting to call Lorraine back, but not wanting to, I think, because she is an eighties woman, and Tim is nothing if not a chauvinist. But he's worried, and so am I.

Lorraine stops when she is about ten yards from the moose, still filming, and finally he puts his head down, gives a few loud slurps to the salt lick, and then turns and stumbles, as if plagued, back into the woods.

When she turns back to face us, Lorraine is radiant, beaming. She is holding the camera against her cheek as if it is a toy. She does a little dance, and then comes over to look at the scarf Elizabeth is painting.

"Tim," she says, "did you see the moose?"

"I did," Tim says. "Why don't you hand me the camera and let me go put it up? Why don't you sit down for a while?"

"I want to film something else," Lorraine says. She looks around, and then focuses on Tim, and starts walking toward him in that same loopy, slinking walk.

"Say something, Tim," she says.

"Something, Tim," he says, covering his face with his arms, all elbows and hands, but Lorraine keeps advancing. Film is cheap.

"Dance," she says. "*Do* something."

There's plenty of film. She can film grass growing, if she wants. There's nothing but time, and they've got boxes and boxes of film. I go out to the greenhouse to work on the novel. I'm too full to bother with lunch; we all are. We'll eat again when we get hungry.

"I want some ice cream," Lorraine says that evening. We're playing an album they brought, a house-warming gift, some kind of Italian music, opera in the wilderness. The sun is low over the mountains, and it's twilight, but it's still a long, long time before darkness.

"No stores," says Tim. "No restaurants. This isn't New York."

"But I want ice cream," says Lorraine. She's pretending to pout, pretending to be cross. Tim is sitting on the couch, thumbing through a magazine.

Soon, we are taking turns grinding on the churn–rock salt and ice, and cream and sugar poured into the bucket; cranking, with the turns becoming harder and harder as the ice cream forms.

"Throw some of these peaches in there," Elizabeth says, handing us a bowl of cut-up peach halves.

Later, we sit out on the porch, stupefied with food, with pleasure, and watch the elk come cautiously out into the meadow. The bulls' antlers are in velvet, and they don't feel like fighting, don't feel like doing anything but grazing in the summer twilight: getting fat, for when lean times come–because for the elk, for the wild animals, they will be coming.

"Is this what it's like all the time?" Lorraine asks.

"In the summer, it is," says Elizabeth. "We'll go up to a lake tomorrow–a lake in the mountains, where you can catch a fish on your first cast."

"Yes," says Lorraine.

We go a whole day without speaking of books, or of writing.

The old man is not coming back.

Our neighbor two miles down the road, Winnie, owns sled dogs, varying crosses of Huskies and Malamutes. All sled dogs are exuberant, slightly loopy, and live for only one reason–to pull sleds.

They've got some biological compass in their heads, I think, some internal motor, that pulls them back to the North Pole, and so when she's not running them, Winnie has to keep them chained (big chains) to trees in her yard–she gives them about fifty feet of chain, tying each dog to one of the big trees in her yard. But the dogs don't use all of this length. Instead, they just lie around in the shadows on the summer pine needles and shed their heavy coats, and try to stay cool. They pant, sip water daintily, and wait to be harnessed so they can pull something, so they can race. Several people up here own sled dogs, and it's nothing to look out the window and see one that has escaped, trotting up the road, heading to Alaska, or farther, even if it wasn't born there. They are more wild than tame.

It's hard to explain how much they love to pull sleds. Anything I say will sound patronizing, or worse; it will sound like the landowner saying of his slaves, "These people *love* to work." And for those who will not believe it, or who cannot believe it, nothing I can say would change your mind–nothing but the sight of the whole yapping, leaping team going berserk when Winnie pulls their sled out of the garage.

The sled, in summer, is more of a go-cart–it's an iron frame mounted above big rubber tires, with rudder-steering foot pedals and a seat for the driver, and a platform behind the driver where one or two brakemen can stand and apply the brakes if the sled gets going too fast.

Winnie's sled dogs have a lot of wolf in them–so much wolf, in fact, that they can't bark, but instead can only howl–but the dog in them, the tamed part, instructs them to bark when they are excited–when they see that sled being hauled out of the barn–and so what fills the air is a hoarse sort of hissing sound, and the sound of teeth snapping–the dogs leaping about on their hind legs and trying to yelp, trying to bark, but physically unable to–this seeming to only further fuel their frenzy, their unbearable wait for Winnie to hook them into their harnesses; and they're small dogs, racing dogs–forty-five pounds, average–but they're much too strong for Tim and me to handle, not being used to them, and so in the darkness, with flashlights, we stand and watch Winnie hook the dogs into their places along the sled line. We were up at four, drinking coffee, and it's 4:45 now, and cold, below freezing. These mountains.

Every dog wants to be the lead dog–the one out in front, with all the other matched pairs running in tandem–three pairs behind the lead dog–and it's all Winnie can do, gripping each dog's collar with both hands, to keep it from dragging her up to that lead spot. Each dog leaps and porpoises, struggling to break free and lunge for that lead spot, or *any* spot–understanding, I think, that Winnie is doing her best to put the dog there, but simply unable to wait–even if the dog's life depended upon restraint, unable to restrain itself–and finally, through muscle and skill, Winnie has the front and rear snaps clipped in place, and the dog is bound, harnessed, but is still hissing and lunging, trying to pull the sled: but Winnie has the sled chained to a big tree, and it's not going anywhere.

She leaves that dog and goes to get another one.

In the summer, this is the only time Winnie can run the dogs–right before daylight–or else they get too hot and suffer heat strokes and end up being even more demented than they already are. They run best at or below zero degrees; this thirty-degree stuff is borderline for them, but Winnie knows we have guests, guests from the city, and also, she likes to run the dogs a little bit, during the summer; it's simply too sad to bear, spending an entire three months watching them watch that barn, waiting for the sled to come rolling out–three months of watching–and so we set the alarm for four, fixed a thermos of coffee, put on our long underwear, heavy coats, mufflers, and gloves (coming down the hills, the dogs hit forty, forty-five miles an hour, dropping the wind chill to near zero)—and we watch, and Winnie finally gets the dogs all lined up—Lightning, the smallest but fastest, in the lead, and male-female pairs behind her—Yodkin, Yukie, Griz, Arthur, Sally, and Elk, who is my favorite, a tag-eared, scarred (the males fight like savages, for dominance), reddish blood-colored eleven-year-old veteran who once ran in the Iditarod—1,100 miles!—and the cart can only hold three of us, so Elizabeth will wait behind.

Lorraine will sit down low, in the driver's seat, right behind the dogs, and work the reins, and Tim and I will ride standing behind her, shouting "mush," and work the foot brakes when we get going too fast down the mountain slopes; on the steepest of hills, the cart can outrun the dog team, and locked into their harnesses the way they are, the dogs are helpless to escape it—they'll try and scatter in all directions, trying to dodge it, but it follows them, what was once their joy is now their pursuer (they've been known to leap off cliffs, trying to elude a runaway cart)—and they can tell by a sudden slackening in the line when this is about to happen.

These are things that Tim should know, that Lorraine should know, before they get on the sled, but there simply isn't time, the dogs are going absolutely bonkers, they're going to injure themselves, leaping and lunging with all their might—the sled's chained and locked to a big larch tree, but still, they're shaking the tree, causing twigs and needles to come drifting down—and Winnie has to turn them loose now or risk ruining their spirit. Tim, looking down at the swarming, surging backs of the hissing animals, barely has time to laugh and say to Lorraine, "This is craz . . ." and then Winnie unlocks the chain, and our heads snap back, it's as if we've been fired from a cannon: the wind is hard in our faces.

There's no barking, just the high speed hum of the wheels down the gravel road; they're just running, we're around the bend already and plunging down the hill, and the sun is beginning to show through the trees, and we are being carried away by wolves.

I'm white-knuckled and crouching low, because the dogs have never gone this fast before, and I'm not wearing a crash helmet, no kneepads, or anything—but Tim's standing straight up and shouting some sort of "Ya-hoo!" sounds into the wind. Our eyes blur because of the speed, the cold, the wind, and the dogs ahead of us are like a wave, we're riding a chariot, they're flowing, and the woods are racing by. Lorraine, I can tell, is sitting hunched up tight, and has her eyes closed. We're out of control, already, and wild dogs have our destiny.

After a couple of quick miles, the dogs stop for a rest at the top of Bunker Hill Mountain. There's a little spring creek there, a shallow pond with morning rim-ice across it, and panting, they trot out into the pond and lie down in the freezing water to cool off, and that's when I realize it's already time to get them back home, that we may be overheating them. Tim and Lorraine and I are cold, almost shivering, but we live in another world from these creatures.

"Gee" means right, and "Haw" means left. We shout "Haw! Haw!" at them, to turn them around in a half-circle and get them pointed back down the road, back to Winnie's, but they know that home means no more running, and they're reluctant to go in that direction. Yodkin, the biggest dog, harnessed in the middle of the line, keeps trying to turn the other dogs back up the mountain, over to the other side–but finally, we have them untangled, and once they start moving, even though it is in a direction they do not want to go, they can't help themselves, and soon we're rocketing down the mountain.

Tim mans the brake pedal above the right rear tire, and I pump the one over the left rear tire. Lorraine, I think, has her eyes shut again.

It's a long way back down to the bottom of Bunker Hill Mountain; coming up, it was so steep that in some places the dogs had slowed from their steady trot to a walk, and then to a leaping, lunging pull; and to help them, Tim and I got off and ran along behind them–but coming down, of course, there's no such problem, and even standing on the brakes, we seem to be going too fast–and the road's bumpier than we remembered, riddled with potholes and craters.

We hit an especially large one midway down the mountain–it jars all three of us up into the air, and for a moment, the cart is brakeless, reinless, out of control–and a crash is imminent. Tim and I are just hanging on, trying to get our feet beneath us again, and the dogs, understandably panicked, break into a hard left turn, scampering, and leap across a small ditch and try to run up into the heavy timber. We see the trees rushing at us, the dark forest, the boulders, and there is just barely time for fear, for worry–we think, *Lorraine*–and then that's it, the sled rams nose-first into the ditch and flips, rolls sideways, and we're launched from it, landing on each other, the sled's rolling over on top of us, and though the last thing we saw was Lorraine tucking, right before the wreck, drawing her arms and legs up around her and tucking like a cannonball, we're still worried. Tim's knee is twisted, his pants legs are torn when he gets up, and my ribs hurt–and we're asking Lorraine how she is, the sled's on top of her, we're lifting it up, and she's dazed–too dazed to feel pain, is my fear at first– but she stands, Tim helping her carefully to her feet, and it turns out she among us is the only one who *is* all right, it's a wild miracle, a cold frosty morning, the sun full up now, and the dogs are sitting up in the woods with their harness scattered and stretched around various limbs, as far up into the woods as they can reach, still attached to the sled, and they're watching us with alarm, still panting.

I leave Tim with Lorraine and the bent frame of the sled and the frightened dogs, and I limp down the road to get the truck. It is not yet quite six o'clock in the morning.

The way you catch trout at Rainbow Lake is to float for them. It's a deep mountain lake, like a crater, with a mat of floating peat moss growing all around it so that you cannot stand at its side and cast into it–you'd fall through the bed of floating peat up to your waist as if in quicksand–and also, beyond the perimeter of peat, there is another, smaller, concentric ring of water lilies, through which you cannot retrieve your spinner, and your dry flies and nymphs get stuck on the lily pads.

You've got to float it. There are no woods, no footpaths–just a steep game trail leading down through the forest. You have to carry your canoe over your head–shoulders cramping, tripping, stumbling, toward the lake, which is sometimes visible, far away, as a glimmer of blue through the trees. Does, with their summer fawns, bound back and forth across the trail ahead of you, and grouse hurry ahead of you, not understanding enough to run left or right into the woods, but merely running ahead of you, certain that you are chasing them. And all the while, as you struggle to bring the canoe down to the lake–a thirty-minute portage–you're wondering, not "Is the fishing going to be good?" but rather, "How are we going to get this back up to the top?"–for it is like a crater, the lake is in a bowl, ringed by mountains, a bowl into which all water drains, and the fishing is good, very good, out in the center, but like the valley itself, like an afterlife, it's very hard to get to.

We can fit three in the canoe, but there's more room for casting, more room for fishing, with just two. "You go, Tim," says Lorraine. Out in the middle, the trout are splashing, leaping at mayflies that hover over the lake's center like a mist. True love: Lorraine watches us push off, poling through the moss, and then out into open water–cold water, clean water, and Tim and I watch a trout take the bright spinner, some ten feet underwater, on Tim's first cast. The rod bows, the line's tight, and Tim's struggling to bring the leaping trout in, a green speckled cutthroat, the orange-red banding beneath its gills like a collar, savage-toothed, big-eyed–Tim's first fish ever, and Lorraine shrieks.

"Y'all can come on in now," says Elizabeth. They've brought their books to read, but there won't be much book-reading today, and there never is, at Rainbow Lake. The fish aren't huge–two pounds is a big fish, and most of them average only a little over a pound–about the size of our largest skillet–but there are too many of them, and it's a good place to get meat.

We catch some for supper and some to smoke and put in the freezer. Toward dusk, a bull moose comes down to the lake and wades out through the chest-high peat and begins grazing on the lily pads. Elizabeth and I are in the canoe, and we paddle over as close as we dare–twenty, twenty-five yards–and float there, watching him–his huge antlers in summer velvet–and we take a few pictures, and then, the thing that the afternoon of warm sun and mild wind and cold water, cold fish, had been able to banish–the thought of the return trip, up through the woods, with the ponderous canoe aloft–finally comes back to mind, to memory. I have made the trip before, and it *can* be done–and the sun is behind the high mountains, an orange glow along the rim to the west, and we paddle back to the meadow, where Tim and Lorraine are waiting.

At the other end of the meadow, a fawn is trying to engage her mother in a game of tag–the doe down at water's edge, knee-deep in peat, drinking, while the fawn races around in circles, leaps and twists, bolts, jags, darts–this is a fawn that needs a twin, a brother or sister–and Lorraine does not want to go, she wants to sit and watch the fawn, but the woods are growing dark, and the feeling is that we've been blessed with this unbelievable bounty of fish, that this day and its stillness, and warmth, was sort of a theft–up in the mountains, and in the woods all around us, coyotes are beginning to laugh and yap–and so, strangely–though this is how it always is–Tim and I suddenly find that we have the energy, that we are *anxious* to muscle the boat up the long steep game trail, and we do so, carrying it over our heads like an offering, stopping to rest often, while Elizabeth and Lorraine, behind us in case a bear charges, carry the big stringers of fish, which have been well-photographed, well-documented, by Lorraine's little pocket camera.

In a week or so, Tim will be going back, but I will not be going back, and could not, even if I wished: I could no more go back than could a dead man come back to life, and like the dead, I think, I have no desire to. It was nice, but all a long time ago, living in the city the way I did–the way Tim does–and this is what I was waiting for, this has it all beat, this is like nothing I've ever seen.

Lorraine goes out to the garden with a flashlight, once we're back home, and cuts some dill, some chives, and with sour cream and mayonnaise makes a sauce for the fish—I'm cleaning them in the sink, simple—one cut, they're all stomach, eating machines, it all comes out with one cut—and we grill them on a fire in the backyard with the moon high above us, bottles of wine opened.

We sit out at the picnic table with a kerosene lantern and heavy jackets and eat the fish, spoon the garden's sauce over them, and it's been a long day, we took it by the heels and carried it home with us, it's a prize we found in the woods, it will fall away into tomorrow, and then into the day after that.

Some mornings I wake up wanting a baby—boy or girl, no matter. Maybe in a year or two. We've been saying that for many years. It's a push and pull, an ocean sort of thing. You can't tell Lorraine's pregnant yet, by looking. But she is. It's in her. Riding around on the dog sled, catching fish in the mountain lake; these are the last things Lorraine will ever do before becoming a mother, the last things she will ever do, childless; but when the child is born, everything will start new, and whatever she does, it will be for the first time as a parent, as a mother. It's the end of one life, but the beginning of another. Nature rolls past, and I want to be in the middle of it, be part of it, wallow in its sweetness and freshness and then decadence; I want to be carried away, swept along with it; I do not want to stand separate from it, living out my cells in a city.

My cells shout to roll in the leaves, to hike down the creek, to sleep outside at night, to set the hook in fish, to catch them, land them, clean them, and eat them; to gasp, and go on.

When I think of a city, I think of buildings, and of concrete. I think that the world—the tiny world of man—is undergoing some tiny reversal, some flip-flop inside its destiny—and that for a while, the peasants, the worker-class, used to be the tools of the rich, the tools of the idle, the force of labor upon which the wealth of the world has been made—but now I think of people in cities as worker ants, who provide me, the peasant, with services.

I go in for the necessary items—photocopies, groceries, dental work—and provide them with paper, dollar bills, with which they build their lives and continue to produce the things I need.

The Kootenai National Forest surrounds us, swallows our sixty-one-acre ranch with its two million acres, we're in its middle, and hidden so well—and there are a couple of abandoned fire lookout towers in the forest, on top of the two highest peaks–Mount Henry and Mount Baldy–towers that rise on sturdy legs into the high winds fifty or sixty feet above the dome-rock tops of these two mountains–Mount Baldy especially bare-rocked–and from Baldy, you can see Idaho, Canada, and Montana in all directions. Glacier National Park, a hundred miles back to the east, looks like someone's backyard.

The fire towers are like lighthouses–surrounded by glass, 360° of glass, and with two cots, a little wood stove, a gas range, a refrigerator, and a sextant in the center of the room for locating fires, with a topographic map pasted to it. Forget computers, graphics, and laser readouts; this is how it was done in the 1930s, and the 1940s, when the towers were built, and for twenty-five dollars a night you can rent the lookout, the highest point in the Purcell Mountains, and you can throw a party, you can light the little hissing propane lanterns and go out on the narrow catwalk deck (with protective guardrails) and dance all night if you wish, a million miles from nowhere; or you can turn all the lights off and sit with your feet dangling over the edge, and sway in the wind, creak and sway, and except for the fact that the stars are all around you, that you're up among them–stars in your hair, stars brushing your wrist–it's hard, sometimes, to tell if you're in the mountains or at sea.

But I am ahead of myself. You want to get there well ahead of dark–around noon or one o'clock, say, while the sun is still climbing and the grass is shimmering, blowing in the forever-wind that sweeps across the top of the mountain–tall grass, through which grouse run back and forth, running in the warmth, and in which deer with their fawns lie, resting, napping–and you can hike in any direction, but it's downhill all the way, and most people are inclined to just stay up top, in the meadow, or up in the tower, and have picnics, or read, or write in the logbook–you'd be amazed at the length of some of the rainy-day entries–and you can sit up on the deck in the sun and drink a beer, and with binoculars watch black bears, glinting like coal in the sun, on far-off hillsides, rooting through old logs for grubs. Sometimes, back in the woods, you can see elk moving. What a place to drink beer!

We didn't get to the lookout tower until close to dusk; we'd been over in the neighboring Cabinet Mountains all day, fly-fishing (nowhere near the luck we had at Rainbow, but it was fun, wading in the river, like a bear, feeling its shudder, being part of the river, like a bear) and we unloaded our sleeping bags and duffel bags, groceries, carrying them up the steep spiral of five flights of stairs–1930s stairs, straight up–and we left the dogs, Homer and Ann, playing in the meadow below.

It has been said many times that there is one sound in nature that you know immediately, instinctively, even if you have never heard it before—the buzz of an agitated rattlesnake—and it's true, you *do* know that one, when you are in rattlesnake country, even that first time—but to this I would like to add a second sound: the sound of your dogs crying and screaming and yelping after biting a porcupine, after being slapped in the face by the porcupine's tail.

I had yet to see a porcupine up in these mountains, but I knew, rushing down the steps—flying down the steps—that that was exactly what it was. I reached the bottom and ran across the meadow in the dusk, calling their names, calling them off—not that they needed any persuasion—such a shrill, frantic, helpless yelp, and pain—my heart was in my throat, even higher, I tripped and stumbled, running so fast—and Homer came out of the brush first, with quills all around her snout—a lot, I thought, at first (I was to find out what a lot was)—and then she turned and ran back into the bushes, more ashamed, I think—knowing she'd done something wrong, big wrong—but I ran after her and caught her by the collar, to keep her from running clear to Canada in her panic—and then I saw Ann, who was trying to stagger over to me, or rather, to the sound of my voice—pawing at her face, sliding on her face, trying to pull quills out, and worse than the shrill yelps, silent now, except for a heartbreaking, breathless panting—panting, I thought, like a woman giving birth, certain that the pain cannot last another moment, and yet it does, and does—and when I got close enough to grab her collar too, I couldn't see her face—there was nothing there but quills. It was one of the most monstrous, shocking things I've ever seen.

A thousand? Five thousand? How many quills can you fit in the face of a big-headed dog?

Elizabeth, followed by Tim and Lorraine, came running down the hill; I was already pulling quills, there was simply nothing else to do. Ann kept trying to run off, making that horrible, frantic wheezing, that hyperventilating panting, and I gave Homer to Elizabeth, and ran and caught Ann. I would say that Homer probably only had about a hundred quills in her.

But Ann! She was choking and gagging, she had them all in her tongue and gums, in the roof of her mouth—so many that she couldn't even close her mouth, and each time she did, she drove them into her mouth again, she was drooling blood and saliva—and Lorraine and Tim held her; there was nothing to do but to start pulling quills.

It was two hours to a vet, but the pain was here and now; there was nothing to do but to pull quills. Lorraine kept closing her eyes and blacking out; fainting, almost, then coming to again—all that blood—

and sitting back up and helping hold Ann, who was whimpering–and we kept telling her, "Lorraine, you take it easy, you'd better not look, you'd better go lie down"–but Lorraine kept coming back and helping hold Ann down–Ann thrashing, stabbing our hands with the quills each time she gasped–and seeing Tim look at all the blood over my hands, my arms–Tim, the good father, looking with concern–not concern for Ann, but for his wife, his child, started to say something, but I interrupted, told him, "It's okay, it's dog blood"–and the relief on his face was something, despite the horror and the trauma, that I still remember.

There were quills deep in Ann's nose, buried an inch, two inches deep. Elizabeth had Homer cleaned up pretty quickly, but we hadn't even begun with Ann; Elizabeth turned Homer loose so that Elizabeth could run back to the truck and get a pair of pliers. Some of the quills simply were not going to come out, not at all. We pulled as hard as we could, but they wouldn't budge–and Homer the madman, Homer the mental case, ran back into the bushes after the porcupine, furious–Tim lunged and grabbed her, caught her by the hind leg, just in time–and Lorraine was sweet-talking Ann, telling her how brave she was, but unable to pet her–still too many quills, all over her face and head–and I remember, the way I remember Tim's look of relief, the way Ann was whimpering but wagging her tail too, while Lorraine was telling her what a brave girl she was.

So much blood! There was barely enough light to see; the sun was long ago down behind the other mountains, and there was nowhere to go, nothing to do but pull quills, and prop Lorraine up every time she fell back and fainted.

The quills in Ann's tongue came out the easiest. Those right below her eyes, and in the end of her nose– and those in the gums, between the teeth, were the hardest to get.

The pliers wouldn't grip them–the quills were too flat, too narrow. I started pulling them with my teeth–putting my face right up against Ann's, staring her eye-to-eye, as animals must do in death-combat–the wolf's teeth and the deer's throat–and I pulled them savagely, because that was the only way they would come out–and Ann was trembling, Tim and Lorraine were trembling, and so was Elizabeth.

I was too frantic to be trembling. It helps, having something to do, in a trauma. There was nothing for me to do but pull quills. Ann's face was puffy and swollen, and she was going into shock–so much pain, each time I pulled one, and I just kept pulling, and pulling–and Lorraine kept talking to her, we all did, trying to keep her from going under into shock, to that place where she could perhaps hear our voices but no longer cared. We tried to keep her on the surface. Homer whined, and tried to get closer to lick Ann.

The old *Boy's Life* horror stories, and the Jack London tales, of the quills working their way into the dog's brain and killing it, madly; it wasn't enough to get most of the quills out, it wasn't enough to get all but one or two out–each was a bullet, each one the possibility of death. We picked by flashlight for an hour and a half; the moon came up, and Elizabeth put a jacket over Ann, who was not wagging her tail, who was not doing anything–she was just lying there, sadly–as if long ago having decided that this was how the rest of her life would be–and around nine o'clock I thought I had them all pulled, so we carried the dogs up the hill to where the truck was parked and loaded them in, and I took off down the mountain, driving hard, too hard, gunning through the gears and sliding on gravel in the switchbacks, plunging down the mountain–but it was different from trembling, because I was *doing* something.

Tim and Lorraine and Elizabeth had to climb the stairs to the lookout tower, and go up there and fix supper, and maybe try to play a game of Scrabble, a hand of cards, and mostly just wait.

Clouds were beginning to blow over the moon, moving past it quickly, streaming across it, the worst of omens, the worst of feelings, and a few big drops of rain began to splatter against the windshield. Lightning cracked through the trees, farther down the mountain, and I worried about the lookout tower, the highest point for a hundred miles or farther. It has been there for sixty years, and there had been summer lightning storms before, thousands of them–and it had a flimsy-looking lightning rod–but still, I worried.

Homer sat in the front seat, with her head against my shoulder, bouncing, as we flew across the rocks. Ann lay on the floorboard, not blinking, not doing anything; she was in shock, and there was nothing I could do about it. I talked to her as I drove, kept the heater on, and asked the time-honored question, "Are you hungry?" but got no response from either of them. I resolved that if they survived, I would–that very night–buy them both a pound, two pounds, of ground sirloin.

I finally got down off the mountain–the rain beating against the truck now, and lightning flashing all around me, scorching the road before me in a shimmering white blaze–deer of all sizes, bucks and does, were running back and forth across the road, hurrying to get out of the rain, and each time the lightning flashed, I could see them, caught, for just a moment, in that quick flash of light–the next time the flash hit, they would be gone–and I roared down Pipe Creek Road, toward my friend the vet's home.

I thought Doug would be asleep–although since it was the weekend, it was also possible that he might be sitting up drinking Glenlivet or Glenfiddich and tying trout flies–and I drove as hard and as fast as the slick water-washing roads would allow me. I was driving down a canyon, and lightning was bouncing all around me, and it could have been the end of the world, my dog dying and my girlfriend and agent and his wife being blown out of the sky by lightning–I could see it being one of those nights, the last night of your life–but I had faith in the afterlife, this new life, and I kept driving, and I drove hard.

Doug was writing letters to the editor on his computer when I drove in. I knocked on the screen door with my foot–Ann in my arms like a big heavy doll, staring blankly at nothing–and Doug was cheerful when he answered the door, having gotten off a good zinger for one or another environmental cause–and he wanted me to come take a look at his letter first before taking Ann next door to his office–he looked at Ann the way he might look at a four-year-old who was playing underfoot on Christmas Day, interrupting two grown-ups from what they wanted to talk about–and I knew then that Ann was going to be all right, and I went and looked at his letter, briefly. Sometimes Doug does not mail, does not even print, the letters that he composes when he has been drinking too much Glenfiddich–only on Friday and sometimes Saturday nights–and this was one of those letters.

"Pretty good, eh?" chuckled Doug.

"I wouldn't send it," I said.

"Oh, I know," he said. "I'm not going to send it–it just makes me feel good."

"Well, then," I said, "yes, it's pretty good."

We took Ann in and he listened to her heartbeat, took her temperature–"She's not in bad shock," he said, "just a little shock"–and he gave her an anti-inflammatory shot, a shot of antibiotics, and a "feel-good" shot–she began wagging her tail almost immediately, and I had the thought that those hypodermic needles must have felt ***good***, compared to the quills–and we examined her throat with a periscope-light, and her gums, and under the high-intensity light, on the stainless steel operating table, Doug found two more half-quills that had been broken off, and pulled them with a pair of surgeon's tweezers. I was worried that Ann might have swallowed one or more quills–they had been all over her tongue, all in her mouth, and she'd been gagging and gulping, swallowing, as I tried to pull them free–and Doug said it was unlikely that she'd swallowed any, but that there was nothing we could do anyway, other than put her out right there—anesthesia—and open her stomach up, and look and see.

Doug was weaving a little from the scotch, and he handed me one of the half-quills and said, "Here, try and swallow that yourself, you'll see how hard it really is"—and I did not want to swallow, or even *try* to swallow the quill, and I also did not want Doug to open Ann up and hunt around for quills. I could tell that Doug did not want to do that, either, and that he was positive she'd not been able to swallow any—and so we lifted her down from the table—her eyes bright, tail wagging, and already, it seemed, her balloon-face beginning to subside—and I brought Homer in then, and we checked her carefully, but she was all right, no swelling, no quill-remnants, and the night seemed to be turning, to be more in hand.

"If Ann did swallow a quill. . . ."

"That would be bad," Doug said. "It could be fatal." I could tell he was annoyed with me for still doubting his diagnosis: that it would be virtually impossible for her to swallow a quill. Doug's a good vet, a great one. He practices in this little town, Libby, because he likes to fish. He could work anywhere, could have a better practice. But the fishing's good here.

"The quill would perforate the intestines and stomach, and there'd be peritonitis, infection, as a result. It would be nearly impossible to treat. Or the quill could go through the heart, through the liver—anything it pierced would be bad. But of all the tens of thousands, hundreds of thousands of dogs that have been slapped by porcupines, there've only been one or two recorded instances, in my journals and medical books, of the quills actually being *swallowed*—and they were both large dogs, German shepherds, I think. Just those two cases, Rick, among thousands, among *billions*."

"But Ann's special," I said. "I could very easily—very easily—see her making the record books, in some way." Ann thumped her tail against the wall and looked up at me appreciatively; her long eyelashes fluttered.

"Very well," Doug said then, tersely, making a motion to roll up his sleeves—though he was already wearing a short-sleeved smock, and couldn't seem to figure out where the sleeves had gone—"You want me to operate, then? If I'm going to look, I need to do it right now, for it to be any good."

I looked up at the clock and saw that it was already past eleven-thirty. "You really think it's unlikely that she swallowed any?" I asked again. Doug relaxed and began rolling his imaginary sleeves down—

again, not realizing they weren't there. "*Highly* unlikely," he said. "Come on back in and help me finish off this bottle of Glenliv . . . Glenfiddich."

We could hear the rain beating down on the roof. Both dogs were healthy and wagging their tails. I really wanted to taste that scotch; to sit in the den with Doug and listen to fish stories, to stories about porcupines–to anything and everything Doug had to say, which could be, I knew from the past, considerable, and always interesting–but I realized this was but the first leg of my journey, and that back in the wilderness, stuck up in the sky, among the bolts of lightning, swaying in the wind, were the rest of my responsibilities–my guests, Tim and Lorraine, and Elizabeth–and so I declined that, too–we could have operated on Ann, and then stayed up drinking all night, after sewing her back up–and I thanked Doug profusely, and gathered the dogs up and took them back out to the truck, into the night, in the rain.

I used to run cross-country, in junior high school and then in high school, and in college–and I remembered, then, what it felt like, to be floating, to be going on forever, and I stood out in the rain, trying to remember something. I had felt this way a long time ago, and it seemed, joyfully, the way I might always feel–always defeating trouble, always running past, and away from, danger. Cars and trucks were driving back and forth on the main road out in front of Doug's office, and I could hear the familiar swish-swish sound of their tires on wet pavement, though it had not rained in a long time before this, we were in our third summer of drought, so that it had seemed it would never rain again, that nothing would ever change–the heat baking the woods dry, but now, a rain–and I got in the truck and drove to the grocery store, which was open until midnight. I got there just a few minutes before midnight, and I petted the girls quickly and then hurried inside to buy the ground sirloin I had promised myself I would give them, if they were all right–their reward for surviving.

I trotted down the aisles, down the walkways of dazzling, artificial light–the floors had been scrubbed and waxed spotless, and I was the only customer in the store. It's amazing how much food is really in a grocery store, when you're the only one in there. There's enough to last you a whole lifetime.

The high school boys in their blue jeans and white short-sleeve shirts and green aprons scurried out of my way, looked askance at me. I had a three-day's beard, was wearing my army camouflage pants and a bloody T-shirt–I'd forgotten there was porcupine and dog blood all over me.

Working in the night, and racing through the night, I'd forgotten–but I could feel it on me now, under all the light; and my hair was wild,

I could see that in the reflections of the freezer-glass windows as I hurried down the frozen foods aisle to the back row, where the raw meat was.

I found the package I wanted—three pounds—and hurried back to the cash register with it. It was straight-up midnight.

The boy who was ringing up my purchase was frightened. I had a lot of blood on me, and there wasn't anything to go with that meat—no milk, no eggs, no lettuce, no hamburger buns, nothing—just meat, and I saw the manager, in his sky box booth over at the other end of the store, studying me closely before picking up the phone and dialing a number—but I was out of there, then, I didn't care, I was a trout running for the sea, and I was back into the night.

I fed the dogs there in the parking lot—tossing them handfuls of meat, which they gulped down with savage, wolfish, choking bites—their eyes sparkled with pleasure—and then, like that trout, or a salmon, or like that free-floating, forever gliding boy I knew in high school and in college, I was traveling on forever again, turning back up the canyon, headed back into the woods, to the north, where I could see it was still lightning, still storming. I was tired and dirty, but my dogs were all right.

I stopped at the base of Mount Baldy around two in the morning and rinsed my hands and arms in the high waters of the fast creek, and took my shirt off, threw it in the back of the truck to be rinsed in the still-falling steady rain—the hair on my head, and on my back, kept rising from all the static electricity in the air—the dogs were napping in the front seat, curled up, their heads over each other's shoulders—and I started up the pitching gravel road, gravel turning to slaughterous mud, to the outlook tower; and when I got there, it was still intact, as it had been for all those sixty years.

I climbed up the steep stairs, trotting (having left the dogs in the truck, with the windows cracked), and I hurried across the deck, my every third step illuminated by the sky all around me opening up with lightning, and I eased quickly (amidst the booms and rolls and echoes of summer mountain thunder) through the screen door, and slipped, damply, into bed with Elizabeth, and fell asleep almost immediately, the end of the day's race, with lightning exploding all around me, and the lookout tower swaying in the high winds like an old tree, a nice sway, a giving sway.

In the morning the sun came up orange over the mountains, taking forever, and Lorraine sat up in bed and filmed it, then went back to sleep. We slept until 7:30, at which point the sun was so high in the sky and bright that it was heating up our lookout, and we had to get out of beds and open the windows and step out onto the windy porch, risen for the day. Instant coffee, and bowls of cereal, with bananas and strawberries cut into them. Bacon, splattering. The day was washed clean by the night's storm, and I went down to check on the dogs. I had a chain in the back of the truck, and I used it to tie them to a tree.

Later in the morning, Tim and I went for a walk, looking for game—deer, elk, even bear. We didn't see anything, but it was good high-altitude exercise, especially coming back up the mountain, and when we neared the lookout tower we saw that the dogs were asleep in the sun, with the wind blowing the grasses flat over them, and that Elizabeth and Lorraine were up on the deck, dropping bread crumbs down to a big mule deer buck that was standing right at the base of the tower, looking up at them. The deer did not run away, but watched us, as we climbed the stairs.

"Let's stay another day," said Lorraine. "I want to watch for fires." We lay on our backs and read for a while, swaying in the wind. It didn't feel like the rest of the world was going on, out there. It didn't feel like we were missing a thing.

Back at the ranch, we spent a day—or perhaps it was two days—hiking in the woods behind the house, and fixing large meals—fish, and elaborate salads from the garden, and golden quiches, and big hamburgers, and appetizers, food everywhere—and also, we sat out on the front porch a lot, with our feet up on the railing, leaning back in our chairs, and read, and watched the deer moving like schooners through the tall grass in the meadow across the road. It was exactly as if they were out at sea: some of them would pause and then lie down, sinking back down into the tall blue-tipped grass, and out of sight—but then others, in other parts of the field, would rise, as if to take their places, and begin walking around, almost strutting, in the warm sunlight. I know that the sun had to feel good on their backs, their faces. It was exactly as if they were at sea.

It felt good for me to be walking around in the cabin, and out in the yard; it felt good, to have my feet set firmly on the land, on the earth.

There's a road up here, or what's left of a road, that goes up over Dodge Summit, up on the Canadian line. It's really just a lane through the thick woods, following a rushing creek—to drive it you need a four-wheel drive, and a chain saw or ax, because trees are forever falling across it and blocking the path—and it's supposed to go all the way up over the mountains and come out on the other side, near a big lake, over by Glacier.

This Dodge Summit Road appears, to the foolish, to be a shortcut–only 40 or so miles, instead of the 120 you have to drive, if you take the other road–the only other road–but it's an impassable jungle, and the best anyone's ever done it in–the few who have–is eight hours. One warm morning we decide that we want to set out for a picnic, up in the woods towards Dodge Summit–we don't fool ourselves, we don't have any pretense of believing we can make it all the way through–and as if to prove our lackadaisicality, the whimsy of our trip, we take the oldest car, our old belly-slung-to-the-ground 1970 Ford Falcon–our picnic car.

It's a small, deep, box-like car with a big trunk, and it will carry six people, or four people and two dogs, easily. It's about the size of a Volkswagen, but it has eight cylinders and drinks old-fashioned regular gasoline. It is like an alligator, going down the road–that low to the ground. It has big goggle headlights and bald tires. It's a good enough car for the jungle. We've used it to haul firewood in before, when the trucks are being worked on–simply stuffed the wood into the trunk, and taken out the back seat and loaded it in there, too. It's a workhorse. It doesn't have a very good muffler.

We follow the Yaak River Road for many miles, driving with the windows down, driving on the luxury of old weed-grown pavement, heading north, and then turning east right below the Canadian border (unmarked, save for a ten-yard stripe of felled timber cutting straight across the mountain's face, unwavering–more like a barrier, even if only psychologically, than a goal, the way most borders are–this one in the jungle, so hard to get to, and then nothing different on the other side, nothing, just more of the same), and we follow our little road east, looking for the unmarked opening in the woods, a little tunnel through the trees, that was the old Dodge Summit trail–the one horses and mules used to use back in the 1920s and 1930s, when they found a little gold in this valley.

We follow the river's rush, and sunlight spreads and falls across our windshield, we're driving into the sun, driving slowly, and the river smells good. Homer is sitting up behind the back seat, in the spot where children on long vacations sometimes ride, up against the back windshield, and she has a fly cornered: she's snapping at it furiously, always missing, and Lorraine's filming the battle.

Ann sleeps peacefully in Elizabeth's lap in the front seat. Are there any quills inside her, working their way slowly through her insides, creeping, trying to pierce soft, important parts? It's an unsettling thought. Doug said we might not know for as many as six months–that if we did miss a quill somewhere–and she had even had them stuck down into her shoulders, all around her, like a shawl–it might take six months to make its journey, its passage through her body, but that after the six-month mark, we would be home free, we would know by then whether we had or had not missed any. There's nothing we can do but wait, and hope, and try not to think about it too often.

December–six months–seems like forever away.

Deer run across the road in front of us. Grouse strut and preen along the side of the road, pecking at gravel. Later in the summer the males will be courting ferociously–as ferocious as grouse are capable of becoming–and they'll stand out in the middle of the road with chests puffed out and wings spread, and will try and keep cars and trucks out of their territory–and traffic is slowed, back in the woods, because it's hard to get around one of these angry male grouse–if you get out and try to shoo them off the road, they'll come running, pecking at your ankles–but that's later in the summer, and we're able to drive, following the rushing river up switchbacks and past unmarked scenic lookouts, the twenty or so miles up to the little dirt road turn-off we're searching for–the beginning of the Dodge Summit Road.

Our picnic lunch is not elaborate–peanut-butter-and-honey sandwiches, and cans of fruit juices–no wine, because of Lorraine–and suddenly we find the turn-off road, it takes a steeper pitch like the up-ramp on a roller coaster ride, but we attack the road with enthusiasm and hunger, and we realize, too, suddenly, that yes, we do want to follow it all the way to the top.

There are cobble-sized stones all over the road, even small boulders, through which we must sometimes thread our way–passages wide enough for two or three horses, perhaps, or for a small Jeep, or, barely, for the Falcon, but nothing wider–and dry weeds brush against the belly of the Falcon, branches scrape against either side, and grouse leap up in front of us and fly into the woods with heavy wingbeats.

We can barely see where we're going; we're mostly just following a path of least resistance, a place where there are no trees, but instead, just heavy brush–rocks clack and clang against the underside, and sometimes the bald tires spin, the trail is so steep–and though we fueled up at the pump in Yaak, I'm horrified to look down and see that the gauge registers empty.

It's a sunny day, and Elizabeth is humming to herself, singing. Lorraine's head is on Tim's shoulder. Anyone else would suspect that the gauge isn't working, but, still used to my city ways, I have to assume the worst—immediately—and when I stop and get out to check, it is true, gas is gushing out of a crease along the gas tank's belly where we bounced off the top of one of the road-buried boulders.

It's such a warm afternoon. The creek by the side of the trail keeps rushing past on its way down, making the most beautiful sound. The leaf-dappling of sunlight coming down through the creekside vegetation is all across us, on our arms, our faces, on the trail. It's just a lovely day. We could gather our picnic baskets and walk away from the dusty, sun-dappled leaking car, and never come back, and we'd be perfectly happy, and I think, too, the tired little car would be perfectly happy too, just resting there forever back in the woods—and perhaps that's what we should have done, but instead we raced around looking for twigs and sticks, with which to try to plug the jagged rend—Lorraine's chewing gum, electrician's tape from the tool box, handfuls of ferns, of grasses—we were no large saviors of the twentieth century, technicians and such, but were suddenly Indians, smearing handfuls of nature over our car—and when it became so soon apparent that nothing our hands could do was capable of stopping the damage, we got in and backed the car up to a wide spot in the trail, turned it around, and then, because we had been nearing the top, the crown of the valley, we shut the engine off, and began coasting. The gas, which was no longer gushing, but merely trickling—having neared the bottom of the tank—was dripping onto the muffler, which we did not want to get overheated. It was easy to picture the muffler beneath us, smoking, smoldering, and then finally, wind-aided, oxygen-rich, fanning to a quick snapping flame, and then the big puffball of our car going up, the inferno of the four of us. . . .

We drove with the windows down, with the tight, slow-to-respond steering of the power being turned off. The smell of the gas fumes was hideous; I was drenched with gas, from crawling under the tank and wrestling with it, and in the back seat, Lorraine had a jacket wrapped around her face, like a turban, over which only her eyes peered.

The brakes in the old Falcon are not so good, but we had to go fast anyway, around the gravel curves and down the steep switchbacks, because there were little flat spots and even rises, for which we had to build up momentum, to carry us across. The valley lay far below us, as if in a cartoon, as we spiraled down toward it, raising dust, but making little, if any, sound—a ghost car, gliding, with just the smack-smack sound of rubber tires skimming warm pavement.

Except for the horrible smell of gas, it was like gliding, like peace;

it raised, for a moment, the question of why we didn't always travel this way–downhill, anyway. The dogs, excited by the wind (or perhaps trying to get away from the fumes) stretched their heads out of each back window, so that their ears flapped like pennants, and Lorraine lowered her head to her lap to keep from gagging and getting sick. Instead of thinning, the fumes were getting stronger. There was dried gas on my arms, in my hair and finally, we had to stop; it was just too much for Lorraine, and not worth the risk.

The valley lay below us. It was like a child's play-farm. We could see the still, winding river, and green meadows, and a few barns. It was still at least another ten miles.

Lorraine asked me to promise to drive carefully, and Tim made me double-promise, and then Lorraine got up on the roof of the Falcon, and lay there on her stomach, as if sunbathing, and with leather and rope we tied her ankles and one wrist to the door handles on either side of the car, tied her down tight–we kept one wrist free, so that she could shield her eyes against the sun, or scratch her nose, or anything like that–and then we started down the mountain again, and we tried to imagine the cool wash of air that was flowing over Lorraine, and we took the corners more slowly, and we were sure that it felt to her as if she *were* the car, as if it were she who was gliding down the mountain, plunging, arms spread out wide, slipping like a knife through the air–and every now and then Tim would lean out the window and look up and ask her how she was doing, and I would too, would ask her if we were going too fast, but she never said anything, she was just grinning.

I kept both hands on the wheel and aimed the car down the center of the lonely road. We were making no sound at all, and it was downhill all the way. We passed the cemetery going forty-five miles an hour. It's a nice place to visit, haunting and romantic, with the graves of the valley's first white settlers, people who died in the 1870s, but we had no time for it.

Up ahead of us, I saw something huge and pale crossing the road–something furtive, something wild, shining in the sun–and I cried, "Grizzly!"–we were coming down off the curve at the base of Caribou Mountain, the long flat stretch, with young cut-over lodgepole on either side, and the way the animal was moving, it looked like a bear, and it was too large to be a black bear, and the color was wrong for any phase of black bear: it was silver.

The animal was walking, moving across the road as if the road were not paved, but some part of the wilderness itself–and we were making no sound at all, running without the engine, and as we drew closer, the bear separated, to my horror at first, into two pieces—and I cried, "Two grizzlies!"—but we were closer then, and could see that they were large silver wolves, almost white—and they stopped, shoulder to shoulder, so much larger and paler than any of the many coyotes we'd been seeing—larger than German shepherds—as large as a grizzly, it seemed, side by side, the two of them combined.

I wanted them to stay there forever, to look at me forever, and we kept coasting toward them, slower now, on the flat stretch, with the speedometer hovering around twenty miles an hour—and you could see their clever minds working, wondering why our car was making no sound—and then they ran into the woods, still heading north, into Canada, I supposed, which, at the base of Caribou Mountain like that, was less than two miles away . . . five minutes away for them, perhaps, running through the woods—and it took us a long time, coasting, to get to the spot where they'd been standing—too long—and we stopped, even though it was on a flat stretch, and looked back through the trees to see if perhaps they were watching us.

Oh, I wanted to see those wolves again!

I started the engine with the brief bit of gas still sloshing around in the belly of the tank—the engine sounded like a cannon, in the silence—and we backed up, pulled forward, backed up again—and I thought I saw some sort of flash, back in the trees, more like a thought or a clairvoyance than any sighting, and Elizabeth cried, "I see one!" and she pointed, but we saw nothing, it was already gone.

"I saw it!" she said, "It was looking at me!"

"Did you see the other one?" Tim asked, craning, peering—but there was nothing but woods.

"Just that one," said Elizabeth. "But it was looking right at me!" The engine was idling, sounding wrong, down in the woods like that, and we had to get going—it was a warm day, and we imagined the muffler getting hot again. Tim and I got out quickly, and while Tim checked on Lorraine—she was fine—I looked beneath the gas tank, as if hoping for some miracle repair—as if perhaps the sighting of the wolves had somehow sealed the leak—but it was still splashing out, coming out in spurts rather than small drips, now that the engine was running—and we got back in the car like gangsters, and were off with a roar, with blue smoke—the wolves halfway to Canada, loping, running wild, but we had taken some of their magic, we had seen them—and we hurried down the road, as rich as kings, as rich as pirates, with our treasure, our friends—

Tim and Lorraine and their unborn child–in our car, and strapped to the roof of the car. I got up to forty miles an hour again, and then quickly cut the engine; and we were gliding again.

We pulled into Crash and Shirley's yard about fifteen minutes later, still talking about the wolves, though we would say nothing of it to anyone else–loose lips sink ships, and while Crash and Shirley were neither trappers nor hunters, they might mention it to a friend who was, or to the friend of a friend–and Crash was out in the yard under a truck, doing something with a wrench–glittering chrome motorcycles, in various states of disassembly, lay about the yard–and Shirley and their two daughters were standing around Crash drinking lemonade, just standing there and watching him: a sort of a cheering section for whatever difficult thing it was he was attempting. Chickens fluttered around in the hayloft of the barn beside their house, and though I had never met Crash before, I knew who he was, and I felt badly, waiting until I needed something from him before coming to visit–but it was also a relief to see a homestead, a family, real people, and a toolbox.

Crash looked pleased to see Lorraine up on the roof like that, but he asked no questions, and he slid out and dusted his hands on his overalls, and I liked the way he shook hands, liked the way he seemed pleased to have visitors. I liked his name, liked him living way up on the North Fork the way he did, the first cabin we came to, coming down off the summit, and a long way, still, away from anyone.

"I smell gas," said Crash.

Lorraine and Elizabeth and Shirley took the dogs down to the river to water them, and the two little girls followed, pulling the dogs' ears and tails and slapping them on the sides, pounding on their backs with their small hands as if playing drums. Lorraine laughed, watching them. Tim and Lorraine aren't going to do the sonogram; or if they do, they're going to ask the doctor not to tell them. I should have mentioned this earlier. I don't know how old Crash's and Shirley's daughters are. They're little, with yellow hair.

Crash didn't have any silicone sealer, no aluma-weld, but he did have some roofing tar he'd been using to chink the logs in his cabin, and so we crawled under the Falcon, all three of us, and smeared it along the rip in the metal. Crash sputtered and blinked whenever gas dripped on his face, and then grinned, wiping it away. I liked the way he stayed calm. It was cool down by the river, in the shade of his yard.

We crawled back out then, after we had it all pasted back together, and Crash went and got us a beer, and he showed us the inside of the new cabin he was building. It was right on the river, and there were big windows, lots of glass. We wanted to leave, after the women came back, but Crash wouldn't let us—he wanted to put another layer of tar over the car's wounds, and so we humored him, and let him fix it properly, and then we were ashamed of having been in a hurry—or if not of having been in some sort of hurry (though there was none), then of trying to take away from the job, trying not to do it perfectly the first time. If we were to rail against other lives, other sins, ranting how quality has been lost everywhere, then surely to earn that right, we must lead the way, must achieve our own perfection, before speaking out.

We waited for the tar to dry, then put a third patch on it—the sun did not appear to have moved, but I know it had been at least an hour—and then, finally, we turned our attention to Crash's old truck—he looked at it with exasperation and fondness both—it was something major, something far beyond either Tim's or my capabilities—and it was time to slip away, to let him go back to work, and to leave him and his family in the peace and silence in which they had been living. Roosters chased chickens around in the dust beneath big trees, and an orange cat slept on the porch, in the sun—and we got back in the car, all four of us this time, and drove back down the dirt road, raising a cloud in the dry summer. We rolled down our windows and were waving out all four of them. No man can keep anything from going wrong—he can only lower the percentages—and the man or woman who can fix them when they do go wrong exercises a control that is rare in this life.

Lorraine aimed the movie camera through the dusty back window and filmed Crash, growing smaller, standing in his yard and waving goodbye to us.

We stop off at the saloon, at the junction of the road that winds back up into the mountains to our house, and we go in for another one, or one more, to cut the heat and the dryness. There's a sign on the door that says "Check your guns," but we're unarmed. I go into the restroom to rinse, with soap and hot water, the last of the gas from my hands and arms. When I come back out, Tim has ordered drinks for us—beer for Elizabeth and me and himself, and grapefruit juice for Lorraine—and we sit in the coolness, in the dark, staring out at the glare of the day, and Jimmy, the bartender, talks to Tim and Lorraine, is courteous, asks them how they enjoy the valley, and then Lorraine asks Tim if she can have a sip of his beer.

"Just one sip," she says. "Not a whole beer—just one sip, just this one day—don't you think?"

There's no telling what Jimmy thinks—Lorraine's not showing at all, it was only just confirmed right before they came out here–but Jimmy's cool as pie, he just smiles and nods, looks out the window, and it's a lovely valley, as long as no harm or evil is done to another, you're free to stay here forever, and whatever you do, however you are, is just fine, just dandy.

"I think so," says Tim, not looking at Jimmy or us, but at his wife: the thing between them, and only their decision. "I think just a sip, just today, will be fine."

"I just want it to wet my lips," says Lorraine, taking the glass mug from Tim, and she holds it for a moment, holds the coldness of it up against her face, and then takes a long swallow.

Her face is sunburned, from riding up on the roof of the car. "Ahhh," she says, when she's finished her swallow, and she sets the glass, still about full, back down in front of Tim.

Back out into the sun then, the day has cooled. It's fresh. Mayflies move in small clouds across the river, and fish are leaping, throwing themselves up into these clouds. It's dramatic and beautiful–life ending, and life going on–and we stand there for a moment and watch it, and wish for our fishing poles, our fly rods.

Driving home, with shadows across the road: driving through long tunnels of tree shade, past open meadows. Deer and cattle stand out in the tall green grasses of summer together; the cows are heavy with calf.

"Poor Ann," Lorraine is saying, holding Ann in her lap and stroking her head. "Do you have a quill somewhere inside you?"

We try to picture it, dark and silent, invisible, working its dark passage through her body, taking no certain route, only traveling at chance, but we're made uneasy by the thought and we try to put it behind us, try to put it out of mind. She seems perfectly healthy.

Tim and Lorraine leave the next day, continuing farther on their journey, after hugs and kisses, handshakes, more neck-hugs–good hard squeezes, good sturdy strength-of-touch, holding each other as if storing ammunition for a battle, though there is none, and will be none–not as long as we hug like that.

There's an ache of loneliness and an ecstasy of being alone, after they're gone, mid-morning, and later in the day, we try, at various times, to imagine how many miles they have made–where they are by lunchtime, and where they are by mid-afternoon, the sights they are seeing, and where they will stop for the day, how far they will have made it, that first day.

It's fun to think of what they're carrying in the front seat with them, of what Lorraine's got inside her–of the certainty of it, and the potential, the future. New life will be born; new life will emerge, later in the winter, must emerge–it will survive, and even conquer, the hazards and dins of old life, of lightning strikes, of wild sled dog wrecks, and of powerless, sliding plummets in old rattling cars down the sides of mountains–life like these things, not yet born, but inside us, survives, surrounds us, and never ends.

That night, as we often do, Elizabeth and I get out of bed, unable to sleep–a dark night, no moon, glittering, frosty stars–and we pull on our robes, and walk barefooted out into the front yard, and stand out there and look at the stars.

Some of them shoot and shriek past us, with whistling, scorching sounds. Are we dreaming? Are we still alive? Sometimes, I think not; I think that we are after-alive; and if the old life ended, then I wonder if this one, too, will someday end and I wonder what it will be like.

I think that if it does–life ends–it might be like driving down a country road, down a road with wind-blown sand snaking across it; driving, perhaps, through dunes of some sort–but that is a faraway thought, and perhaps not a thought at all.

We stand there as long as we can, and watch the stars.

Apologia

BARRY LOPEZ

A few miles east of home in the Cascades I slow down and pull over for two raccoons, sprawled still as stones in the road. I carry them to the side and lay them in sun-shot, windblown grass in the barrow pit. In eastern Oregon, along U.S. 20, black-tailed jackrabbits lie like welts of sod–three, four, then a fifth. By the bridge over Jordan Creek, just shy of the Idaho border, in the drainage of the Owyhee River, a crumpled adolescent porcupine leers up almost maniacally over its blood-flecked teeth. I carry each one away from the tarmac into a cover of grass or brush out of decency, I think. And worry. Who are these animals, their lights gone out? What journeys have fallen apart here?

I do not stop to remove each dark blister from the road. I wince before the recently dead, feel my lips tighten, see something else, a fence post, in the spontaneous aversion of my eyes, and pull over. I imagine white silk threads of life still vibrating inside them, even if the body's husk is stretched out for yards, stuck like oiled muslin to the road. The energy that held them erect leaves like a bullet; but the memory of that energy fades slowly from the wrinkled cornea, the bloodless fur.

The raccoons and, later, a red fox carry like sacks of wet gravel and sand. Each animal is like a solitary child's shoe in the road.

Once a man asked, Why do you bother? You never know, I said. The ones you give some semblance of burial, to whom you offer an apology, may have been like seers in a parallel culture. It is an act of respect, a technique of awareness.

In Idaho I hit a young sage sparrow–*thwack* against the right fender in the very split second I see it. Its companion rises a foot higher from the same spot, slow as smoke, and sails off clean into the desert. I rest the walloped bird in my left hand, my right thumb pressed to its chest. I feel for the wail of the heart. Its eyes glisten like rain on crystal. Nothing but warmth. I shut the tiny eyelids and lay it beside a clump of bunchgrass. Beyond a barbed-wire fence the overgrazed range is littered with cow flops. The road curves away to the south. I nod before I go, a ridiculous gesture, out of simple grief.

I pass four spotted skunks. The swirling air is acrid with the rupture of each life.

Darkness rises in the valleys of Idaho. East of Grand View, south of the Snake River, nighthawks swoop the road for gnats, silent on the wing as owls. On a descending curve I see two of them lying soft as clouds in the road. I turn around and come back. The sudden slowing down and my K-turn at the bottom of the hill draw the attention of a man who steps away from a tractor, a dozen yards from where the birds lie. I can tell by his step, the suspicious tilt of his head, that he is wary, vaguely proprietary. Offended, or irritated, he may throw the birds back into the road when I leave. So I wait, subdued like a penitent, a body in each hand.

He speaks first, a low voice, a deep murmur weighted with awe. He has been watching these flocks feeding just above the road for several evenings. He calls them whippoorwills. He gestures for a carcass. How odd, yes, the way they concentrate their hunting right on the road, I say. He runs a finger down the smooth arc of the belly and remarks on the small whiskered bill. He pulls one long wing out straight, but not roughly. He marvels. He glances at my car, baffled by this out-of-state courtesy. Two dozen nighthawks career past, back and forth at arm's length, feeding at our height and lower. He asks if I would mind–as though I owned it–if he took the bird up to the house to show his wife. "She's never seen anything like this." He's fascinated. "Not close."

I trust, later, he will put it in the fields, not throw the body in the trash, a whirligig.

North of Pinedale in western Wyoming on U.S. 189, below the Gros Ventre Range, I see a big doe from a great distance, the low rays of first light gleaming in her tawny reddish hair. She rests askew, like a crushed tree. I drag her to the shoulder, then down a long slope by the petals of her ears. A gunnysack of plaster mud, ears cold as rain gutters. All of her doesn't come. I climb back up for the missing leg. The stain of her is darker than the black asphalt. The stains go north and off to the south as far as I can see.

On an afternoon trafficless, quiet as a cloister, headed across South Pass in the Wind River Range, I swerve violently but hit an animal, and then try to wrestle the gravel-spewing skid in a straight line along the lip of an embankment. I know even as I struggle for control the irony of this: I could pitch off here to my own death, easily. The bird is dead somewhere in the road behind me. Only a few seconds and I am safely back on the road, nauseated, light-headed.

It is hard to distinguish among younger gulls. I turn this one around slowly in my hands. It could be a western gull, a mew gull, a California gull. I do not remember well enough the bill markings, the color of the legs. I have no doubt about the vertebrae shattered beneath the seamless white of its ropy neck.

East of Lusk, Wyoming, in Nebraska, I stop for a badger. I squat on the macadam to admire the long claws, the perfect set of its teeth in the broken jaw, the ramulose shading of its fur—how it differs slightly, as does every badger's, from the drawings and pictures in the field guides. A car drifts toward us over the prairie, coming on in the other lane, a white 1962 Chevrolet station wagon. The driver slows to pass. In the bright sunlight I can't see his face, only an arm and the gesture of his thick left hand. It opens in a kind of shrug, hangs briefly in limp sadness, then extends itself in supplication. Gone past, it curls into itself against the car door and is still.

Farther on in western Nebraska I pick up the small bodies of mice and birds. While I wait to retrieve these creatures I do not meet the eyes of passing drivers. Whoever they are, I feel anger toward them, in spite of the sparrow and the gull I myself have killed. We treat the attrition of lives on the road like the attrition of lives in war: horrifying, unavoidable, justified. Accepting the slaughter leaves people momentarily fractious, embarrassed. South of Broken Bow, at dawn, I cannot avoid an immature barn swallow. It hangs by its head, motionless in the slats of the grill.

I stop for a rabbit on Nebraska 806 and find, only a few feet away, a garter snake. What else have I missed, too small, too narrow? What has gone under or past me while I stared at mountains, hay meadows, fencerows, the beryl surface of rivers? In Wyoming I could not help but see pronghorn antelope swollen big as barrels by the side of the road, their legs splayed rigidly aloft. For animals that large people will stop. But how many have this habit of clearing the road of smaller creatures, people who would remove the ones I miss? I do not imagine I am alone. As much sorrow as the man's hand conveyed in Nebraska, it meant gratitude too for burying the dead.

Still, I do not wish to meet anyone's eyes.

In southwestern Iowa, outside Clarinda, I haul a deer into high grass out of sight of the road and begin to examine it. It is still whole, but the destruction is breathtaking. The skull, I soon discover, is fractured in four places; the jaw, hanging by shreds of mandibular muscle, is broken at the symphysis, beneath the incisors. The pelvis is crushed, the left hind leg unsocketed. All but two ribs are dislocated along the vertebral column, which is complexly fractured. The intestines have been driven forward into the chest. The heart and lungs have ruptured the chest wall at the base of the neck. The signature of a tractor-trailer truck: 78,000 pounds at 65 mph.

In front of a motel room in Ottumwa I finger-scrape the dry stiff carcasses of bumblebees, wasps, and butterflies from the grill and headlight mountings, and I scrub with a wet cloth to soften and wipe away the nap of crumbles, the insects, the aerial plankton of spiders and mites. I am uneasy carrying so many of the dead. The carnage is so obvious.

In Illinois, west of Kankakee, two raccoons as young as the ones in Oregon. In Indiana another raccoon, a gray squirrel. When I make the left turn into the driveway at the house of a friend outside South Bend, it is evening, hot and muggy. I can hear cicadas in a lone elm. I'm glad to be here.

From the driveway entrance I look back down Indiana 23, toward Indiana 8, remembering the farm roads of Illinois and Iowa. I remember how beautiful it was in the limpid air to drive Nebraska 2 through the Sand Hills, to see how far at dusk the land was etched east and west of Wyoming 28. I remember the imposition of the Wind River Range in a hard, blue sky beneath white ranks of buttonhook clouds, windy hay fields on the Snake River Plain, the welcome of Russian olive trees and willows in creek bottoms. The transformation of the heart such beauty engenders is not enough tonight to let me shed the heavier memory, a catalog too morbid to write out, too vivid to ignore.

I stand in the driveway now, listening to the cicadas whirring in the dark tree. My hands grip the sill of the open window at the driver's side, and I lean down as if to speak to someone still sitting there. The weight I wish to fall I cannot fathom, a sorrow over the world's dark hunger.

A light comes on over the porch. I hear a dead bolt thrown, the shiver of a door pulled free. The words of atonement I pronounce are too inept to offer me release. Or forgiveness. My friend is floating across the tree-shadowed lawn. What is to be done with the desire for exculpation?

"Later than we thought you'd be," he says.

I do not want the lavabo. I wish to make amends.

"I made more stops than I thought I would," I answer.

"Well, bring this in. And whatever I can take," he says.

I anticipate, in the powerful antidote of our conversation, the reassurance of a human enterprise, the forgiving embrace of the rational. It waits within, beyond the slow tail-wagging of two dogs standing at the screen door.

The Abstract Wild

JACK TURNER

The tigers of wrath are wiser than the horses of instruction.
–WILLIAM BLAKE, *The Prophetic Books*

The mountains have many moods. Even under clear summer skies I require my clients to pack warm clothing, to be prepared for the worst. I am a mountain-climbing guide, and like all mountain-climbing guides I am a skeptic about mountain weather. We abide by a local adage: only fools and newcomers predict the weather in the Tetons. If someone does not have the right equipment–a hat or a pair of warm pants–I send them to Orville's, a nearby army surplus store that sells cheap wool clothing. Once, however, I sent a client to Orville's for pants and he came back without them, although he did not reveal this until later, after the climb was well underway. Since he was ill-prepared for our venture I was annoyed, and said so. He replied that the only pants available at Orville's were old German army pants; he would not wear them.

My client was Jewish. He offered no further explanation, no list of principles; he expressed no hate. The decision was visceral, as private as the touch of fabric and skin.

His action suggests a code: if justice is impossible, honor the loss with acts of remembrance, acts that count for little in the world, but which, if sustained, might count for oneself, might shore up a portion of integrity. Refuse to forgive, cherish your anger, remind others. His code was old-fashioned, almost Biblical. A less impassioned attitude, indeed, an almost indifferent one, was expressed by Vice-President Bush when he visited Auschwitz in September, 1987: "Boy, they were big on crematoriums, weren't they?"

I understood my client. His conviction opposes our tendency to tolerate everything, to accept, to forget, to forgive, to get on with life, to be realistic, to get over our losses. We accept living with nuclear weapons, toxic wastes, oil spills, rape, murder, starvation, smog, racism, teenage suicide, torture, mountains of garbage, genocide, dams, dead lakes, and the daily loss of species. Most of the time we don't even think about it.

I, too, abhor this tolerance for anything and everything. My client's refusal stems from the Holocaust; mine started with the damming of the Glen Canyon of the Colorado River and its tributaries, especially the Escalante River, and specifically Davis Gulch, which I visited twice in 1963 just before it was drowned by the waters of Lake Powell. Visitors now houseboat and water-ski hundreds of feet above places where I first experienced wilderness. It broke my heart then; I am still angry about it now. I am angry that Wallace Stegner and the late Edward Abbey would boat around Lake Powell as guests of universities and the U.S. government, I am angry with those who vacation on houseboats there, I am angry with friends who kayak and skin-dive its waters. I make a point of being nasty about it.

Some find it obscene to mention the loss of six million people and the loss of one ecosystem in the same breath. I am not ignorant of the difference in magnitude, but I refuse to recognize a difference in causation. In the *High Country News* of September 11, 1989, there is a picture of eleven severed mountain lion heads stacked in a pyramid at the base of a cottonwood tree. You can see the details of their faces; they are individuals. The association with death camps is involuntary. These are only eleven of the 250,000 wild predators killed by the U.S. government in 1987. No one raised a voice to the Animal Damage Control division of the U.S. Department of Agriculture. No one got angry. These deaths, the destruction of the rain forest, and the death of two million Cambodians have a common source, a source that deserves our rage, but a source that we do not yet comprehend.

It is now often said (ever since Wendell Berry stated it so clearly and forcefully) that our ecological crisis is a crisis of character, not a political or social crisis. This said, we falter, for it remains unclear what, exactly, is the crisis of modern character; and since character is partly determined by culture, what, exactly, is the crisis of modern culture. Answers to these questions are not to be found in the writings of Thoreau, or Muir, or ecologists ("deep" or otherwise). Answers, always controversial, are found in the study of the Holocaust, the study of "primitive" peoples untouched by our madness, and in the study of the self.

Although the ecological crisis appears new (because it is now "news"), it is not new; only the scale and form are new. We lost the wild bit by bit for ten thousand years and forgave each loss and then forgot. Now we face the final loss. Although no other crisis in human history can match it, our commentary is strangely muted and sad, as though catastrophe was happening to us, not caused by us. Even the most knowledgeable and enlightened continue to eat food soaked in chemicals (herbicides, pesticides, and hormones), wear plastic clothes (our beloved polypropylene), buy Japanese (despite their annual slaughter of dolphins), and vote Republican—all the while blathering on in abstract language about our ecological crisis. This is denial, and behind denial is a rage, the most common emotion of my generation; but it is suppressed, and we remain silent in the face of evil.

Why is this rage a silent rage, a quiet impotent protest that doesn't extend beyond the confines of our private world? Why don't people speak out, why don't they *do* something? The courage and resistance shown by the Navajos at Big Mountain, by Polish workers, by blacks in South Africa, and, most extraordinarily, by Chinese students in Tiananmen Square render much of the environmental protest in America shallow and ineffective. With the exception of a few members of Earth First!, Sea Shepherd, and Greenpeace, we are a nation of environmental cowards. Why?

Effective protest is grounded in anger, and we are not (consciously) angry. Anger nourishes hope and fuels rebellion; it presumes a judgment, presumes how things ought to be and aren't, presumes a care. Emotion is still the best evidence of belief and value.

Our most recent conceit is that certain places and animals and forests are "sacred." We have forgotten that sacred is a social word and that "sacred for me" is as absurd as "legal for me." We ignore that our culture is as sacred as any other, because we do not distinguish between formal and popular religion. If it is true that our national parks are sacred, it is also true that Disneyland is sacred, and that the location of President Kennedy's assassination is sacred. But these pilgrimage sites are sacred because of the overwhelming importance of commercial entertainment and tourism in our culture, not because of formal religion. In a commercial culture, the sacred will have a commercial base. If you wish to discover what is sacred in America, try eliminating the Super Bowl.

We have also forgotten the relation between violence and the sacred, forgotten that the wars in Ireland, Palestine, and Kashmir are, in part, about sacred land (and, in part, as Joseph Campbell points out, about mistaking a piece of real estate for the "Kingdom of God"). If you go to Mecca and blaspheme the Black Stone, the believers will feed you to the midges, piece by piece. Go to Yellowstone and destroy grizzlies and grizzly habitat and the believers will dress up in bear costumes, sing songs, and sign petitions. This is charming, but it is not rage, and it suggests no sense of blasphemy.

It would be helpful to acknowledge that we fear our rage for two reasons: it might lead us to do something illegal, thus threatening our freedoms, and it might lead to violence. This fear is justified. Any form of resistance to public or private authority that is *effective* (e.g., spiking trees) must of necessity become a felony. Historically, continued effective disobedience has been met with violence. At Amritsar, India, in 1919, the British slaughtered 379 nonviolent demonstrators in cold blood and wounded more than 1,000. In 1930 they murdered 70 more at Peshawar. The nonviolent demonstrators in Norway who successfully resisted German attempts to teach Nazi ideology in Norwegian schools were sent to concentration camps. Remember Kent State?

Violence breeds violence. In demonstrations at the Pentagon in October of 1967, protesters were nonviolent until U.S. marshals began dragging women by their hair and beating them in the groin with clubs. Only then did the demonstrators riot. The cant of messianic humanism conceals our culture's highest command: thou shalt not defy authority. To effectively protest the destruction of the earth we will have to face these facts, surmount these fears.

A *sacred* rage does often surmount these fears. The belief, emotion, and action of the little old Christian lady arrested for protesting abortion can reasonably be connected to the sacred. So can the nonviolent protest of a Buddhist peace activist. So can the terrorist activities of a Moslem fanatic. Whether we like or dislike these acts, think them good or bad, right or wrong, is irrelevant to their being sacred. They are sacred because of their origin. For the believer, the sacred is the *source* of belief, emotion, and action, what is good and what is right; it *determines* life and is immune to merely secular legal and ethical judgments. This is vital religion, lived belief. Old forests will be sacred, and their destruction blasphemous, when we demonstrate that *our* rage is immune to secular judgment. The hard question is this: do we seek a religious culture of sacred nature? We should perhaps recall the ambivalence Thoreau, Melville, and Jefferson felt toward religious cultures. As the anthropologist Rene Girard says, "'Conservative' is a word too weak to describe the rigidity of spirit and terror of change that characterizes those societies in which the sacred holds sway." That's the problem: rigidity of spirit–the exact opposite, I think, of the freedom inherent in wildness. I am inclined to agree with Dogen Zenji: "Truly nothing is sacred, hard as iron."

Effective protests are grounded in a refusal to accept what is normal. We accept a diminished world as normal; we accept a diminished way of life as normal; we accept diminished human beings as normal. What was once considered pathological becomes statistically common and eventually "normal"–a shift that veils an absurdity. Decayed teeth are statistically common, just like smog and environmentally-caused cancers. That a statistically common decayed tooth is also an abnormal tooth, a pathological tooth, a diminished tooth, a painful, horrible, mind-bending tooth, is a fact we ignore. Until it is our tooth. At present most of us do not experience the loss of the wild like we experience a toothache. That is the problem. The "normal" wilderness most people know is a charade of areas, zones, and management plans that has driven the wild into oblivion, a wilderness without wildness, a placebo. But we deny this, accepting the semblance instead of demanding the real. The real loss is not experienced.

Effective protests are grounded in a coherent vision of an alternative; we have no coherent vision of an alternative to our present maladies. Deep Ecology does not, as yet, offer a coherent vision. Our main resources for Deep Ecology, the books by Sessions, Devall, and LaChapelle, are hodgepodges of lists, principles, declarations, quotations, clippings from every conceivable tradition, and tidbits of New Age kitsch. The authors do not clearly say what they mean; they do not forcefully argue for what they believe; they do not create anything new. That some are professional philosophers is all the more confounding. Presented as revolutionary tracts aimed at subverting Western Civilization, these works embarrass us with their intellectual timidity and flaccid prose. Compare them with other revolutionary works–*Leviathan*, the *Social Contract*, the *Communist Manifesto*–or even the work of contemporary European thinkers such as Foucault or Habermas and we glimpse the depth of our muddle.

Deep Ecology is suspicious. It lacks passion, an absence that is acutely disturbing given the current state of affairs. A reading of Marx's theses on Feuerbach is in order, especially the eleventh: "Philosophers have only interpreted the world in various ways; the point, however, is to change it." If we do not change the world soon, Deep Ecology will become an obtuse form of necrophilia.

Our apathy, complacency, docility, and cowardice are not new; they were, for instance, major subjects of both *Walden* and "Resistance to Civil Government." (It is always helpful to recall that for most of their lives, Thoreau and Muir were considered maladjusted failures, even by those who knew and loved them.) But for the present let it be, at best, controversial, and at worst, improper, to have strong moral feelings about the treatment of animals, plants, and places–an emotional mistake–like being in love with the number 2. Let the case for the destruction of the earth rest–we are smothered with facts; they are both depressing and endless. What is shocking is that we are all "good Germans." That is *our* problem, and a problem we can attempt, at least, to solve.

The social reasons for our apathy are numerous: religious traditions (Christian and Buddhist) that glorify acceptance and condemn emotion (particularly anger) and judgment; a political ideology that extols relativism, pluralism, tolerance, and pragmatism in internal affairs (although not in external affairs–until recently it was all right to hate the "Commies" and be enraged at *their* "evil"); the inertia of any social structure; a claustrophobic conformity behind a mask of individualism; and a love of expediency that is short-sighted and self-serving. The most readily accepted social criticism in our society is cloaked in humor–the political cartoons of Garry Trudeau and Gary Larson, for example. Ordinary people don't talk of normal and abnormal. We no longer talk of good and evil; we talk about what we like and dislike, as if discussing ice cream. To defend our likes and dislikes we quote opinion polls and surveys that track the gentle undulations of the true, the good, and the beautiful.

There are also private reasons for apathy and indifference. As Marcuse noted twenty-five years ago, "The intellectual and emotional refusal 'to go along' appears neurotic and impotent." Even as citizens of the alleged high point of Western Civilization, we are ridiculed for connecting public pathology and personal tragedy. Criticize the greed of the rich and you are *envious;* become enraged at the killing of a hundred thousand dolphins every year and you are *infantile;* protest the FBI's harassment of dissident organizations and you *have a problem with authority;* condemn the state for exposing citizens to radiation from nuclear arms testing and you are *unpatriotic*. This reduction of social criticism to private defect is incessant in our culture; it cripples our outrage and numbs our moral imagination. The result is a palsied moral being, no longer astonished by evil and oblivious to the living nightmares of our daily life. We are put down, so we shut up, abandoning the prospect of autonomy, self-respect, and integrity.

Signing more petitions, giving money, or joining another environmental organization helps some, but is too abstract to help *us* and *our* problem. These means are too far from the end, the intention unachieved. Indeed, our apathy and cowardice stem, in part from this: these abstractions *never* work; they *never* achieve for us a sense of power and fulfillment; they correct neither the cause nor the effect. We end up feeling helpless, and since it is human nature to want to avoid feeling helpless, we become dissociated, cynical, and depressed. Better to live in the presence of the wild—feel it, smell it, see it—and do some small thing that is real and succeeds, such as Gary Nabhan's preservation of wild seeds or Doug Peacock's study of grizzlies. Thoreau's "In Wildness is the preservation of the World" is exact truth. We know that in the end moral efficacy will manifest knowledge and love—our intimacies. We only value what we know and love. We no longer know or love the wild. So we no longer value it. Instead, we accept substitutes, imitations, semblances, and fakes—the diminished wild. We accept abstract information in place of personal experience and communication. This removes us from the true wild and severs our recognition of its value. Most people don't even miss it. Most people *literally* do not know what we are talking about.

In 1928, Walter Benjamin sadly remarked, "The earliest customs of peoples seem to send us a warning that in accepting what we receive so abundantly from nature we should guard against a gesture of avarice. For we are able to make Mother Earth no gift of our own." Now a gift is possible: knowledge, passion, courage, and a long list of heresies (often called felonies). We must become so intimate with wild animals, with plants and places, that we answer to their destruction from the gut. Like when we discover the landlord strangling our cat.

If anything is endangered in America it is our experience of wild nature – gross *contact*. There is knowledge only the wild can give us, knowledge specific to it, knowledge specific to the experience of it. These are its gifts to us. In this, wilderness is no different from music, painting, poetry, or love: concede the abundance, respond with grace. The problem is that we no longer know what these gifts are. In our noble effort to go beyond anthropocentric defenses of nature, to emphasize its intrinsic value and right to exist independently of us, we forget the reciprocity between the wild in nature and the wild in us, between knowledge of the wild and knowledge of the self that was central to all primitive cultures.

Once the meaning of the wild is forgotten, because the relevant experience is lost, we abuse the word, literally, misuse it. The savagery and brutality of gang rape is now called "wilding," and in New Age retreats men search for a "wild man within." It is doubtful these people have been in a wilderness. They don't know what wild means. They don't know in the sense of having experienced it, though they may know it abstractly. (Bertrand Russell put the difference nicely: knowledge by acquaintance and knowledge by description.)

Why do we associate the savage, the brutal, and the wild? The savagery of nature fades to nothing compared to the savagery of human agency. The most civilized nations on the planet killed sixty million to seventy million of each other's citizens in the thirty-year span from the beginning of World War I to the end of World War II. Dante, Shakespeare, Goethe, Kant, Rousseau, Dogen, Mill, Beethoven, Bach, Mozart, Manet, Basho, Van Gogh, and Hokusai didn't make any difference. The rule of law, human rights, democracy, the sovereignty of nations, liberal education, tradition, scientific method, and the presence of an Emperor God didn't make any difference. Protestantism, Catholicism, Greek and Russian Orthodoxy, Buddhism, Shintoism, and Islam didn't make any difference. How can we, at this time in history, think of a bear or a wolf as savage? Why laugh at the idea of the noble savage when we have discovered no "savage" as savage as civilized man?

Why equate the wild only with the masculine, as though the feminine were not also wild? The wild is neither and both. The easiest way to experience a bit of what the wild was like is to go into a great forest at night alone. Sit quietly for a while. Something very old will return. It is well described by Ortega y Gasset in *Meditations on Hunting:* "The hunter . . . needs to prepare an attention which does not consist in riveting itself on the presumed but consists precisely in not assuming anything and in avoiding inattentiveness. It is a 'universal' attention, which does not inscribe itself on any point and tries to be on all points."

This is very close to a description of certain meditation techniques, especially *shikantaza*, a practice of the Soto sect of Zen. (It is not an accident that Lama Govinda believed meditation arose among the hunting cultures of the Himalayan foothills; it is not an accident that the Balti and the Golok handle utensils like masters of the Tea Ceremony.) Alone in the forest, time is less dense, less filled with information; space is very close; smell and hearing and touch reassert themselves. The experience is keenly sensual. In a true wilderness we are like that much of the time, even in broad daylight. Alert, careful, literally "full of care." Not because of principles or practice, but because of something very old.

The majority of Americans have no experience of the wild. We are surrounded by national parks, wilderness areas, wildlife preserves, sanctuaries, and refuges. We love to visit them. We also visit foreign parks and wilderness; we visit wild, exotic cultures. We are deluged with commercial images of wildness: coffee-table books, calendars, postcards, posters, T-shirts, and placemats. There are nature movies. A comprehensive bibliography of nature books would strain a small computer. There are hundreds of nature magazines with every conceivable emphasis: yuppie outdoor magazines, geographical magazines, philosophy magazines, scientific magazines, ecology magazines, and political magazines. Zoos and animal parks and marine lands abound, displaying a selection of beasts exceeded only by Noah's.

From this we conclude that modern man's knowledge and experience of wild nature is extensive. But it is not extensive. Rather, what we have is extensive experience of a severely diminished wilderness animal or place—a *caricature* of its former self; or, we have extensive indirect experience of wild nature via photographic images and the written word. This is not experience of the wild, not gross contact.

The national parks were created for and by tourism, and they emphasize what interests a tourist—the picturesque and the odd. They are managed with two ends in mind: entertaiment and preservation. Most visitors rarely leave their cars except to eat, sleep, or go to the john. (In Grand Teton National Park, 93 percent of the visitors never visit the backcountry.) If visitors do make other stops, it is at designated picturesque "scenes" or educational exhibits presenting interesting facts—the names of the peaks, a bit of history—or, very occasionally, for passive recreation, a ride in a boat or an organized nature walk. None of this is accidental. It results from carefully designed "management plans" that channel the flow of tourists according to maximum utility—utility defined by the ends of entertainment, efficiency, and preservation.

The problem is not what people do in the parks; it is what they are discouraged or prevented from doing. No one, for instance, is encouraged to climb mountains, backpack, or canoe alone. Hikers are discouraged from traveling off-trail, especially in unpatrolled areas with difficult rescue. They are often prohibited from remote areas where they might encounter bears, or else travel is restricted to groups. Their movements are always tracked. It is *illegal* to wander around the national parks without a permit defining where you go and where you stay and how long you stay. In every manner conceivable national parks separate us from wildness.

If we go into a designated wilderness area, say the Bridger-Teton, we are slightly less restricted, but we find as much degradation of the wild environment. We see signs and hike horse trails and cross sturdy bridges and find maps on large boards at trail junctions. We meet patrolling rangers, Boy Scout and Girl Scout troops working on character, and Outward Bound teaching "wilderness" skills in a corporate management seminar. We meet trail crews, pack trains, and hikers galore.

At night we see the distant lights of cities and highways and sodium-vapor lamps in the yards of farms and ranches. Satellites pass overhead. By day, contrails from commercial jets mar the sky; military planes, private jets, small aircraft, and helicopters are a common presence. We camp by a lake, the outlet of which is filled with spawning golden trout. We notice they are thin as smelt. They are not indigenous to these mountains. Around camp, many small trees have been cut down by Basque sheepherders. The trails of their herds are ubiquitous; domestic sheep still graze this wilderness. In autumn we find hunting camps the size of military installations, the hunters better armed than Green Berets. Many of the camps use salt licks to lure the elk, deer, and moose. If we wander out of this narrow "wilderness zone," we walk straight into clear-cut forest, logging roads, and oil wells.

This is no longer the wild, no longer a wilderness, and yet we continue to accept it as wilderness and call our time there "wilderness experience." We *believe* we make contact with the wild, but this is an illusion. In both the national parks and wilderness areas we accept a reduced category of experience, a semblance of the wild nature, a fake. And no one complains.

We visit the zoo or Sea World to see wild animals, but they are not wild; they have been tamed, rendered dependent and obedient. We learn nothing of their essential life in nature. We do not see them hunt or gather their food. We do not see them mate. We do not see them interact with other species. We do not see them interact with their habitat. Their numbers and their movements are artificial. We see them controlled. We see them trained. In most cases they are as docile, apathetic, and bored as the people watching them. If we visit wild animals in sanctuaries we are protected by buses and Land Rovers and observation towers. We are separated from any direct experience of the wild animals we came to visit. With no contact, why call it a visit?

The majority of people who feel anguish about whales have never seen a whale at sea; the majority who desire to reintroduce wolves to Yellowstone have never seen a wolf in the wild, and some, no doubt, have never been to Yellowstone. We feel agony about bludgeoned seal pups and shredded dolphins without every having touched one or smelled one or watched it swim. However much these emotions promote environmental causes, they remain suspect, for the object of the emotion is experienced through a *medium*, via movies, television, the printed word, or snapshots. They pass as quickly as our feelings about the evening news or our favorite film. They are the emotions of an *audience,* the emotions of *sad entertainment*. We cry our hearts out about "Old Yeller"; the Humane Society has to destroy thousands of dogs and cats because homes cannot be found for them.

Dissatisfied with the semblances and imitations at home we travel abroad in a search for the real thing. But there isn't anything different out there, no *exotic* context by which to judge the absence of context in our lives. The context remains, in the apt phrase of George Trow, "the context of no context." We do not find the Other. We can spend a lifetime in parks and wilderness areas and on adventure travel trips and remain starved for wild country and wild people.

Forty years ago no foreigner had set foot in Khumbu, the beautiful valley that approaches Everest from the south. When I started going there thirteen years ago it was advertised as a remote wilderness, despite the presence of thousands of Sherpas in dozens of villages. Sometimes it is still advertised that way—an exotic Shangri-la. That this is false is not the point; it is the form and magnitude of the con that is important, the size of the illusion.

Now, tens of thousands of foreigners visit the region every year. Most arrive by plane at the village of Lukla. The trail from there to the old Everest Base Camp—Interstate E—is always crowded with tourists, many of them in shorts and sandals with Pan Am flight bags over their shoulders containing all they need for several weeks in this wilderness.

In Namche Bazaar I recently stayed at a hotel owned by a Sherpa

I worked with years ago. I slept in one of the special rooms separated from the dorm used by most tourists. On the wall are two scribbles. One is the signature of former president Jimmy Carter. The other is the signature of Richard Blum, husband of former San Francisco mayor Diane Feinstein. Both needed to let us know they slept in this special room in this remote wilderness. In the morning I was served the first omelette prepared in the hotel's new microwave oven, the first microwave in Khumbu. It was so hard I barely got it down. The cook, who happens to be the owner's wife, said, "Sherpa way better" and headed back to the kitchen in disgust. Right! That next winter electricity came to Thyangboche Monastery and promptly burned it down.

At the old British Base Camp in Tibet, on the north side of Everest, is a bare concrete platform awaiting a communications satellite dish that will improve weather predictions for climbing expeditions. Soon there will be a hotel.

The north side of K2 is more difficult to reach. Fly to Beijing. Fly from Beijing to Urumchi. Fly from Urumchi to Kashgar. Drive two days by Toyota Land Cruiser or Mitsubishi bus to Mazar on the long road between Kashgar and Lhasa. Ride camels for a week (they are required for the many fordings of the Shaksgam River). Walk for several days up a glacier. What do you find? Skeletons of tents, with pieces of nylon flapping in the breeze. Inside are boxes of unused stainless steel pressure cookers, cases of antipasto, and Italian magazines. On a ridge above the glacier is a concrete platform with a radar dish.

Tibet is still described as wild, exotic, and forbidden. When in Lhasa, I stay in a large, modern hotel operated by Holiday Inn. The manager meets me at the door. He is an Englishman dressed in an impeccable three-piece Saville Row suit and speaks with an Oxford accent. My room is like any other Holiday Inn room. It has closed-circuit television. In the lobby, during cocktail hour, there is a string quartet that plays Mozart and Beethoven. I drink Guinness Stout and Courvoisier Cognac. I dine on pasta and yakburgers.

In the streets I see a Red Army soldier driving a lime green Mercedes Benz; another soldier drives a cobalt blue Jeep Cherokee. Golok nomads wander the bazaar wearing yak-skin boots, woolen breeches, and cloaks (Tibetan "chuba") fringed with snow leopard fur. Their hair, entwined with scarlet cloth, is gathered on top of their heads. One carries a ghetto blaster the size of a small suitcase. The volume makes me wince. He is playing Bruce Springsteen.

The preferred style of dress for young male Tibetans in Lhasa is called "Kathmandu Cowboy": black Hong Kong cowboy boots, stone-washed Levi's, a black silk shirt, gold necklace, and Elvis Presley haircut. Young Tibetan women date Chinese soldiers.

I am thankful for the small things. Once, at a monastery outside of Lhasa, I witnessed a senior monk debating with a large gathering of students. He shouted his questions, clapping and stomping to an eight-count beat. His students shouted their answers trying to keep up with his furious pace, and he continued at the same furious pace. When they failed to answer correctly he would brush the back of one hand with the back of the other, dismissively smiling and laughing. The students, animated and responsive, would try again.

Once I saw a pilgrim circumambulating the Jokhang monastery through the Barkhor bazaar. He was wearing only yak-skin boots and woolen breeches; in the middle of his back, a gilded prayer box the size of a gallon of milk hung from a thick leather strap slung over one shoulder. He chanted continuously in a strong voice, first holding his hands in prayer high over his head, then bowing hard to the ground in the middle of the bazaar—first knees, then chest, then elbows, his hands still held in prayer over his head. Then he would rise, take one step to the left, and repeat his prayer. Though the bazaar was packed with people there was a forty-foot circle around him. No one interfered; very few tourists had the temerity to photograph him, and then only from a great distance. He is the only wild human being I have seen during fifteen years of travel in Asia. A modern Milarepa.

At the Dalai Lama's old summer palace—the Norbulingka—there is a zoo, his private zoo. There are high enclosures for deer and buffalo; all they see is the sky. There are small cages for wolves and foxes and lynx and bears. In one of the cages there is a bear the Chinese call *ma-shang*. We would call it a grizzly. I think of Buddhism's first vow—"Beings are numberless: I vow to enlighten them"—trying to discover the proper relation between the Dalai Lama, enlightenment, and a caged grizzly. I think of the Buddhist nuns in Bangkok selling the freedom of trapped birds to raise money for gilding a Buddha. I think of Kafka's saddest sentence: "A cage went in search of a bird."

These places *are* beautiful; these people *are* wonderful. I continue to go there and always will. There are small pockets of wilderness left, and a few wild people, but, in general, the wilderness and the people of the wilderness are gone; wild things cannot necessarily be reached by travel. We perpetuate the idea that it is out there, we console ourselves with feeble imitations, we seek reassurance in nature entertainment and outdoor sports. But it is nearly gone. Unless we change the world soon, the wild will be but a memory in the minds of a few people. When they die it will die with them, and the wild will become completely abstract.

What is wrong with all this fun and entertainment, with this imitation of what was once a real and potent Other? Nothing, if it is recognized for what it is—a poor substitute. But we do not note that the wild is missing, and it is not clear how we might reestablish contact with wild things. It is probably best to begin now with what we are emotionally closest to—animals. Plants can come later, places last. Despite all the ecobabble to the contrary, at present we do not understand what it might mean to communicate with a plant or a place as Native Americans did. Unfortunately, the conditions under which we might form a relationship with wild animals are also diminishing.

The story is repeated daily in the media. A natural habitat is eroded or lost, a species suffers, becomes endangered, or is lost. Efforts are made to save it, study it, and arouse public sympathy for its plight. This always sounds so inevitable, as though the loss of habitat is as incorrigible, as implacable as fate. There is no mention of human agency, no suggestion that we are responsible for the loss of wilderness habitat, no possibility that we could have done otherwise, that we could reverse this horrible situation, no suggestion that we have this power, no realization that the abstract language of wildlife management aids and abets the continued loss of wild habitat, no acknowledgment that a zoo, a circus, a Sea World, a national park, is *a business.* Reading these articles, hundreds of them, we never discover why an orca like Shamu has to jump through ten thousand hoops next year to help make $338 million for the parks division of Harcourt Brace Jovanovich, Inc.

Zoos are getting bigger and more "natural"; wildlife sanctuaries and national parks are "islands," too small and increasingly artificial. Yellowstone National Park is really a megazoo. *Everything is exploited and managed, now; it's just a matter of degree. Accept this. It's normal. Nothing to be done.*

When we deal in such abstractions boundaries are blurred, between the real and the fake, between the wild and the tame, between independent and dependent, between the original and the copy, between the healthy and the diminished. Blurring takes the edge off loss and removes us from our responsibilities. *Wild nature is not lost; we have collected it; you can go see it whenever you want.* With the aid of our infinite artifice this fake has replaced the natural. It's not really *very* different from the original! Why worry? As Umberto Ecco observes in *Travels in Hyperreality,* "The ideology of this America wants to establish reassurance through imitation." And that ideology has succeeded; we are reassured, we are not angry, we are not even upset.

Abstraction masks horror. A zoo is a very different kind of place from the wild; a caricature requires an original. A zoo, a Sea World is (at best) a fake habitat presenting pseudo-wild animals to the public for entertainment and financial reward. The wild is the original, the wild is home. The bigger and more naturalistic the megazoo, the "better" the fake. But it is still a fake. And why we should or should not accept this fake is a subject that cannot be addressed by the abstractions of wildlife management.

Abstraction displaces emotion, constraining us to relate to the "problems" of wild animals rationally—the excuses of scientific knowledge, commerce, and philanthropy. It leaves us without an explanation of our emotional relations to animals. It cannot explain why I went berserk, amok, at the zoo in Mysore, India, at the sight of a crowd pelting an American mountain lion trapped in a cage on a small wooden platform. This animal was suffering due to a very un-abstract cause. She had been sold to a foreign business for purposes of amusement and profit, and human beings there were mistreating her. Nothing unusual here. *Normal.*

Her suffering was obscene, the solution simple: she needed to get home. To run along rims through piñon and cedar and crouch and leap and dance on her toes sideways, her tail curled high in the air to seduce a mate and then hunt with him in the moonlight and eat deer and cows and sheep and make little pumas and die of old age on warm sandstone by a clear spring at the end of a gulch dense with cottonwood and box elder.

The condors need to get home, too. So do the orcas. That they no longer have a home is not their problem. (That homeless humans no longer have a home is not their problem.) It is our problem; *we* have done it. The solution is to give them their home. (The solution for the homeless is equally simple.) Why is this so difficult to conceive or act upon? Part of the answer is this: *we* no longer have a home except in a brute commercial sense; home is where the bills come. To seriously help homeless humans and animals would require a noncommercial sense of home. The Eskimo, the Aranda, the Sioux belonged to one place. Where is our *habitat?* Where do *we* belong?

"All sites of enforced marginalization—ghettos, shanty towns, prisons, madhouses, concentration camps—have something in common with zoos" (John Berger, "Why Look at Animals?"). If we add Indian reservations, aquariums, and botanical gardens to this list, then a pattern emerges: removed from their home, living things become marginal, and what becomes marginal is diminished or destroyed. Of bedrock importance is community, for humans, animals, and plants.

We know that the historical move from community to society proceeded by destroying local structures–religion, economy, food patterns, customs, possessions, families, traditions–and replacing these with national, or international, structures that created modern "individuals" and integrated them into society. Modern man lost his home; in the process everything else did, too. That is why Aldo Leopold's Land Ethic is so frighteningly radical; it renders this process *morally wrong*. "A thing is right when it tends to preserve the integrity, stability, and beauty of the biotic community. It is wrong when it tends otherwise." Apply this principle to people, animals, and plants, and the last ten thousand years of history is *evil*.

We are repeatedly told that the nature entertainment and recreation industries help the environment. After an orca killed another orca at Sea World, the veterinarian responsible for the whales claimed that children often "come away with knowledge they didn't have before and a fascination that doesn't go away . . . they become advocates for the marine environment." We hear the same general argument about national parks and wilderness areas; they must be entertaining and recreational or the public will not support environmental issues. And contact with exotic cultures is defended by saying it is required to save them.

This argument is no different from the one given by the Marine officer in Vietnam who explained the destruction of a village by saying, "We had to destroy it in order to save it." The first "it" here is real–people, plants, animals, houses: what was destroyed. The second "it" is abstract–a political category: the now nonexistent village we "saved" from the Viet Cong.

What, *exactly*, is the "it" we are trying to save in all the national parks, wilderness areas, sanctuaries, and zoos? What are we traveling abroad to find? I suggest that part of the answer is this: something connected with *our home*.

That, of course, is not the usual answer. The usual answer is mass recreation sites and mass entertainment programs. We have succeeded admirably. Nature recreation and entertainment is a multibillion-dollar business–the Nature Business. Hundreds of thousands of people in the government and in the private sector depend on the nature business for their livelihood, *depend* on a caricature defended by obscure abstractions.

If the answer is wild nature and the experience of wild nature, then we have failed miserably, for intimacy with the fake will not save the real. Many people believe that continued experience with caricatures creates a desire to experience the real wild. In my experience it is more likely to produce a desire for more caricatures.

The illusion of contact with the wild provided by national parks, wilderness areas, and Sea Worlds actually *diverts* us from the wild. Knowledge gained from these experiences creates an *illusion* of intimacy that masks our true ignorance and leads to complacency and apathy in the face of our true loss. We are inundated by "nature," but we do not care about nature. We do not care that Shamu is in exile from a home in the sea.

We might call this failure "Muir's Mistake." He did not see clearly enough, if at all, that his experience of the wild–intimate, poetic, and visionary–*could never* be duplicated by Sierra Club trips. In 1895 he told the Sierra Club, "If people in general could be got into the woods, even for once, to hear the trees speak for themselves, all difficulties in the way of forest preservation would vanish." They got into the woods, but they did not hear the trees speak. Muir could not understand then that setting aside a wild area would not, in itself, foster intimacy with the wild. Yosemite Valley is now more like Coney Island than a wilderness. He could not know that the organization and commercialization of anything, including wilderness, would destroy the sensuous, mysterious, empathic, absorbed identification he was trying to save and express. He could not know that even the wild would eventually succumb to commodicide–death by commodification.

The world of Thoreau and Muir–the mid-nineteenth century–was bright with hope and optimism. In spite of that, these men were angry and expressed their anger with power and determination. Thoreau went to jail for his beliefs. Our times are darker; such optimism seems impossible at the end of this century. Our world looks backward, obsessed with nostalgia, with memory and forgetting. Something vast and crucial has vanished. Our rage should be as vast. Refuse to forgive, cherish your anger, remind others. We have no excuses.

> *It was a place for heathenism and superstitious rites–to be inhabited by men nearer of kin to the rocks and to wild animals than we. We walked over it with a certain awe . . . it was a specimen of what God saw fit to make this world. What is it to be admitted to a museum, to see a myriad of particular*

> *things. compared with being shown some star's surface, some hard matter in its home! I stand in awe of my body, this matter to which I am bound has become so strange to me. I fear not spirits, ghosts, of which I am one—* that *my body might—but I fear bodies, I tremble to meet them. What is this Titan that has possession of me? Talk of mysteries!—Think of our life in nature—daily to be shown matter, to come in contact with it—rocks, trees, wind on our cheeks! the* solid *earth! the* actual *world! the* common sense! Contact! Contact!
>
> –Thoreau, "Ktaadn"

Undressing the Bear

TERRY TEMPEST WILLIAMS

He came home from the war and shot a bear. He had been part of the Tenth Mountain Division that fought on Mount Belvedere in Italy during World War II. When he returned home to Wyoming, he could hardly wait to get back to the wilderness. It was fall, the hunting season. He would enact the ritual of man against animal once again. A black bear crossed the meadow. The man fixed his scope on the bear and pulled the trigger. The bear screamed. He brought down his rifle and found himself shaking. This had never happened before. He walked over to the warm beast, now dead, and placed his hand on its shoulder. Setting his gun down, he pulled out his buck knife and began skinning the bear that he would pack out on his horse. As he pulled the fur coat away from the muscle, down the breasts and over the swell of the hips, he suddenly stopped. This was not a bear. It was a woman.

Another bear story: There is a woman who travels by sled dogs in Alaska. On one of her journeys through the interior, she stopped to visit an old friend, a Koyukon man. They spoke for some time about the old ways of his people. She listened until it was time for her to go. As she was harnessing her dogs, he offered one piece of advice.

"If you should run into Bear, lift up your parka and show him you are a woman."

And another: I have a friend who manages a bookstore. A regular customer dropped by to browse. They began sharing stories, which led to a discussion of dreams. My friend shared hers.

"I dreamed I was in Yellowstone. A grizzly, upright, was walking toward me. Frightened at first, I began to pull away, when suddenly a mantle of calm came over me. I walked toward the bear and we embraced."

The man across the counter listened, and then said matter-of-factly, "Get over it."

Why? Why should we give up the dream of embracing the bear? And what do these bear stories have to do with writing about the natural world? For me, it has everything to do with undressing, exposing, and embracing the Feminine.

I see the Feminine defined as a reconnection to the Self, a commitment to the wildness within—our instincts, our capacity to create and destroy; our hunger for connection as well as sovereignty, interdependence and independence, at once. We are taught not to trust our own experience. The Feminine teaches us experience is our way back home, the psychic bridge that spans rational and intuitive waters. To embrace the Feminine is to embrace paradox. Paradox preserves mystery, and mystery inspires belief.

I believe in the power of Bear.

The Feminine has long been linked to the bear through mythology. The Greek goddess, Artemis, whose name means "bear," embodies the wisdom of the wild. Christine Downing, in her book *The Goddess: Mythological Images of the Feminine,* describes her as "the one who knows each tree by its bark or leaf or fruit, each beast by its footprint or spoor, each bird by its plumage or call or nest. . . ."

It is Artemis, perhaps originally a Cretan goddess of fertility, who denounces the world of patriarchy, demanding chastity from her female attendants. Callisto, having violated her virginity and becoming pregnant, is transformed into the She-Bear of the night sky by Artemis. Other mythical accounts credit Artemis herself as Ursa Major, ruler of the heavens and protectress of the Pole Star or *axis mundi.*

I saw Ursa Major presiding over Dark Canyon in the remote corner of southeastern Utah. She climbed the desert sky as a jeweled bear following her tracks around the North Star, as she does year after year, honoring the power of seasonal renewal.

At dawn, the sky bear disappeared and I found myself walking down the canyon. Three years ago, this pilgrimage had been aborted. I fell. Head to stone, I rolled down the steep talus slope stopped only by the grace of a sandstone boulder precariously perched at a forty-five degree angle. When I stood up, it was a bloody red landscape. Placing my hand on my forehead, I felt along the three-inch tear of skin down to the boney plate of my skull. I had opened my third eye. Unknowingly, this was what I had come for. It had only been a few months since the death of my mother. I had been unable to cry. On this day, I did.

Now scarred by experience, I returned to Dark Canyon determined to complete my descent into the heart of the desert. Although I had fears of falling again, a different woman inhabited my body. There had been a deepening of self through time. My mother's death had become part of me. She had always worn a small silver bear fetish around her neck to keep her safe. Before she died, she took off the bear and placed it in my hand. I wore it on this trip.

In canyon country you pick your own path. Walking in wilderness becomes a meditation. I followed a small drainage up one of the benches. Lithic scatter was everywhere, evidence of Anasazi culture, a thousand years past. I believed the flakes of chert and obsidian would lead me to ruins. I walked intuitively. A smell of cut wood seized me. I looked up. Before me stood a lightning-struck tree blown apart by the force of the bolt. A fallout of wood chips littered the land in a hundred-foot radius. The piñon pine was still smoldering.

My companion, who came to the burning tree by way of another route, picked up a piece of the charred wood, sacred to the Hopi, and began carving a bullroarer. As he whirled it above our heads on twisted cordage, it wailed in low, deep tones. Rain began–female rain falling gently, softly, as a fine mist over the desert.

Hours later, we made camp. All at once, we heard a roar up canyon. Thunder? Too sustained. Jets overhead? A clear sky above. A peculiar organic smell reached us on the wind. We got the message. Flushed with fear, we ran to higher ground. Suddenly, a ten-foot wall of water came storming down the canyon filling the empty streambed. If the flood had struck earlier, when we were hiking in the narrows, we would have been swept away like the cottonwood trees it was now carrying. We watched the muddy river as though it were a parade, continually inching back as the water eroded the earth beneath our feet.

That night, a lunar rainbow arched over Dark Canyon like a pathway of souls. I had heard the Navajos speak of them for years, never knowing if such magic could exist. It was a sweep of stardust within pastel bands of light–pink, lavender, yellow, and blue. And I felt the presence of angels, even my mother, her wings spread above me like a hovering dove.

In these moments, I felt innocent and wild, privy to secrets and gifts exchanged only in nature. I was the tree, split open by change. I was the flood, bursting through grief. I was the rainbow at night, dancing in darkness. Hands on the earth, I closed my eyes and remembered where the source of my power lies. My connection to the natural world is my connection to self: erotic, mysterious, and whole.

The next morning, I walked to the edge of the wash, shed my clothes, and bathed in pumpkin-colored water. It was to be one of the last warm days of autumn. Standing naked in the sand, I noticed bear tracks. Bending down, I gently placed my right hand inside the fresh paw print.

Women and bears.

Marion Engel, in her novel *Bear,* portrays a woman and a bear in an erotics of place. It doesn't matter whether the bear is seen as male or female. The relationship between the two is sensual, wild.

The woman says, "Bear, take me to the bottom of the ocean with you, bear swim with me, Bear, put your arms around me, enclose me, swim, down, down, down, with me."

"Bear," she says suddenly, "come dance with me."

They make love. Afterwards, "She felt pain, but it was a dear sweet pain that belonged not to mental suffering, but to the earth."

I have felt the "dear sweet pain" that belongs to the earth, pain that arises from a recognition of beauty, pain we hold when we remember what we are connected to and the delicacy of our relations. It is this tenderness born out of a connection to place that fuels my writing. Writing becomes an act of compassion toward life, the life we so often refuse to see because if we look too closely or feel too deeply, there may be no end to our suffering. But words empower us, move us beyond our suffering, and set us free. This is the sorcery of literature. We are healed by our stories. To articulate what we know in our hearts is never easy. Solitude is required in order to listen, courage in order to speak.

By undressing, exposing, and embracing the bear, we undress, expose, and embrace our authentic selves. Stripped free from society's oughts and shoulds, we emerge as emancipated beings. The bear is free to roam.

If we choose to follow the bear, we will be saved from a distractive and domesticated life. The bear becomes our mentor. We must journey out, so that we might journey in. The bear mother holds the secrets of regeneration within her body. She enters the earth before snowfall and dreams herself through winter, emerging in spring with young by her side. She not only survives the barren months, she gives birth. She is the caretaker of the unseen world.

As a writer and a woman with obligations to both family and community, I have tried to adopt this ritual in the balancing of a public and private life. We are at home in the deserts and mountains, as well as in our dens. Above ground in the abundance of spring and summer,

I am available. Below ground in the deepening of autumn and winter, I am not. I need hibernation in order to create.

We are creatures of paradox, women and bears, two animals that are enormously unpredictable, hence our mystery. Perhaps the fear of bears and the fear of women lies in our refusal to be tamed, the impulses we arouse and the forces we represent.

Last spring, our family was in Yellowstone. We were hiking along Pelican Creek, which separated us from an island of lodgepole pines. All at once, a dark form stood in front of the forest on a patch of snow. It was a grizzly, behind her, two cubs. Suddenly, the sow turned and bolted through the trees. A female elk crashed through the timber to the other side of the clearing, stopped, and swung back toward the bear. Within seconds, the grizzly emerged with an elk calf secure in the grip of her jaws. The sow shook the yearling violently by the nape of its neck, threw it down, clamped her claws on its shoulders, and began tearing the flesh back from the bones with her teeth. The cow elk, only a few feet away, watched the sow devour her calf. She pawed the earth desperately with her front hooves, but the bear was oblivious. Blood dripped from the sow's muzzle. The cubs stood by their mother, who eventually turned the carcass over to them. Two hours passed. The sow buried the calf for a later meal, then slept on top of the mound with a paw on each cub. It was not until then that the elk crossed the river in retreat.

We are capable of harboring both these responses to life in the relentless power of our love. As women connected to earth, we are nurturing and we are fierce, we are wicked and we are sublime. The full range is ours. We hold the moon in our bellies and fire in our hearts. We bleed. We give milk. We are the mothers of first words. These words grow. They are our children. They are our stories and our poems.

By allowing ourselves to undress, expose, and embrace the Feminine, we commit our vulnerabilities not to fear but to courage–the courage that allows us to write on behalf of the earth, on behalf of ourselves.

Cryptic Cacti on the Borderline

GARY NABHAN

Hide and Seek

While driving along the U.S.-Mexico border one scorching summer day, I caught myself being lured by mirages. I had been wishing too much for the cooling relief of rain and for better luck in finding a rare, night-blooming cereus cactus.

That cactus was playing hide-and-seek with me in the thorny brush on either side of the border. It was winning. In the previous ten months, I had found only seven individual plants of the Sonoran Queen of the Night in northern Mexico, after more than fifty hours of diligent inspection of their presumed desert habitat. During the dry season, they are often obscured in the canopies of desert shrubs, such as the creosote bush, because the pencil-thin stems of this night-blooming cereus have the same gray color and same diameter as the branches of the bushes. This sort of plant mimicry functions primarily to confuse herbivorous desert mammals that mistake the cactus for unpalatable shrubs, but it works on omnivorous, cosmopolitan biologists as well.

I was not the only human who had been hoodwinked by this coevolved crypticity. A couple of my botanical colleagues had been surveying rare plants on the U.S. side of the international boundary, where this frost-sensitive cereus reaches its northern limits. They had encountered only fifty individuals, after hundreds of hours of scrutinizing the lands along the two hundred miles of U.S.-Mexico border that runs through the Sonoran Desert. Because 90 percent of the Sonoran Desert lands adjacent to the border in Arizona are managed by U.S. government agencies, my colleagues had federal funds to underwrite their frequently fruitless searches.

My own research eventually came part of the FLORUTIL rare plant project, a cooperative effort between Mexican, Navajo, and Anglo-American botanists in the borderlands. However, my initial searching was simply a masochistic pastime. At the onset, I supported the research myself, out of pure curiosity. The costs included ice cream, cold drinks, and fruit shared with the children of the Mexican ranchers and farmhands who gave me permission to wander their lands; wear and tear on my car as it bumped along the border; time spent peeking under the skirts of shrubs; and patience, a resource I could well learn to cultivate. For that investment, a mere seven plants wasn't much to write home about.

That August day, I was to have my wishes granted, both for rains and for discovering more cereus. By the time my Jeep had bounced down the rutted borderline road to the rocky knoll where the seven Sonoran cereus cacti grew, a stray storm cloud had come along to dump a half inch of rain. Though not enough to turn the road into a running arroyo, the downpour was sufficient to moisten the earth and drop the air temperature below a hundred degrees for the first time in hours.

Exhilarated by the sudden rush of fresh air and the relative coolness, I decided to walk around the knoll once more rather than visit with the plants I had already encountered. I found the entire scene transformed. The brief deluge had darkened the lead-colored stems of the creosote bush to a charcoal black, and beneath them, the Sonoran cereus cacti were showing their true colors as well. A glaucous or powdery bloom had been washed away from the cactus stems, revealing a brighter green. When water reached their root tips ready in bud below the rocky surface, the cacti had instantly broken dormancy and activated their photosynthetic machinery.

As the green stems revealed themselves against a black background of wet bushes and trees, I added plant after plant to my cactus count. In forty-five minutes, I spotted eleven additional night-bloomers, some of them under creosote, but others beneath small ironwood and palo verde trees. With the help of the rain, I became a hundred times more efficient at cactus hunting than in all the previous months of the dry season. I had finally encountered enough of the cacti on the Mexican side of the line to compare their status with that of their Arizona brethren a few hundred yards away.

Different Sides of the Fence

Once, when pondering the causes of cereus cactus rarity, I paused and stared at the fence between my two study sites. It shimmered in the desert heat. Intended as a political boundary, it cross-cut an ecological edge created from different desert management traditions. This edge was not identical to the line of the fence, but reverberated around it, like the afterimage of a plucked guitar string. I was beginning to sense the dynamics of the borderlands–how phenomena on one side of the fence affected those on the other–rather than simply seeing a static partition.

I realized that the plants on both sides of the border began their lives in one thinly distributed population, now fragmented by the fence and the roads that run on either side of it. When the Gadsden Purchase in 1849 drew a line down the middle of the population, perhaps half of the cereus plants had became U.S. citizens, while the others remained under the flag of Mexico.

Before then and for some time after, I suspect that the plants and the people around them were not much affected by international politics. The local Indians and mestizos, who dominated the sparse human population in the area, occasionally used the underground tubers as a medicine. These desert people knew how to harvest a couple of the numerous "sweet potatoes" out of the rocky ground without permanently injuring the plant.

For centuries, land uses on opposite sides of the border were not much different. Some of the same families ran cattle in both countries and collected plants in much the same way wherever they were. Gradually, however, the U.S. and Mexican desert economies diverged and left their distinctive imprints.

I initially expected that overgrazing would have made the deepest imprint on the cereus populations. In the United States, government agencies have periodically promoted livestock reductions, whereas overgrazing in Mexico has continued unabated. Sonoran cowboys typically run stock in densities two to five times higher than the desert's carrying capacity. I could plainly see some effects of Mexican cattle on the vegetation where the cereus grew. The beeves had browsed back much of the shrubbery that usually buffers sensitive seedlings from temperature extremes. At the northern edge of its range, cereus cactus needs more cover than it does farther south in frost-free areas.

I am willing to bet any cowboy that the plants will face increasingly stressful conditions if high stocking rates continue. In response to evaporation changes resulting from this overgrazing, wind speeds have increased and temperatures have risen at least four and a half degrees on the Mexian side of the fence. Infrared photos taken from satellites show reduced vegetative growth just over the line.

I soon found out that ranching was not the only force throwing local desert dynamics out of kilter. One day on my seven-acre Sonoran study site, I counted forty-eight legume trees—ironwood, mesquite, and palo verde—with scars of woodcutting on their trunks and branches. Just a week later, I returned to find that nine more ironwood trees had been cut, some of them to the ground. My heart sank, for woodcutting decreases the amount of protective cover available to cacti. Desert cereus seeds have never been known to germinate in the open. Since 90 percent of all mature cereus grow beneath woody cover, the density of trees and shrubs is critical to habitat health.

It dawned on me that deforestation in deserts can be as devastating as in rain forests. I initially assumed that all the wood was being cut for the grills and hearths of low-income Mexican households. As Mexico's poor have gravitated to the U.S. borderlands in hope of better economic opportunities, bordertowns in the Sonoran Desert have grown sevenfold since 1950. Most low-income residents rely on local wood for cooking their food and keeping their adobe homes from freezing during winter months. The stumps I saw bleeding out their last sap seemed victims of the ecological fallout from the borderland's demographic bomb.

Where the cereus grow, I observed that 60 percent of the legume tree stumps showed signs of the ax, and 30 percent of the living trees had at least one branch lopped off by woodcutters. What surprised me was the discovery that woodcutters were creeping across the border, even into areas ostensibly protected as U.S. wildlife refuges and parks. In desert watercourses near the night-bloomers within two hundred yards north of the borderline, 41 percent of the mesquite and ironwood trees have been scarred by woodcutters and 73 percent of the stumps have been hacked by axes.

The campesinos use a variety of desert legumes for firewood, but I was puzzled to hear that palo verde had become one of their mainstays, commanding prices of eighty-five dollars a truckload along the border. As one Mexican cowboy grumbled, "I'd never buy it if I had a choice. Palo verde is so punky, it burns as fast as paper." Where were the prime woods going, then? While shooting the breeze with several bordertown woodcutters, I learned that local families were not burning as much mesquite and ironwood as in the past, because new markets had developed. Both trees were being cut locally to make charcoal for sale to steak houses in the United States. Although advertised as flavorful mesquite charcoal, tens of thousands of tons of carbonized ironwood have been mixed into the mesquite shipments crossing the border. In addition, the slower-growing ironwood was being cut clear up to the border to make "Seri Indian" wood carvings of animals to sell to American tourists.

"But the Seri villages are 150 miles to the south. Why do the Seri need wood from up here on the border?" I asked.

They don't, a Mexican friend explained. The Seri have to go only half that far to find good ironwood these days. But then, he added, smiling, "there are at least 750 other people making carvings like theirs to sell to the tourists. An awful lot of Indians, no?"

Most American tourists have no idea that the animal figurines they buy are destroying wildlife habitat. The carvings are not made by the Seri, but they are often advertised as Indian handcrafts. The market is booming, and nearly every tourist trap up to the border has non-Indian craftsmen who chainsaw, then carve and sand ironwood by machine. Usable ironwood is becoming scarce everywhere within a hundred miles of the Sea of Cortez and the international border. Woodcutters can now demand $200 for six giant ironwood trunks, killing trees that were four hundred to seven hundred years old. At $250 a ton, ironwood is now as expensive as any wood has ever been in Mexico.

As these desert trees are destroyed, night-bloomers and a variety of other cacti—from towering saguaros to picturesque pincushions—have been left without the camouflage of thorns and shade required to protect them. For a Sonoran cereus, having a woodcutter blow its cover means certain death.

What Flows Across the Border?

I remember the day I stumbled over a hacked-up ironwood and found a heavily browsed cereus exposed beneath it. The stems of the young cactus were beaten back almost to ground level. The next month, they were gone. Such premature deaths have become an unfortunate fact of life on the Mexico side of the border. But it is not as if cereus plants on the American side are necessarily safer. To the contrary, I am no longer complacent that the cacti in our "protected areas" are any less vulnerable.

It took me a while to accept that night-bloomers are in demand in the north. When I first began working with them, during the winter and then a drought that followed the cold, they were dormant, with all the appeal of dead sticks. I dismissed the idea that anyone would want them as an ornamental or greenhouse plant, let alone be able to find them if they did.

Then in late August, not too long after the rain with its revelation, I stumbled into the cereus population just after dusk. At first, from a distance, I thought there were people out in the shrub cover shining flashlights. As I came closer, the flashlights turned into flowers. I had happened on one of the four or five nights of Sonoran cereus blooms that would occur that entire summer.

The flowers were gorgeous! The ugly ducklings had metamorphosed into swans. The silky white flowers exuded a perfume that I could smell from five to ten feet away. The way the delicate buds and flowers were distributed upon the stems reminded me of a Japanese floral arrangement.

In fact, the loveliness of cereus blooms has not been lost on Japanese horticulturists. Illegally trafficked cereus plants sell for upwards of ten thousand yen, over seventy dollars, among Japanese cactus fanciers. Exported out of the United States in violation of CITES—the Convention on International Trade in Endangered Species—night-bloomers regularly reach Japan as well as Germany and other northern European countries.

Ironically, cacti are most frequently removed from U.S. lands stewarded by the government agencies with the strongest conservation messages–the National Parks and Monuments and the National Wildlife Refuges. Visitation is higher in these places than on Bureau of Land Management or state lands, and tourists to parks and refuges are responsible for many more cactus thefts, despite concerted educational efforts to discourage native plant removal. Tourists to Sonoran beach towns also bring cacti back across the border, hidden beneath seats, in boats, or under luggage.

Recently, I became aware of thievery even more disconcerting to me. On a nearby Indian reservation along the border, tribal officials told me of the wholesale removal of all transportable cacti from dozens of acres of Indian lands in remote areas. Hole after hole can be seen as you walk around the reservation. Some were damaged so badly during removal attempts that they were left, half-uprooted, to die. The theft prompted the Indians to begin rewriting their native plant protection law to offer stiffer penalties for outsiders caught taking cacti from their lands. In helping them toughen up their law, I came to understand that nowadays a cactus needs a human community willing to protect it as much as it requires the concealing cover of a nurse tree or shrub.

For plants living on a border, it may not matter who now owns or manages the land. Cereus growing near the boundary of one landholding are dependent on the land uses on the other side.

The Sonoran cereus is seldom found in densities greater than five plants per acre, and often the plants are spread as thinly as a single plant per acre. Their habitat may only cover forty or fifty acres per square mile. In the population I have been studying, sixty cereus plants occur on the Mexican side of the border and nearly as many grow on the U.S. side. Outside of the few hundred acres that these hundred-some cacti inhabit, there is no good habitat for several miles in either direction.

The small population size and low density of Sonoran cereus are of particular concern because this cactus appears to be obligately cross-pollinated. This means that if a pollinator does not find two plants blooming the same night within close proximity of one another, the plants will not set fruit. About a third of the mature plants in the population bloom simultaneously on any single night, then their flowers permanently close before the next morning. Over the entire season, a single plant may bloom on four to six nights, but hardly more than half of all the plants set fruit, and not all of those mature.

Put yourself in the plant's position: If you were a cereus flower, you would have less than eight hours of your whole blooming existence to attract a pollinator that had already visited one of twenty to thirty other bloomers scattered over hundreds of acres of desert lands. If you were a U.S. cereus and half of your potential mates on the other side of the border were wiped out, your chances of producing progeny would be slim.

And what if the pollinators are being wiped out as well? At one time, the cereus's most frequent floral visitor was a common desert dweller, the white-lined sphinx moth. In larval form this moth mobs irrigated fields as a notorious summer feeder on foliage. The cereus population sits adjacent to a valley of twenty-two thousand acres of irrigated cropland, some thirty-five hundred acres planted in cotton. To control sphinx moth larvae, thirty-two hundred gallons of pesticides are sprayed within drift's distance of the cereus habitat during the flowering season. This was another notion that had at first escaped my notice—that having a normally abundant pollinator may work against the cereus, if the pollinator's abundance attracts pesticide sprayers. When spraying precedes blooming by a day or two, few moths remain to haul pollen from one plant to the next. The flowers fade, and their fruits abort.

The night I finally caught sight of a few sphinx moths buzzing from one cereus flower to the next, zooming in on the fragrance from yards away, I had reason to jump for joy. At least I could be sure that during that summer, on that particular night, active pollinators were splashing about in this small binational gene pool. The sphinx moths had not yet all drowned in the local bath of pesticides. There was still hope, perhaps, that the uncultivated desert nearby was extensive enough to allow the recruitment of new moths into the service of the night-bloomers.

Elated, I took my friends and children out to see the last bloom of the season. They were dazzled by the floral flashlights shining up from under the desert bushes. Once again, patches of gray, static shrubs had been transformed by the fragrant, freshly opened blossoms, which were attracting a frenzy of insect activity. As the moths zipped around us, we spotted several additional cereus plants now in flower that we had walked past numerous times but not seen.

By nine in the evening, it looked as though most of the pollen presented that night had already been spent. Exhausted ourselves, we began the bumpy ride down the puddled, muddy Mexican road, overwhelmed by the chimeric nature of the desert. Had I been sleeping, or had the desert? Had the vivid scene we had just witnessed been a dream?

A haze hung in a cool air pocket where the Sonoran road crossed a muddy arroyo. As my Jeep lumbered up out of the depression, through the mist I thought I saw a cluster of men in the middle of the road. With instruments? In the heavy air and in the beam of headlights, the men looked as though they held trumpets, violins, *bassos sextos,* and *guitarrones*.

"Mariachis!" I cried, startling the half-asleep passengers in the Jeep. As we peered through the windshield into the haze, the trumpets turned into pistols, the *guitarrones* into Uzi machine guns–an anti-drug patrol, well-armed, on alert for loads of cocaine and marijuana.

"What are you Americans doing down here?" the head of the *Federales* asked. He seemed bewildered by the presence of children in the vehicle.

"We've been out smelling the cactus flowers . . ." I tried. The chief grimaced, unconvinced.

Where cultures collide on the border, even cactus-sniffing carries its own risks. As the odor of road dust and firearms filled the Jeep, the fragrance of the cereus flowers vanished like a mirage.

From "Here/Now": Mostly on Place

SHERMAN PAUL

During the summer of 1980, when we were building an addition to our cabin in the Minnesota woods, I kept a journal, "Here/Now," from which I have garnered the following entries, mostly on place. I have omitted the dates of the entries but have kept their chronology. Had Robert Duncan written the following lines by 1980, I would have added them.

In the wide Universe
  emptying Itself into me, thru me,
In the myriad of lights falling,

let us speak of the little area of light
  this lamp casts.
Let us speak of what love there is.
Let us speak of how these perishing
  things
uphold me so that
  I fall
    into *Place*.

The Idea of Landscape and the Sense of Place: The title of John Barrell's book makes distinctions, of great historical importance, between concept and percept, observing from without and participating from within. Though he doesn't use *space* as the polar word to *place,* as in the title of Yi-fu Tuan's recent book, the fascination of "landscape"–certainly for Americans in the great age of landscape-painting and -viewing when painting taught one what to view–was with space, and spaciousness: with the liberation of visually searching out space in the joyful security of knowing it "composed," readily conformed to aesthetic expectations and was as ready to conform to economic ones. Space seen is not the same as space sensed. The latter is *place.* Thoreau, himself given to romantic viewing, knew the difference and practiced it by wedding the mind to Nature, by knowing, as he said, by "direct intercourse and sympathy." He knew with all of his senses–"he will smell, taste, see, hear, feel better than other men"–and knowing in this careful, attentive, intimate way, he familiarized space, made it *familial,* or place. His journals report this lifetime work of familiarization. *Walden, or Life in the Woods*–he wished to omit the subtitle but it has stuck–fables a representative action of human history and of nineteenth-century America; clearing the wilderness, building a homestead, beginning to farm. The Homestead Act. And primarily because it involved homesteads, space may be said to have been conquered. Thoreau's distinction is that in the course of doing these things he also created a sacred space, the place of places. Walden is cosmologically central, but this clearing beside Wolf Lake is not and most homesteads are not. I was about to say in defense that Thoreau's greatest achievement was an act of imaginative arrogation–arrogant imagination, isn't that the romantic hubris?–but I believe otherwise, that only an imagination of cosmos, of cosmological scope, will transform our places, make us at home where finally we most wish to be, in the universe.

Self-subsistence is not the goal. That would indeed be subsistence living. We require more than a place provides. We bring it in, so that place *becomes* the navel of the world, opens to it and takes nurture from it. Perhaps by being cosmopolitan it may become cosmological?

Primordial Acts. Clearing, building, farming (gardening). Emerson puts it in a more sophisticated way than Thoreau; his eye is on the village, not his woodland by the pond, and he knows that place is generational. He says that we should build a house, plant a tree, beget a child. He probably meant fruit trees, since there was no need to plant other kinds and he was an orchardist. He did not sanction Thoreau's experiment perhaps because he considered Walden a place away from home and not a home-place. Did he realize the extent to which Thoreau achieved cosmicity or dismiss it as brag? And did Thoreau finally leave Walden—as he frequently did during his stay there—because it was not *everything* a place should be?

To open up and to enclose: both acts are needed to make a place. Having found space for a place, you must make it place. Places belong to human geography, and they may be the supreme human art. Small as my transformative acts have been, I have come to appreciate landscape architecture and to see the considerable justice of those critics at the beginning of this century who, looking back to the transformation of nineteenth-century America, thought Frederick Law Olmsted our greatest artist.

In this beginning to begin again are we building in Heidegger's sense—creating a *location,* making a *space,* a *clearing,* an *open,* in which the fourfold—earth, sky, divinities, and mortals—may *gather,* come to *dwell,* have their *dwelling?* Of all the essays I have read recently in *Poetry, Language, Thought,* none has spoken so directly to me and found me so responsive as "Building Dwelling Thinking." Yet Heidegger, himself a deconstructionist, overlooks the destructiveness of building, and this does not accord with his recognition of *dwelling* as *sparing, preserving, nurturing.* But certainly he is right when he says that we must be capable of dwelling before we can (truly) build. For then the buildings we erect will be complemented by the *building that cultivates growing things. Bauen,* to build, derives from *bhu,* to be, to grow. A dwelling place is a place where one grows things. It is also a place one grows into and from; it is the place one is, has being.

Topography: to describe a place. According to the aeronautical map, we are located 95°45′ W, 47°27′ N, elevation, 1,140 ft. But also from *graphien,* to carve. The place you carve out is the place you write about.

Jim Summerville, in Nashville, recently reminded me that down there some people are quietly marking the fiftieth anniversary of *I'll Take My Stand.* He did not mention Wendell Berry, who more than anyone I know has kept Southern Agrarianism alive. He has done this as much by his example as by modifying it, by eliminating the defensive regionalism and pressing the national claims of agrarianism. His misgivings about political action and his sense of the human situation ("these separate problems are merely aspects of the human problem, which never has been satisfactorily solved") are those of the Southern Agrarians, but his moral stance is Thoreau's, that the problems and their solution are, at bottom, personal and that social reform begins (and ends) at home. We create the energy problem (and the building of the nuclear power plant he protests), and we can solve it by reducing our energy needs, by gardening, for one thing. Gardening is a good example, a diminutive agrarianism, and the argument for it goes beyond Borsodi's economic appeal to home production. It is good for body (countervailing "the obsolescence of the human body"), mind ("an agricultural and ecological education"), and soul (by such work we rejoin the human race). "A garden," he says, "gives interest to a place, and it proves one's place interesting and worthy of interest."

Places are important because all we *really* have are our particular places, our localities. We do not live in the universal, only in our small portions of the universe. In fact, it is the universal that keeps us from our places, that estranges us, as Olson says, from that with which we are most familiar. He says in *Causal Mythology* that "where we are has a particularity which we'd better use because that's about all we got" and that everyone has such "absolute place[s] . . . places and things that are theirs."

Farrell may be said to have a country house, a handsome estate of more than a hundred acres, with a fine house and "barn," lawns, garden, orchard, groves, plantations of pine, and its own interior roads. He has built it all himself, over a period of forty years, the life-work, his serial poem, which has satisfied an otherwise unfulfilled desire to be a landscape architect. Of everything involved in all of this he has practical, technical, and theoretical knowledge, and no one I know is better able and more willing to teach one to live a good life, what in the sixties we talked of in terms of self-subsistence and survival. He calls to mind Scott Nearing, and though he is a Hoosier is still very much an intrepid Yankee. Making his place has been an act of fierce independence, but knowing that place is also a matter of dependence: he has acquired an intimate knowledge of flora, fauna, geology, and former inhabitants. In this exemplary way he has located himself. Still, making a place may keep one in place and may not, finally, be the same as dwelling there. I'm not sure that this applies. But "Hoosier" now suggests the imperial design of Faulkner's plantation owners and how such designs (desires) get translated to the north woods.

Buber addresses me, but I do not find myself in any way better able to acknowledge his truth than I was before. I understand it better and appreciate it more, this great work of poetry, this fable of our estrangement from nature, man, and God (the mystery), and desire for (re)union. I recognize the human predicament of which he speaks: it is accounted for in much advanced criticism of Western thought. The very idea of "relational event" stirs me, perhaps because the term brings together much of what I have been thinking about and because he says that it transforms the cosmos into "a world that is homely and houselike, man's dwelling in the world." It may be that his confident use of "God" and "center" makes me–now perhaps too much aware of the work of *deconstruction* in our time–distrustful. Yet I trust him–it is for me a signature of his thought–when he speaks of the glance in the eyes of his cat and claims that "an animal's eyes have the power to speak a great language." And I think he speaks the truth when he says, "but look! round about you beings live their life, and to whatever point you turn you come upon being." We *are* surrounded, environed by being.

In the beginning, Buber says, is relation. And in the middle, and at the end.

No one has understood so well as the well-digger our deep concern here, appreciated it, and said so. Perhaps it's in the nature of his calling. Or maybe it is because he is neither envious nor invidious (envy is not invidiousness, though it may be at the root of it; my use of invidious is taken from Veblen). Only once before in all the years we have been here has anyone seen the place as we do and spoken of it. That involved water too. There was a drought, and we had advertised for sale a troublesome but reparable gasoline-driven pump, which we had replaced. The suburban shopper (yes, even up here) came out on Thursday, but no one inquired (appeared: we have no phone) until Sunday, and in the meantime we had given the pump to someone who needed it and could repair it. Two young people came that Sunday morning; young people like those we had met in the late sixties at the commune of the Free Folk, serious, committed, clearly familiar with the hard work of subsisting here, finding sustenance in sand, a veritable labor of organic gardening. (The ecstasy when an earthworm finally appears!) They stood just within the gate, where we had gone to meet them, and took in, in an opening perspective, the lay of the land, the disposition of buildings, the evident achievement of clearing: mowed grass, trimmed trees, plantings. In their exclamation–"What a place you have here!"–you could hear their realization of what they wished to realize. Sunday morning.

In sketching a philosophical anthropology, Buber notes epochs of habitation and homelessness. Ours, he says, writing during the rise of Nazism, is special in its human homelessness. The poets as well as theologians testify to this: to what is lost when one no longer has the sense of having a place in an ordered universe, when the community, as Paul Goodman said, is "missing." Yet Buber would not have us "housed and unproblematic," since only in homelessness and solitude do we ask the essential question about ourselves.

The large machinery—a Cat and a backhoe—sat here all weekend. Their keys had been left in them, enticing me (in fantasy anyway) to wonderful deeds of earth-shaking and earth-moving. Why, in minutes I could transform the place! But prudence prevailed when I remembered the sorcerer's apprentice.

Place is not a refuge from despair, because you despair of a place when you are despairing. This is a measure of despair.

I have been pondering this approvingly for days—it is the assumption upon which this work rests—and now, a bad back, got while sailing yesterday, provides an emphatic occasion to mention it. Buber says that "thought cannot authorize itself but is authorized out of the existence of the thinking man." He means actual concrete particular existence in the world.

Isn't this a way in which a place may reconstitute the family? A "starting place," as when Buber says that "to be able to go out to the other you must have the starting place"—the place where you are "with yourself," the place where true dialogue takes place.

I am filled with spiritual yearning. This is not unusual but it surprises me, probably because the depth of feeling answers to a perennial youthfulness. I recognize my sentiment of being as youthful, and as one known in youth. I can understand how men of advanced years give over one life and begin another. The concept of *turning* calls me to attention, and I know, as Buber says in *The Way of Man,* that the power of self-renewal is at the center of the way of man. This little book of Hasidic teaching kindles me. The zaddik addresses me when he explains God's question to Adam: "Where art thou?" I ask myself: "You have lived nearly sixty years. How far along are you?" With Rabbi Bunam, I would like "to become a little more myself." I would like to hallow my life. I do not seek transcendence but transformation. It makes me glad to know that religious yearning is of this world, of one's concrete destiny, and best fulfilled in this world by giving thought not to the self but to the world; that the "fulfillment of existence"–the great treasure–is to be found "in the place where one stands." Here/now.

I am rereading Wendell Berry's *The Unsettling of America,* a jeremiad of the first order, which makes me realize, as with Lasch and Mumford, that the most radical (to the roots) and revolutionary (turning, turning back) perspective today is conservative (conserving). Nothing less than saving the earth and the human legacy of our culturation, the immemorial affair of land and life, of the culture that once respected agriculture. Speaking of houses, which are very much on my mind, Berry locates in the household the habits of consumption that make us so destructive of the world. He says that "the modern house is not a response to its place, but rather to the affluence and social status of its owner." That answers to what I noted earlier of houses being built here, but doesn't exactly exonerate me. Berry defines place in relation to work and responsibility: you live where you work. Our cabin might be said to express the conservation ethic of the wilderness movement: it modified nature as little as possible and provided shelter for the enjoyment of sacred space. It was only a wooden tent, as we are reminded by our attempts to keep out wind and water, to make it more substantial. Still, we alter and add to it, don't abandon it or build from scratch because, for us, it is of the place, "organic." We have done nothing to the cabin for twenty years–just added a porch. And our out-buildings are the response to need, to the work made possible by settling in a wooden tent. Studying and gardening, varieties of nurturance. Our addition, with its expensive, dressy triple-pane windows, its better building, is "modern" and "suburban," though its modesty (it is inset and of lower roofline than the cabin) and tie-in with the cabin (by uniform cedar siding) perhaps subdues that impression. Both buildings are very much the products of the carpenters who built them; in that respect they are local. Now the addition of a large kitchen over a basement fitted to the functions of storing and canning food is the direct result of land use. We have moved beyond but not abandoned the wilderness ethic, incorporated it–if our buildings tell the story–in an ethic of land use, of caring for and building up the soil, of planting trees, of gardening. Our gardens could easily sustain us, and perhaps they will if–again, the future–we *ever* live here and have the strength and energy to do so. "This is no country for old men." Except Scott Nearing! Shouldn't the enterprise toward which we advance be the life-work of the young? The extent to which this is impossible suggests to me a meaning Thoreau never had in mind when he wrote that "America is still unsettled and unexplored." We may have missed "America" entirely.

I am especially sensitive to Berry's argument because, for good and ill, it focuses on the household, the place of ecos/eros. His heavily ironic description of the suburban household as the private locus of all that is dismaying in our civilization – and especially of the consumerism that makes it so destructive of the earth – is matched by the exalted description of the productive (farm) household, whose very economy (ecos) is one of nurturance (eros), restoring us to *health,* healing and hallowing us. "It is possible," he says in respect to the imprisoning suburban household, "to imagine a more generous enclosure – a household welcoming to neighbors and friends; a garden open to the weather, between the woods and the road." Such a household is the formal bond between marriage and earth, human sexuality and the fertility of the earth, and to live in it – to live in this connected way – is, Berry believes, a responsible way, a religious way (from *religio,* from *religare,* to reconnect, connect back) to live in the world, and something we can do. I think, of course, of the centrality of the household in Duncan's poetry, of his association of *heart/hearth* (which incorporates *earth*), and, with it, his restoration of the communal, even the ring dance, also cited by Berry. And when Berry speaks of communion and nurturance, of "the sexual feast and celebration that joins them [us] to all living things and the fertility of the earth," I think of Duncan's great poem, "The Feast."

The measure of success: when I pause in my shoveling and look out over the lake, now dark with scud, and note the reeds – the natural beauty of natural things, this landscape – I know that what I build must conform to this, must belong to this composition.

The Woman Who Married a Bear

GARY SNYDER

Once there was a little girl, about ten years old. She used to go pick berries every summer. Every summer she would go with her family and they would pick berries and dry them. Sometimes they would see bear droppings on the trail. Girls had to be careful about bear droppings, they shouldn't walk over them. Men could walk over them, but young girls had to walk around them. But she loved to jump over the bear droppings, and kick them. She would disobey her mother. All the time she would see them and kick them and step over them. She kept seeing them all around her. She did this from childhood.

She grew up. One summer they were all going out to pick berries, dry fish, and camp. She was with her mother and aunts and sisters all day picking berries. It was toward the end of the day, and she saw some bear droppings. She said all kinds of words to them, kicked them, and jumped over them. The ladies were getting ready to go home, lifting up their burden baskets of blueberries. The young woman saw some extra-good berries and was picking them as the others went ahead. As she started to catch up she slipped, and spilled some of her berries on the ground. So she was bending over and picking them off the ground. The others went on down.

A man was standing there, dressed up fine, his face painted red. She saw him in the shadows. She had never seen him before. He said, "I know where there are lots of big berries, better than those. Let's go fill your basket. I'll walk you home." And they picked a while. It was getting dark. But he said, "There's another good place"–and soon it was dark. He said, "It's too late to go home. Let's fix a dinner." And he cooked over a fire, it looked like a fire. They ate some gopher. And then they made a bed in the leaves. When they went to bed he said, "Don't lift your head in the morning and look at me, even if you wake up before I do."

Next morning when they woke the young man said to her, "We can go on, we'll eat cold gopher. We won't make a fire. Let's get lots of berries." The young woman talked about going home, about her father and mother, and he said, "Don't be afraid. I'll go home with you." Then he slapped his hand down right on top of her head and put a circle around the woman's head with his finger, the way the sun goes. Then she forgot and didn't talk about home any more.

Then she forgot all about going home. She just went about with him, picking berries. Every time they camped it seemed like a month to her, but it was really only a day. They kept traveling from mountain to mountain. Finally she recognized a place. It looked like a place that she and her family used to go and dry meat. He stopped there at the timberline and slapped her head, and made a circle sunwise, and then another on the ground where she was sitting. He said, "Wait here. I am going hunting gophers. We have no meat. Wait till I come back."

Then he came back with the gophers. In the evening they made camp and cooked.

Next morning they got up and traveled on. At last she knew. It was getting near fall, and it was cold. She knew he was a bear. He said, "It's time to make a home" and started digging a den. She really knew he was a bear then. He got quite a ways digging the den and then he said, "Go get some fir boughs and some brush." She broke the branches from up high and brought him a bundle. He saw that and said, "Those limbs are no good. You left a mark and the people will see it and know we were here. We can't stay here." So they left.

They went up to the head of a valley. She recognized this valley. It was where her brothers used to go to hunt and eat bear. They would take the dogs there in April and hunt bear. They would send the dogs into the bear den, and then the bear would come out. That's where her brothers used to go. She knew it.

Her husband dug a den again and sent her out for brush. He said, "Get some brush that is lying on the ground—not from up high. No one will see where you got it, and it will become covered with snow." She did break it from low to the ground, but she also bent some high-up branches too. She let them hang down so her brothers would know. She rubbed sand on herself too—all over her body and limbs. And then she rubbed the trees around, so that the dogs would find her scent. Then she went to the den with her bundles of brush.

When the man was digging he looked like a bear. That was the *only* time. But the rest of the time he looked like a human being. The woman didn't know how else to stay alive, so she stayed with him as long as he was good to her.

"This is better," he said, and he carried the brush inside and fixed the den. After he fixed the den, they left. The Grizzly Bear is the last to go into the den; they like to go around in the snow. So then he spent more days hunting gophers for the winter. She never saw him do it; she sat in the late autumn sun and looked down the valley. He didn't want her to see him digging up gophers like a grizzly bear. Nearly every day he hunted gophers and they picked berries. He was just like a human to her.

It was really late in the fall. He said, "Well, I guess we'll go home now. We have enough food and berries. We'll go down." So they went into the den and stayed there and slept. They woke once a month and ate, and then went back to bed. Each month seemed like another morning, just like another day. They never really went outside, it just seemed like it.

Soon the woman found she was carrying a baby. And then in the middle of the winter, in the den, she had two little babies—one was a girl, and the other was a boy. She had them when the bears have their cubs.

Her husband used to sing in the night and she woke up to hear him. The bear became like a shaman when he started living with the woman. The song just came upon him, like a shaman. He sang it twice. She heard it the first time. The second time he made a sound, "Wuf! Wuf!" and she woke up.

"You're my wife, and I am going to leave soon. It looks like your brothers are going to come up here soon, before the snow is gone. I want you to know that I am going to do something bad. I am going to fight back!"

"Don't do it! They are your brothers-in-law! If you really love me you'll love them too. Don't kill them. Let them kill you! If you really love me don't fight! You have treated me well. Why did you live with me, if you are going to kill them?" "All right," he said. "I won't fight, but I want you to know what would happen!" His big canine teeth looked like swords. "These are what I fight with," he said. She kept pleading. "Don't do anything. I'll still have my children if they kill you!" She really knew he was a bear then.

They went back to sleep. When she woke again he was singing his song. "It's true," he said. "They are coming close. If they do kill me I want you to get my skull and my tail from them. Wherever they kill me build a big fire, and burn my head and tail and sing this song while the head is burning. Sing it until they are all burnt up!" And he sang the song again.

Then they ate some food and went back to bed. Another month went by. They didn't sleep well that month. He kept waking up. "It's coming close," he said. "I can't sleep well. It's getting to be bare ground. Look out and see if the snow is melted in front of the den." She looked out, and there was mud and sand. She grabbed some and made a ball and rubbed it over herself. It was full of her scent. She rolled it down the hill—then the dogs could smell it. She came in and said, "There is bare ground all over in some places." He asked her why she had made the marks. "Why? Why? Why? They'll find us easy!"

They slept for half a month, and then they woke. He was singing again. "This is the last one," he said. "You will not hear me again. Any time now the dogs will be at the door. They are close. Well, I'll fight back! I am going to do something bad!" His wife said, "You know they are my brothers! Don't do it! Who will look after my children if you kill them? You must think of the kids. My brothers will help me. If my brothers hunt you, let them be!" They went back to bed for just a little while. Next morning he said, "Well, it's close! It's close! Wake up!"

Just when they were getting up they heard a noise. "The dogs are barking. Well, I'll leave. Where are my knives? I want them!" He took them down. She saw him putting in his teeth. He was a big Grizzly Bear.

"Please don't fight. If you wanted me, why did you go this far? Just think of the kids. Don't hurt my brothers!" He said, "You won't see me again!" At the entrance he growled, and slapped something back into the den. It was a pet dog, a little bear dog. When he threw the dog in, she grabbed it and shoved it back in the brush under the nest. She put the dog there to keep it. She sat on it and kept it there so it couldn't get out. She wanted to keep it for a reason.

For a long time there was no noise. She went out of the den. She heard her brothers below. They had already killed the bear. She felt bad, and she sat down. She found an arrow, and she picked it up. Then she fitted the little dog with a string around his back. She tied the arrow on the little dog and he ran to his masters. The boys were down there dressing out the bear. They knew the dog. They noticed the arrow and took it off.

"It's funny," they said. "No one in a bear den would tie this on!" They talked about it and decided to send the youngest brother up to the den. A younger brother could talk to his sister, but an older brother couldn't. The older brothers said to the young one, "We lost our sister a year ago. Something could have happened. A bear might have taken her away. You are the youngest, don't be afraid. There is nothing up there but her. You go and see if she is there. Find out!"

He went. She was sitting there crying. The boy came up. She cried when she saw him. She said, "You boys killed your brother-in-law! I went with him last summer. You killed him, but tell the others to save me the skull and the tail. Leave it there for me. When you get home, tell mother to sew a dress for me so I can go home. Sew a dress for the girl, and pants and a shirt for the boy, and moccasins. And tell her to come and see me." He went back down and told his brothers, "This is our sister. She wants us to save the bear's head and tail."

They did this and they went home. They told their mother. She got busy and sewed. She had a dress and moccasins and clothes for the children. The next day she went up there. The mother came to the place, and put clothing on the little kids. Then they went down to where the bear was killed. The boys had left a big fire. The woman burned the head and the tail, then she sang the song, until all was ashes.

Then they went back to her home, but she didn't go right in. She wasn't used to the human smell. She said, "Get the boys to build a camp. I can't come right into the house. It will be quite a while." She stayed there a long time. Toward fall she finally came and stayed with her mother. All winter the kids grew.

Next spring her brothers wanted her to act like a bear. They had killed a female bear that had cubs, one male and one female. They wanted their sister to put on the hide and act like a bear. They fixed little arrows. They pestered her to play with them, and they wanted her two little children to play too. She didn't want it. She told her mother, "I can't do it! Once I do it, I will turn into a bear. I'm half there already. Hair is already showing on my arms and legs–it's quite long." If she had stayed there with her bear husband another summer she would have turned into a bear. "If I put on the bear hide, I'll turn into one," she said.

But they kept telling her to play. Then the boys sneaked up one day and threw the bear hides over her and her little ones. She walked off on four legs! She shook herself just like bear–it just happened! She was a Grizzly Bear. She couldn't do a thing. She had to fight against the arrows. She killed them all off, even her mother. She didn't kill her youngest brother, not him. She couldn't help it. Tears were running down her face.

Then she went on her own. She had her two little cubs with her. They walked up the slope and back into the mountains.

So a Grizzly Bear is partly human. Now people eat Black Bear meat, but they still don't eat Grizzly meat, because Grizzlies are half human.

1. *On "The Woman Who Married a Bear"*

Salmonberries, Crowberries, Nagoonberries, Cloudberries, High Bush Cranberries, Low Bush Cranberries, Thimbleberries, Raspberries, Soapberries, Blackberries, Serviceberries, Manzanita Berries, Red Huckleberries, Blueberries . . .

The salmonberries ripen early, and most of the others toward the end of summer. The berries' sheen, aroma, little spike of flavor, sweetness, all handed down from long ago. Who is it for? The berries call the birds and bears to eat. It's a gift, but there's also a return, for now the seed will be moved away. The little seeds buried in the sweet globules will go traveling in birds' craws, in raccoon bowels, across the rocks, over the river, through the air, to be left on other forest soils to sprout anew.

Picking berries takes patience. The bears draw over the shoots and delicately rake through the clusters with their claws. People make wooden rakes that look like bear-claws and gather them into a basket, or beat the bushes with a wooden spoon toward a winnowing basket held in the other hand. Some women are fast! Picking with all the fingers of both hands, never bruising the berries. When the berries are ripe people go out picking every day, and then dry or pickle them with sourdock for the winter. Eating them does no harm to the bush or the seed. Maybe this story starts with berries.

From long ago the Brown Bears, the Grizzlies (but we wouldn't speak of them directly by such blunt names), have come to the berry fields. They have been out ranging and feeding since spring, ranging dozens or hundreds of miles, often alone. When they gather to the best slopes for berries, there may be many bears picking berries close together, so they manage not to wrangle.

They eat all summer building fat for winter. If for some reason they don't put on enough weight by late fall, the mothers' bodies will abort the little fetus, since midwinter nursing might draw down her strength. After they are done with the soapberries and blueberries on the mountains they go to the streams and rivers for the fall-run salmon.

(Chinook or King, Sockeye or Red or Nerka, Pink or Humpbacked, Dog or Keta, Cherry or Masu, the salmon come into rivers from as far south as the Sacramento and go all the way around the North Pacific to Korea. At every river on the rim there are bears.)

For a long time only the bears and birds were at the berry thickets and the rivers. The humans arrived later. At first they all got along. There was always a bit of food to share. Small animals might be as powerful as big ones. Some, and a few humans, could change skins, change masks. From time to time they all would cross into the spirit world for a Big Time or a contest. The human beings in the original time weren't so bad. Later they seemed to drift away. They got busy with each other and were spending all the time among themselves. They quit coming to meetings, and got more and more stingy. They learned a lot of little stuff, and forgot where they came from.

Some animals started avoiding human beings. Others were concerned because they liked the human people and enjoyed being near them for their funny ways. Bears sort of cared. They still wanted to be seen by people, to surprise them sometimes, even to be caught or killed by them, so they might go inside the houses and hear their music. Maybe that's why bears leave droppings in the trails. It's a way to warn people that they're near, and avoid scaring them. If bears or people get a fright, someone might get hurt. When people see scats they can study them and see how new they are, and check what's being eaten. If it's berries this week, you should know. Scats are a window into a bear's life: they show where she's been. Then when the people go to the mountain they can whistle and also mind their minds, because everybody knows what humans are thinking.

Young girls like to run and jump and sing. Some of them like to poke fun, but it's not usually mean. Jump-rope, they jump and sing– hopscotch, they jump and sing. Still, a girl or woman shouldn't jump over bear droppings, or any droppings really, and neither should men. It's fine to look at them and think about such signs, but it would be foolish to have opinions about them. But this girl always stepped over them and kept talking about it. Perhaps she was being naughty, but we also have to say that she was an exceptional little girl who somehow felt drawn to the wild place.

Drawn to the wild. Bears are so powerful and calm. At the same time, they are the closest of all animals to humans. Everybody says, "after you take a bear's coat off, it looks just like a human." And they act human: they fool, they teach their cubs (who are rowdy and curious), and they remember. They are confident. They will eat little trifles, or knock down a moose, with equal grace. Their claws are delicate and precise: they can pick up a nut between two tips. They make love for hours. They are grumpy after naps. They can lope a hundred miles overnight. They seem to be indestructible. They know what is happening, where to go, and how to get there. They are forgiving. They can become enraged, and when they fight it's as though they feel no pain. They have no enemies, no fears, they can be silly, and they are big-hearted. They are completely at home in the world. They like human beings, and they decided long ago to let the humans join them at the salmon-running rivers and the berry fields.

This girl must have known some of that, and in a way she was calling to the bears. Most people know that breaking rules is bad, and when they do it in a sneaky way they feel they're doing wrong. Some people break the rules because of muddy hearts and greed. Certain people are clear, and break the rules because they want to *know*. They also understand that there's a price to pay, and won't complain.

The rules are matters of manners that have to do with knowledge and power, with life and death, because they deal with taking life and with one's own eating and dying. Human beings, in their ignorance, are apt to give offense. There's a world behind the world we see that is the same world but more open, more transparent, without blocks. Like inside a big mind, the animals and humans all can talk, and those who pass through here get power to heal and help. They learn how to behave, and how not to give offense. To touch this world no matter how briefly is a help in life. People seek it, but the seeking isn't easy. Shapes are fluid here. For a bear, all the beings look like bears. For a human, they all look like humans. Each creature has its stories and its oddities–all the animals with their funny natures acting out different roles. "When dragons and fish see water as a palace, it is just like human beings seeing a palace. They do not think it flows. If an outsider tells them, 'What you see as a palace is running water,' the dragons and fish will be astonished, just as we are when we hear the words, 'Mountains flow.'"–Dōgen. And sometimes those who have the power, or a reason, or are just curious, walk across the borderlines.

So this young woman was grown now, and was picking berries with her family. The bears knew she was there. When she happened to fall behind to pick up the berries she had spilled from her basket, a young man stepped forward from the shadows to introduce himself and help her out. He was in his finest clothing, dressed like one who was going visiting. He was a human to her. And so she entered the in-between world, not exactly human, not exactly animal, where rain might look like fire, and fire might be rain. And he put her more sharply, more solidly, into it, patting her on the head so she forgot. They went under the tangled windfalls, and when they came out they had passed beneath a range of mountains. Each day is a month, or years.

But she didn't entirely forget. We are always in both worlds, because they aren't really two. But even though she remembered that she had a family and a home behind her, it was not too strong a pull, because she was in love. He was a strong, handsome man, and he loved her too. They were in the most beautiful of mountains, in the grand golden weather of late summer, with ripe berries on every slope. Her young maiden dreams were fulfilled. If she has learned to love a bear, he has had to overcome his prejudice against humans, who are weak, light, unpredictable, smelly. So they join in passion and conversation. They live at timberline.

But winter comes. Bears put on weight and grow thick coats. If they are making a new den, they select a place on a slope, dig downward and then up, putting the chamber under a mat of alpine tree roots or under a great slab of rock. The entrance passageway may be three to ten feet long and the chamber eight or ten feet wide. And then the bears break off limbs: they bend them over one arm and break them off with the other and so they gather bedding and place it up in the den. With the den made, the Grizzlies walk around, still hunting, as long as the weather's mild. When snow comes down in earnest, right while it's falling hard, the bear goes into the den, and the falling snow will cover up its tracks.

In the den bears cease to drink or eat or urinate or defecate for four or five months. They are alert and can wake up fairly quickly. Their bodies somehow metabolize their own waste. Though losing fat they increase their lean body mass and conserve their bone volume as though they were awake and active. They dream. Perhaps their dreams are of the gatherings in the Inner Mountains where Bear as "Lord of the Mountain" hosts a great feast for all the other animals.

For the young woman, this is a time of flashing back and forth between selves. The landscape reenters her story: she recognizes a valley. She sees her lover, her husband, first as a bear digging the den, then as a human who sits and chats with her. She helps him gather Balsam Fir boughs for the den and cannot keep herself from leaving marks, leaving signs, for her brothers who will seek her. With annoyance, sadness, and a certain fatalism, he sees this, and without growing angry with her, simply moves on and digs a new den, where she still leaves her scent.

And so they go down into the den. She's not a bear yet, so they put up food for her need. She gives birth to babies in the winter just like bears do. And then it comes that they must grapple with their fates, with their task. He "became like a shaman when he started living with the woman." He was no ordinary bear to be able to change forms and accept humanity, but the power is still coming on him. Elder bears watching over him from afar? Knowing that powers would be needed? A shaman sings songs of power. He sang such a song. If he hadn't known before what was coming, he senses it now: her brothers, and a battle. He could kill them certainly, and keep his wife and children, and move deeper into the mountains and be safe. That is a temptation: he flashes between realms with the huge grizzly canine teeth that are swords/teeth/ swords/teeth to her eyes.

But having come this far into the human realm, he has obligated himself to human custom too, and there is a firm rule which says that brothers-in-law must never fight. The children's name passes down on the mother's side, and the children will be raised by her brothers more than by their father. If they could only accept him as a brother-in-law! That would be an ideal family unit, odd only in that half the unit would be bears (for she is changing into one) and the other half human! What a moment of utopian dream it must have been for him.

She is practical. She knows her brothers will never accept him, and she feels her children must be raised as human. But she loves her husband—not just the handsome human, the bear body. She is getting hairy herself. For several weeks they must live with these choices and the fate that approaches them. He sings in the night again. It is the song that must be sung when a bear has been hunted and killed. He gives the instructions to her: "Wherever they kill me build a big fire, and burn my head and tail and sing this song while the head is burning. Sing it until they are all burnt up!"

So that is the reason they came together: for him to pass this instruction from the bear realm to the human, via her. They both know it now. But he can't quite let it go—he says, "Why? Why?"—and even the final day there's one more thought of fighting back. She always stresses *brothers* and he can't go against that. Out the door he goes on the way to his death, knocking the little Tahltan bear dog behind him with a swipe of the paw. The pet dog is somewhere between wild animal and human, and helps prepare her to rejoin the human. Her husband dies out of sight, but she can hear the barking of the dogs. She sits and weeps, letting the loss and sorrow she was holding back come forth: she pours it out on her younger brother—"You boys just killed your brother-in-law!" which is a grievous thing for them, as well.

(Bears emerge from the den in the spring gaunt and hungry, and fill up on Spring Beauties or such if they can't find a winter-killed elk or moose or caribou carcass.)

She burns the head and tail and sings the song.

She cannot go back to her mother's house. She spends all summer getting used to the human smell—and mourning. That fall and winter, living in the village, she is teaching her relatives what she learned—to burn the skull and tail of a bear after you kill it—and she teaches them the song. There is much more that she learned from her husband about the proper hunting and the ceremony of the bear, and she teaches it all—to be indirect, not to boast, not to point at a bear, to talk slow.

It's not an easy winter. The children don't fit it, nor does she. People don't talk comfortably to her. The brothers are carrying dark and difficult thoughts about their sister who knows so much about bears. They set out the following spring on their annual bear-hunt and come back with the pelt of a female and two cubs. They push, push, their sister to play bear. Secrets not to be told are bothering them: their sister, a bear. What did they eat? What did they speak of? What does she dream? What was it like? How much power does she have now, can she be trusted? What will her children become? Her power and the mystery that surrounds her now go beyond what is comfortable for the humans.

She tries to get her mother to stop them, knowing what will happen, her hair already growing longer. But it happens: the brothers cannot stand this ambiguity: they push her over the line. She turns back into a bear and kills them all except the younger brother. So now they have paid for killing their brother-in-law, and paid for teasing and pushing, and the mother has died too. The young woman and her children are irrevocably bears now: the human world will not accept them. They must return to the wilderness, having accomplished their task—to teach humans the precise manners in regard to bears. Perhaps all this was planned by the Bear Fathers and Mothers, who chose an intrepid young male to be the messenger. For each of the actors there was a price: the bear and the woman's family lost their lives. One cannot cross between realms without paying a high price. She lost her lover and her humanity to become a bear with two rowdy cubs alone in the wild.

That was very long ago. After that time human beings had good relations with the bears. Around the top of the world many peoples have hunted and celebrated and feasted with the bears outdoors in the snow every year in midwinter. Bears and people have shared the berry fields and the salmon streams without much trouble summer after summer. Bears have been careful not to hunt and kill humans as prey, although they would fight back when attacked.

Their story had further consequences: the bear wife was remembered by human beings as a goddess under many names, and there were many stories about her children and what they did in the world.

But that period is over now. The bears are being killed, the humans are everywhere, and the green world is being unraveled and shredded and burned by the spreading of a gray world that seems to have no end. If it weren't for a few old people from the time before, we wouldn't even know this tale.

II. *Maria Johns and the Telling of This Story*

This version of "The Woman Who Married a Bear" is based on a telling by Maria Johns to Catherine McClellan, an anthropologist and ethnohistorian. There are many versions of this story, and eleven of them are examined in McClellan's study, *The Girl Who Married the Bear: A Masterpiece of Indian Oral Tradition* (1970). Of Maria Johns she wrote:

> Maria Johns was born probably some time in the 1880s. The first time she saw a white man was when she and her family challenged the coastal Chilkoot and crossed the Chilkoot Pass to trade at Wilson's store in Dyea. This was in the eighties, and Maria was a young woman. Maria belonged to the *tuq'wedi* or *decitan* sib, and she traced her ancestry ultimately to the coastal Tlingit town of Angoon. While her first language was the Tagish dialect of Athapascan, she also spoke a good deal of Tlingit, which became, in fact, the chief native language of Tagish. She had little command of English.
>
> Although she seems to have led a rather rich, full life, she was in poor health and partly blind during most of her adult days. When I met her in 1948 she was totally blind and spent most of her days in bed covered with a gopherskin robe. Maria composed at least three songs of her own and she evidently told a great many stories to her children, judging by the repertoires of her two grown daughters.
>
> Maria volunteered the bear story on the morning of July 16, 1948. I had visited her in her daughter Dora's house, and had been asking if there were any ritual observances for bears.
>
> Maria was obviously a good raconteur. She pantomimed frequently, changed her voice to indicate that different characters were speaking, and imitated the sounds of the dogs and bears. She hurried the tale a bit at the end for she was worried that I might miss the train taking me from Carcross.
>
> Dora Austin Wedge, the interpreter, had been to school, and she speaks excellent English. Dora's daughter, Annie, was the only other person present. She was much interested in the story, which she evidently had not heard before.

III. *Arkadia*

Brown Bear, *Ursus Arctos.*

Arktos, Greek for bear, in Latin called *urs,* in Sanskrit *rksha,* in Welsh *arth* (King Arthur)–the Sanskrit probably yields *Rakshasas,* night-wandering demons who roar and howl and eat corpses. The proto-proto root, D. Padwa suggests, is "Rrrrrr!"

The "arctic" is where the bears are.

Arkas was the son of Zeus and the Bear-goddess Callisto. He was supposedly progenitor of the Arkades, people of Arkadia, "Bear People." They were worshipers of Pan and Hermes and Artemis, lady of wild things, also associated with bears.

Arkadia: the inland upland plateaus and ranges of the central Peloponnesus, with seven-thousand-foot peaks along the northern edge. Originally it was pine-oak forest and grassland. The other Greeks thought of the Arkadians as an aboriginal population who had always been there, and in fact they remained a tough and independent people throughout Greek history. They were not affected by the Dorian invasions. They were gardeners, herders, and hunters. Urban Greeks and Romans took them as the model of a resilient vernacular subsistence culture that did not lose its connection with nature. In the early centuries A.D., deforestation and soil exhaustion reduced the population, and in the eighth century Slavic immigrants brought something of an end to the old culture. Some of the original Arkadians doubtless knew and told some version of the story of "The Woman Who Married a Bear."

IV. *At the Bear Dance*

A grandmotherly woman in a print dress is speaking to a grizzled hard-worn elder in logger jeans and suspenders: "There are spirits in everything, right?" He nods. She smiles, "You don't look too convinced."

The old man is tall and powerful, though a bit stooped. He has curly steely-gray shoulder-length hair, pants half out of ten-inch ranch boots, heavy rough hands with a broken thumb. He says, "The old-time people didn't have all the right words we have now from science, so they just called the sun's rays 'spirits.' They called a lot of things 'spirits.' It wasn't that they were dumb, but they called these power-things and energy-things 'spirits.'"

A young Anglo is listening in. The woman is intense, clear-eyed, good-humored, and continues her own exposition: "There are a lot of things forgotten. I found a lot of it out. It's not for everybody, it's for our people. We need to teach the young ones."

In the dusty dance area, a circle of children is being formed. Marvin Potts in old felt hat, denim work jacket and jeans, scuffed work boots, is shaping them up, explaining gently. An eight-foot pole is set up in the dance area, with a bear-pelt hanging from it. At the base of the pole is a heap of freshly gathered, still-damp-from-rinsing, sagebrush (artemisia) stems and leaves. Everyone is helping themselves to little bundles of it. A ways up the slope is a shade-shelter with a handgame in progress, the constant rhythm of the drumming on the logs, and the singing rising and falling.

The woman and the two men stand on and on in the hot sun, the crowd washing around them, the older man's voice so soft we can barely hear. The younger man listens and only occasionally questions.

"Science went up so high," the old one says, "that now it's beginning to come back down. We're climbing up with our old-ways knowledge, pretty soon we'll meet science coming down." A young native woman has joined the group, and the older woman is saying, "Don't call me a Maidu or a Concow, I'm a Tai. That's our name for ourselves." The old man turns back to her and says, "What's a Tai?" "That's what I am," she says, "but you don't know it."

"Well, I'm a Maidu just like you," he says. She laughs easily, says, "You're really a ———," and speaks a rich native word. "It means Middle Mountain." He repeats the word easily; he clearly knows it: "Yes, it means Middle Mountain. So that's what we were?"–"Yes, your group. The white anthropologists gave us all the name Maidu."–"OK," he says, and he turns back to the younger man. "I'll go dance now. Come see us some time. We have a lot of trouble keeping people from robbing our graveyard." "What do you do?" the white man asks. "I work parttime in a sawmill." And he departs, gathering three tiny grandchildren and leading them into the children's inner circle of the Bear dance.

Marie Potts is in her wheelchair by a standing pole adorned with strips of maple bark that dangle down around it. A portable PA system is now working and Frank begins to sing: "*Weda . . . weda . . . weda . . .*" There are two circles, an inner one of children and an outer ring of adults. Both begin to revolve. Slowly, going clockwise, people waving their little bundles of artemisia in rhythm. Young and old, lots of whites, lots of native people, lots of colors in between.

Pretty soon the Bear Itself comes forth, the great head held far forward, the thick black pelt covering the back. The two front legs are arms with canes. The lower body of the Bear is wearing cut-off white jeans with the seams half open. He moves well, truly bearlike, weaves in and out through the dancers, goes in circles between them, cutting through, going backwards. He takes a child and leads it along with him under the bearskin, and then turns the child free. A little one bursts into tears as he comes near, while a small boy behind him whops his back with artemisia. He runs up at women, bothers them, they squeal and slap the artemisia at him. At times the song stops for a moment, and the singer gets a few breaths. The Bear goes over to Marie in her wheelchair, puts his paw around her shoulder and nuzzles her. Her eyes glisten, her smile is intense and delighted.

Marvin meanwhile leads the circle of dancers holding the maple-bark streamer pole aloft. (He had said that the twisted curls of bark are to be rattlesnake rattles, and that we play with Rattlesnake and Bear and give them good spirit and humor, so that we'll all get along through the summer.)

The round dance continues in its stately revolutions. Finally Marvin leads the circle out and away from the dance ground. The line of dancers, native men and women, children, middle-aged white ranchers in Wranglers and Resistols, weaves through the densely parked cars and pickups. It goes down between the cinnamon-brown trunks of shady Jeffrey Pines and around the handgame ramada (songs still going strong side by side with the music of the Bear dance), and then over a grassy slope to a fast-running stream where everyone spreads out along the banks and washes their hands and face with cool water. They let their bundles of artemisia float free with the creek. The bundles will flow through the pine forest, back down to the sagebrush, and disappear into the Great Basin.

This is the end of the Bear dance. The bearskin is hung up on the pole again, the people drift toward the whole-steer barbecue pit and the salmon that was a gift from some people on the coast. The power songs of the handgame players continue without break.

At Wepamkun, in Notokkoyo, Shasta, June of 40077

White Wilderness

JEAN CRAIGHEAD GEORGE

This wilderness in which I stand will not be here long. Its white ridges and hummocks, its pale blue chasms, magenta holes and ponds will disappear in less than three weeks. Its demise will not be acid rain or bulldozers, but its own intrinsic self.

I am on the arctic sea ice, a 5.5-million-square-mile parkland of frozen water. It is May 19 and cold. The sun has been up night and day since May 9, and I, like the mammals and birds, am charged with sunlight. Like them I sleep little, a nap at midnight and noon. Bombarded by constant sunlight, we all move with exhilaration: birds, beasts, fishes, and people.

I am standing on a tower of ice looking down on an open lead, a blue river-like break in the white icescape. Leads appear in the solidly frozen ocean several weeks after January 28, the day the sun comes up for the first time after November 16. They mark the beginning of the breakup, when the longer hours of sunlight, the stresses of wind and water, the Coriolis effect of the spinning Earth, and the internal banging and crashing of floes, put the sea ice in motion and turn it back into water.

The opening of the leads forespeak doomsday for the white wilderness and birthday for spring. Migrating birds come up over the globe flying just above the ice in rippling ribbons. Seals dive under the ice and climb up to their pups in glassy, turquoise nurseries in the snowdrifts behind blocks of ice. And the magnificent bowhead whales leave whale tracks on the surface of the water as they migrate through the leads on their way to the Beaufort Sea from the Bering Sea.

It's a strange feeling to stand on this solid wilderness, knowing that if I stay here until the end of June there will be nothing under me but water. It is also strange to know that an entire vocabulary of ice words—pack ice, landfast ice, thin ice, pressure ridges, pans, new ice, rough ice, ice apron, ice holes, first-year ice, freshwater ice, crack in the ice, old crack in the ice, grease ice, plus one hundred and forty more—will be dropped from Eskimo conversations for the summer.

Not until the sun sets in late September will the bell-toned Inupiat ice words be heard again. At that time the hunters will talk about *saalguaq*, the black-colored young ice among heavier ice, which can be penetrated by one thrust of an *unaaq*. They will begin to look for *piqaluyak*, very old ice that has lasted through many summers and is salt free and potable, drinking water for home and ice camp. The Eskimo children will talk about the ice foam, frozen bubbles that roll up on the shore and mark the beginning of the "freeze up," the first stage in the life history of the white wilderness. Like the end of the breakup, the early stages of the freeze up are dangerous. Hunters do not venture far from shore. Instead, they wait for the second stage, the December stillness, when temperatures of forty-five degrees below zero, and lower, thicken the landfast ice—ice frozen to the bottom of the ocean—and hold it steady. In this month the ice topography is set. The landfast ice that I am standing on is edged with mountainous pressure ridges. Drifting icebergs and ice islands are frozen still, forming great shiplike landmarks for the hunters to steer by. The pan ice, flat plains like skating rinks, is six to eight feet deep, ninety feet where it's two or three seasons old. The December stillness is a twilight lit by the stars and the moon, which does not set but circles the top of the world showing off all its phases like a demonstration in a planetarium. The North Star gleams directly overhead to say that there are no directions here but south.

Then comes the sun, and the great white wilderness cracks near shore and moves as it begins the process of destroying itself.

On this day I am some eleven miles from Barrow, Alaska. The midnight sun is coloring the lead purple. A smoke-colored cloud formed by the evaporating sea hangs above it. Called "water sky," it can be seen from miles away, guiding hunters to the leads where the seals and whales are swimming. An eerie red shadow falls at my feet. The colors, like the ice itself, are always changing. In a few hours the icescape may be baby blue, the lead steel gray.

The sea ice is both glorious and terrifying. Glorious when I look out on the pile-ups of sky-blue monoliths of ice ten to twelve feet thick looming above silver pools, terrifying when I stop to think that I am in an environment so unstable it has carried people out to sea, dumped them in the ocean, and crushed them to death.

Like everyone else who comes out on the ice, my fear is that I will be carried off toward Siberia on a floeberg that will slowly dissolve beneath me. This is arctic reality, not paranoia. Before helicopter rescue planes came to the Arctic, many Eskimo hunters were swept out to sea when the wind and currents broke off the ice they were standing on. A few were lucky enough to come back. An elder, one of the old men of Barrow, told of his friend, a whaling captain who looked up to see the ice he was on speeding away from the land, carrying him and four of his crew to sea. They drifted for three months, living on seals and a polar bear whose hide they used for shoes. As their ice island melted, they waited for death in a dark blue sea on a ship of ice going where they did not know. One morning the whaling captain awoke to see the two distinct hills outside the village of Wainwright. His island had docked on the shore. He leaped to the beach, fell to his knees, and cried.

I am in this white wilderness at the invitation of my son, John Craighead George (Craig), coordinator of three bowhead whale studies – behavioral, physiological, and a census. We are with the crew of the census study, which was initiated by the Eskimos after they were told by the International Whaling Commission that they could no longer harvest the endangered bowhead whale. The Eskimos, who practically live on the ice, had seen an abundance of whales and believed they could take the thirty-five animals they needed for their nine whaling villages without changing the upward trend of the population. The bowhead is not only an important food for the Eskimos, but it is the cement that holds their culture together. In the hopes of proving them right, the Eskimo Whaling Commission employed scientists from Alaska and the lower forty-eight states to census the bowhead whale. The first counts were discouraging–only about a thousand were estimated to exist. When both scientists and whaling captains felt the visual count of the whales was unsatisfactory, Craig and his boss, Dr. Tom Albert, brought acoustic experts to the Arctic. Sound gear was dropped beneath the ice. When the "moos" of the great black behemoths were tallied, the Eskimos were proven right. The bowheads, which were all but eliminated by the Yankee whalers in the last century, numbered over six thousand animals.

The census crew lives on the sea ice during April, May, and June, when the bowheads are on their spring migration. Life is dangerous out here. Currents and winds break off floes, storms toss waves up on the ice, and hungry young polar bears swim in from floes looking for food, be they seals or people. Everyone, including myself, must carry a gun–we hope to scare them off by shooting skyward. Survival is as thin as new ice, as tentative as the wind and current, and as erratic as the temperature. The scientists observed the Eskimos, with their four thousand years of experience, to learn how to stay alive on the ice. Like them, they set up tents that can be packed up and put on sleds in ten minutes, wear clothing designed by the Inupiat whalers to cope with the wind, snow, and ice, and never take their eyes off the clouds, water, and ice as they watch for signs of impending disaster.

One disaster is *migalik,* a slushy ice caused by the movement between floes. *Migalik* looks solid but is not. Several years ago a seal hunter ran his snowmobile onto the *migalik* in a fog and lost his machine, his sled, and nearly his life. Another ice to be feared is the "ice override," sheets four or more feet thick that do not break and pile up on the shore as they should, but instead advance up the beach and over barrier islands in a continuous slab that has bulldozed down buildings and is always a threat to oil rigs.

This morning we are watching the most fear-inspiring ice phenomenon–the pack ice, that permanent mass that covers nearly five million square miles of this, the smallest and shallowest of the four oceans. The pack ice drifts, even in December stillness, on a clockwise gyral course, moving three to five kilometers a day, or in a storm, four hundred. The Eskimos call it the *sarri* or "mother ice" because it stays out in the sea at all times and is "the place where the animals always live."

It is indeed. Eight marine mammal species utilize the pack ice: the bowhead and beluga whales, who move along the edges as they swim from sea to sea; the walrus; the ringed, spotted, ribbon, and bearded seals; and the arctic fox, who is not considered a marine mammal but ranges over the pack ice, gliding like a phantom as it tracks down birds. It is the polar bear, however, who is the sovereign of this realm. Astride great white floes, the bear drifts the polar circle all year. Several years ago, one big male white bear with a radio collar placed around his neck by scientists at the Naval Arctic Research Lab touched land in Siberia and was held by the Russians under the suspicion that he might be an American spy.

Although polar bears are residents of the pack ice, they are usually born on the land. In November and December pregnant females come ashore and dig dens in the deep snowdrifts in ravines, where they give birth in late December. After three or four months the mothers move their cubs onto the drifting pack ice, and together they begin to circle the top of the world.

Each of the eight species of marine mammals finds its own ecological niche in the white wilderness. The ringed seals invade the landfast ice, where they can construct their lairs in drifted snow. Spotted and ribboned seals settle in the front line of the ice, and the bearded seals, the seals of the Eskimo skin boat, take up residence wherever the waters are shallow enough for bottom feeding. Sharing their habitat are the gregarious walruses, who ride the floes like mythical gods.

At this moment, the *sarri* is moving toward us like a freight engine without brakes. Craig and the census crew watch it approach. If it strikes the landfast ice where we are, it will pile up the ice and demolish our camp. It can even trap individuals. In the Eskimo book *Puiguitkaat* (pwe-weetkaht), a recounting of old days, an elder tells the story of Aana, who was caught in a such a pile-up.

"After it 'bit' Aana in its grip," the storyteller relates, "the people tried to remove him, but he told them, 'I don't think you can take me off from here with those little penknives, do you?'

"Immediately after Aana had finished saying that, all of a sudden, without warning he was taken down under holding his pipe in his mouth. When he was about to go out of sight he just smiled at those people there."

Most people do not smile even at the merest thought of a pile-up, never mind being "bit" by one. We are grim-faced. Then, "all of a sudden, without warning," the pan ice where our snowmobiles are parked, cracks like a shattering windshield.

"Off the ice!" Craig calls. Instantly young men and women leave the observation ice tower, drop tents, pick up the floorboards, and secure equipment, stoves, and bedding on the six waiting sleds. Within fifteen minutes we are racing the sleds and snowmobiles over upthrusting mountains toward stable ice nearer land. I am on the back of a speeding sled, watching the topography change. The driver, a young Eskimo woman, Elaine Potkotak, steers around a ridge as fog rolls in. Whiteness surrounds us. No sea, sky, or snow exists, just sparkling fog crystals gleaming like sequins. Hoar frost grows on my clothing, changing me into a white-feathered ice person. It is cold and tomblike inside the ice fog.

Leaning over the side of the snowmobile, Elaine follows bright green flags set out along the snowmobile trail for just this purpose. After an interminable time she stops. The other sled drivers hear our motor go off and pull around us.

The wind reverses. The pack ice drifts away. The fog lifts. We are on a pan surrounded by newly erupted ridges as blue as new turquoise, and, because Elaine knows her ice, we are stable. I step off the sled, and the ice turns to snow as I walk.

While Craig and the camp leader scout for a new location to set up the tents, I climb an iceberg to look for our abandoned campsite. I cannot recognize one landmark in the landscape once as familiar to me as my backyard. Unnerved, I look back toward the wires and towers of Barrow, eager to see something permanent. I see only endless miles of sea ice, now cut with sky-blue cracks and crevasses, and I wonder if it isn't time for me to leave the frozen Arctic Ocean to self-destruct.

Suddenly Craig is beside me pointing to a black mass coming toward us.

"King eider," he says and presses his stopwatch. I hear the loud throbbing of wings as a twenty-foot-deep ribbon of birds shoots past heading for the Canadian barrens to breed and raise young before the sun sets. They come on and on, flying just over the ice, skimming hummocks, valleys, icebergs and pans. The topography is outlined in bird wings, an otherworldly sight.

At last the flight ends. Craig clicks the stopwatch.

"Ten minutes," he says. "Probably more than one hundred thousand birds!"

I ask about the birds of the ice, for although there are millions and millions, they represent only a few species.

"I can count them on my fingers," Craig says. "There is the black guillemot. It is to the birds what the polar bear is to the mammals. It can stay out here all winter by going under the ice to keep warm and by surfacing in seal holes to breathe. In spring the guillemot is joined by four eiders, the king, common, spectacled, and Steller's, the glaucous gull, the long-tailed and pomarine jaegers, and the beautiful white arctic tern that flies the leads. And that's just about it, except for a stray or two."

I slide down the iceberg. My fear of the pack ice and of the "bite" of the pile-up tells me to join Elaine and go back to Barrow. But I cannot move. I am caught in a different bite than the one that killed Aana. This one has my mind. I cannot leave. Instead, I stand transfixed, watching the sun circle the icy top of the world and listening to the boom and snap of the sea ice as it turns back to water.

Craig pulls me onto Elaine's sled, and I am sped away from the bite of the vanishing wilderness.

Meeting the Tree of Life

JOHN TALLMADGE

A pine cone sits on my desk in southern Ohio. It is not large–less than two inches long–and it has no decorative value. I have seen other pine cones handsomely displayed, singly or arranged with flowers, nested in Christmas wreaths or heaped in baskets on end tables. Foxtail pines from the High Sierra, ponderosa pines from the Rockies, or piñon pines from the canyonlands all grow beautiful cones in the familir beehive shape. Up close, their radiating scales have the carved elegance of Scandinavian furniture.

But this cone of mine has neither symmetry nor grace. In fact, "cone" is hardly the proper word: it looks more like an oversized cashew. Pick it up, and it feels surprisingly heavy. Drop it, and it clatters like a stone. The bumpy, irregular scales overlap like shingles, and you would be hard put to pry them apart, even with a knife. This cone has a clenched, impenetrable look, as if it had no interest in promoting the future.

Such cones belong to the jack pine, a prolific and weedy tree that grows across North America in a broad band stretching from northern Alberta to Nova Scotia between Hudson Bay and central Minnesota. The jack pine thrives in the poorest soil–rock outcrops, sandy moraine–and it tolerates extremes of heat, cold, and drought that discourage more popular trees. Loggers have little use for it, except occasionally for pulp. If you drive through a northern town, you will not see it growing in many front yards. It lives on the edge of society, a fact suggested by its common name.

The cone on my desk came from a jack pine that grows on a rock overlooking the northwest arm of Horse Lake, two miles from the Canadian border, in the Boundary Waters Canoe Area of Minnesota. How I came by it is a story of unlooked-for transformation, about learning to teach and seeing the unseen.

The first time I encountered jack pines, I was not impressed. I had moved to Minnesota from Utah, following my teaching career to a small liberal arts college of excellent reputation set in the corn and soybean prairies south of Saint Paul. I had fallen in love with the West, and, after three years of roaming the Deep Creek Mountains, the High Uintas, and the Wind River Range, Minnesota hardly seemed like the promised land. The tallest thing in sight was always a grain elevator, and what passed for "wilderness" in these parts was a two-section county park where the land was too steep to plow. I had a couple of colleagues from the West, and they noticed that every ten weeks I would jump on the plane for Salt Lake, right after turning in my grades. So they invited me along on their next trip to the Boundary Waters.

I remember putting in at Basswood Lake, near the small town of Ely, and paddling north into Canada. Jack pines were growing on the shores. Here and there a statelier white or red pine would tower above them. The border lakes were intricate, rockbound, and clean as those in the mountains, but with no commanding summits, it was the tall pines that drew the eye. Along with occasional rocky bluffs, they provided the only sublimity one could find in this country. The white pines were smooth and dark, with feathery needles and haunting, irregular crowns that suggested a character both ancient and oriental. The reds were more rugged and western in appearance, with long, stiff needles and coarse, brick-red bark that broke off like pieces of jigsaw puzzle. The red pine looked like an American tree. With the white pine, it dominated the open, virgin forests of the border lakes.

The jack pines were far less interesting. We found them crowding the rocky bluffs as we slowed toward portages, scrawny trees seldom a foot in diameter, with shaggy bark that curled and broke like weathered shingles. Threadbare twigs dangled from the branches, a cluster of small, coarse needles at each end. We noticed the odd cones that clung to the twigs like lumps of dough. Some were green, some tan, and some bleached to a driftwood gray. It was no fun camping under jack pines, for the sharp needles pierced our tent floors and our clothes. We found ourselves looking for campsites in white or red pine groves, where the ground was soft underfoot and we could look out at evening waters framed by massive pillars and brushstroke foliage, serene as the view from a Japanese temple door.

That was the lake country—beautiful, surely, but not the mountains that I had learned to love. As we drove back home through flat, cut-over forest and small, dead-end towns, I wondered what I was going to do in Minnesota. Ever since college I had dreamed of living an integrated life. In my graduate work and early teaching, I had managed to combine the two things I loved best, literature and wilderness. My students and I had read the great nature writers and then sought out the places that had inspired them, following Thoreau to the summit of Mount Katahdin and Abbey into the maze of the canyonlands. In those days I saw the experience of great literature and the experience of great places as all of a piece. I had chosen to teach for the same reasons that everyone does: something in the material had reached in to change my life. In the giddy, confusing years of the 1960s, I had been drawn to literature because I loved words and hungered for wisdom. The visionary poets of the twentieth century had inspired me with their prophetic certainty. They spoke the truths needed to change our life, to thread our way through the mazes of sex and politics, the clashing horrors of Vietnam, the cloying idolatry of drugs, cults, and patriotism. Reading them was like cupping your hands in a snowmelt stream.

Then, too, I had shared an Edenic view of university life. In those days, so many of us believed that the campus embodied a nobler set of values than the culture at large. It seemed like a perfect community, dedicated to truth, wisdom, and personal fulfillment. Knowledge and insight counted for more than wealth. Passion and creativity were valued above status and power. Politics was ennobled by virtuous ideals. Best of all, there was a place for everyone. It was up to the campus, then, to set an example for society as a whole. To participate in the academic life was an act of public service.

Unfortunately, our government did not share this view. After one year in graduate school, I was moved out smartly for basic training. After that I was posted to language school in Monterey, California, to train as a Russian interrogator in case we should go to war. Ironically, it was there that I discovered nature writers. A weekend pass was good for a lot in California, and the Pacific coast was more inviting than any bar or strip joint in Monterey. Two days on the beach or the trail gave me enough "tonic of wildness" to offset the numbing effects of a week of drill. I remember lying awake in the midnight barracks, feeling the images of those weekend trips return: a necklace of blue surf boiling around a rock, the flint-black silhouettes of cormorants skimming the waves, mint-blue anemones in tide pools, dark, hieroglyphic cypresses spun from the rock. It was the portentous quality of these images that first drew me toward the works of the nature writers. I discovered the bitter elegies of Robinson Jeffers, who had lived on the Big Sur. At first, I read only about places I had seen. But soon his poems drew me out toward other places–Point Lobos, the Sur Rivers, and the Ventana Mountains–and I would arrive feeling the landscape already beginning to glow from within, as if the poetry had given me a sixth sense unknown to the tourists or casual hikers I often met.

That spring in California, I discovered that writing was not just a means of expression: it was a way of seeing the unseen. Poetry could make visible the hidden web of ecological, historical, and spiritual relations that give each place its distinctive presence. A conversation began in my mind between the poetry and the land, and before long I had found other writers and begun traveling farther and wider, into the redwood forests of Gary Snyder and up to John Muir's Yosemite. By summer's end I knew why Jeffers had written of Big Sur crying out for tragedy like all beautiful places, and why Muir had named the Sierra the Range of Light.

Back in graduate school, I was surprised to find that no one had heard of the nature writers, so I made them the focus of my research and teaching. In those days, I saw teaching as an improvisational performing art. My goal was to capture my students' imagination through a combination of wit, empathy, awesome knowledge, and sheer entertainment. I was not a naturalist: I saw wilderness as a scene for heroic action. In my classes I concentrated on the literature of adventure–writers like Muir, Clarence King, and John McPhee–with an admixture of natural history and vision quests, as represented by Abbey, Thoreau, and Annie Dillard. I could not imagine taking students anywhere but into the mountains. In literature and in landscape, I was devoted to the sublime.

All this I pondered in the fading light, as we drove south away from the Boundary Waters. What was I going to do in Minnesota? That canoe trip had been like no other journey: it had had no center, no peak experience, no moment of vision. Yet it had made an undeniable impression, like my first trips along the Big Sur coast. There was, after all, some sublimity in the virgin woods. Perhaps I could make do with the Boundary Waters in some way or other. As we sped into farm country at last, I composed my mind to remember the tall pines. When jack pines appeared, silhouetted against the burning dusk, I put them out of my mind.

Inevitably I became a naturalist, for the essence of a country like the Boundary Waters lies in its details. I took my first class to Horse Lake because it was convenient: five portages in, with two neighboring campsites shaded by red and white pines. The approach could not have appeared less promising: five miles of slow paddling down a twisted, muskeg stream lined with anorexic spruce and thickets of alder. The water was dark as molasses and frothed over rapids like so much root beer. Yet, here and there, a cluster of jack pines would appear on a rock, and we would catch the flutelike call of a white-throated sparrow. Steering close to shore, we often struck sweet gale bushes, releasing a startling fragrance of camphor. We saw mink weaving among the rocks, dark and sinuous as the stream itself. On portages, we found red knots of bunchberries shining like buttons. And then the woods would open onto a new lake with its own distinctive character—light, scent, color, and shoreline texture all accentuating the spirit of the place.

Travel here was intimate and absorbing, without drama yet subtly transforming. Each time I returned, I became more attuned to small things: the canoelike shape of a spruce needle, the coralline branching of reindeer moss, the frosty tartness of blueberries. I learned that the small herbaceous plants on the forest floor, like trillium and wild sarsaparilla, come up each year from the same root, leaving annual rings that show they are often older than the trees above them. They flourish in old soil with a thick layer of duff, but they cannot compete in disturbed areas, where raspberry, fireweed, and poison ivy take over. I learned that loons, sleek as torpedos in water, can hardly move on land. Once I chanced upon one of their shallow nests built in some reeds less than a handsbreadth from the lake. In it were two eggs the size of avocados, colored the same dull green as an army jeep. I got out of there fast, for the parents were surely close by. Loons mate for life and spend their winters along the Florida coast—not unlike some rich Minnesota farmers. I loved them for their constancy, their beauty, their heroic journeys. They come north to breed, each pair claiming a lake and defending it with their wild, ecstatic cries that shimmer long afterward in your mind, like some sound equivalent of the northern lights.

Returning to the same place again and again was a new experience for me. All my previous trips had been explorations: in fact, I had never taken a class to the same place twice. Therefore, the details had often escaped me. I had been satisfied to encounter the landscape as scenery that presented itself in the most blatant, romantic terms. But getting to know a place is a slow process, like making friends, and each time I went to the Boundary Waters I discovered a deeper layer of detail. The accumulation of chance encounters led me gradually toward an ecological view, with a new feeling for subtlety and a deeper sense of participation.

Not surprisingly, my taste in literature began to change. I drifted away from prophetic and visionary writers toward those who celebrated relationship and community. I began to prefer the understated, laconic sketches of Aldo Leopold and the calligraphic epiphanies of Snyder, both of which seemed to mirror the ways in which the land presented itself. The land does not speak, yet it hides nothing: to be there is to listen, to become involved. So too with writers like these. The sense of beauty depended on coming to see relationships between imagery, allusions, point of view, and the character of the speaker. Here was an aesthetic of nuance, not the alpine sublimity of high peaks, but the variety and intricacy of moss, the dipping sine curve of a woodpecker in flight, the artless art of symbiosis enabling lichen to feed on rock. The beauty of these texts, like that of the Boundary Waters itself, was always just coming into view. It was easy to miss, like a mink disappearing. Reading these texts and reading the land required the same poised alertness and imagination.

This ecological sense also began to influence my teaching. In canoe country, everyone depends on everyone else. One ankle sprained on a portage means the end of the trip, no matter whose ankle it is. To launch canoes, therefore, is to begin a study in ethics. A canoe trip is not like a logging drive: the leader is not the boss, but rather the guide who facilitates the adventure. I found that, despite my familiarity with the place and experience in dealing with emergencies, I was no more likely to spot a moose than the greenhorn (or sophomore) in the bow. Nor could I, in my role as guide, take credit for any such sightings. This may be bear and wolf country, but the animals appear by grace: they are not found by seeking. All learning comes as a gift to the prepared mind. The best memories of these trips always turned out to be things I had least expected.

I soon noticed similar processes at work in my classes back home. Try as I might, I could not control what my students learned. As a young teacher, I had prepared assiduously, arriving with sheaves of notes and a clutch of books, well-scuffed, which I would pile conspicuously on the floor. (I had seen this done in graduate school, with its culture of "esoterrorism.") After some brief opening remarks, I would try to lead the class through a series of key insights. My students, however, proved much less compliant than Socrates'. They were always running off on a tangent or seizing on wacky ideas that had no place in my lesson plan.

I would nod politely, glance at my watch, and then wrench the discussion back to its formal course. This worked only about half the time. I began to sympathize with my middle-aged colleagues, who stood around the coffeepot complaining that their students were getting more sullen and ignorant by the year.

After several canoe trips, however, I began to think there might be a better way. I realized that my students were bringing to literature the same beginner's mind that all of us brought to the woods. Each kind of expertise, after all, imposes its own limits on the imagination. So I began to experiment. I arranged the chairs in a circle, which encouraged open discussion. I came to class without books, which forced me to listen to what the students were saying, as if we were all encountering these texts for the first time. Initially it was an act, but it got results. Discussions took off. I no longer left class exhausted. Instead of bringing notes, I began to take them. Gradually, the act became a genuine style. I found myself changing from a performer and impresario to a plain member and citizen of the learning community. As a teacher, I had gained strength by giving up control.

I suppose it was natural to begin seeing my whole career in ecological terms as well. In fanciful moments, I imagined a kind of "professional succession" beginning with the wastelands of the army. First came the brushed-in heaths of graduate school, where big minds lumbered among the lush growth, browsing on new ideas. This soon gave way to deciduous thickets of temporary jobs, where we all struggled to publish, designing new courses and jostling for a place. Over time, the real work made itself known: nature writing and wilderness travel emerged like evergreen saplings under the pale, leggy birches of freshman English. This was the mixed, transitional woods of assistant professorship, tough going if you were on foot, yet evolving steadily toward the light-filled climax of tenure, where everyone would be guaranteed a place in the sun. In the white pine forests of the border lakes, the air was sweet and quiet as a church. You could sit down anywhere and feel at home. I wanted my life to be like this too. I wanted to realize the dream of a community where the order and decency of human relationships mirrored the beauty of nature itself.

Blithe as this vision was, I did not see it just as a dream of the 1960s. It had been preached, in one form or another, by all the great nature writers. Even Leopold had used the harmony and integrity of nature as a standard against which to measure both social and individual character. He had written that one of the banes of an ecological education was to live alone in a world of wounds. People abused the land because they had not come to love it. They could not love it until they had learned to see the unseen. The role of the teacher, therefore, whether enacted in class, in print, or in the woods, was vital to healing both society and the earth. I felt very good about what I was doing. My life seemed all of a piece.

But, we are made a little lower than the angels and cannot imagine paradise without overlooking some vital piece. In this particular case, it was the jack pine. Five years after moving to Minnesota, I discovered that, despite my newfound reverence for detail, I had not been paying close enough attention. That summer I was teaching my course at a field station near Ely, and one evening I heard a visiting scientist named Bud Heinselman lecture on forest fire. I was astonished by his perspective. To my untutored eye, this country had always seemed wonderfully lush and green. Yet, incredibly, its character has evolved through periodic destruction by fire. Despite the abundance of surface water in lakes, swamps, and streams, the land dries out in August, and fires are ignited by "dry lightning" from thunderstorms that move on before dropping their rain. Fires sweep along the ground, destroying the duff and leaving a mineral soil enriched with ash. It kills the tall pines, though some may survive on the edges to seed in a new generation. The versatile aspens send up clones from underground roots that survive periodic burns: what appears as a grove may in fact be a single plant of great antiquity. The aspen saplings provide abundant food for deer, moose, and beaver, all of which multiply after a fire. Since fires bring on lush growths of blueberry and raspberry, bears increase as well. The Ojibway Indians, who lived here before us, were known to set fires to increase the berry crop. The old-growth forests of tall pine may be pleasant and admirable, but they do not support much wildlife, since they offer so little food. This was not the paradise of which we have heard, where all creatures thrive in the abundance of the Lord.

Because of fire, what we humans perceive as a timeless, enduring wilderness is really no more than a wave in the stream of life. The pattern of succession, so evident in clear-cut and burnt-over areas, does not actually lead to a stable, perennial state. In the Boundary Waters, a "climax community" does not exist. What we think of as climax forest is only a forest waiting to be burned. The longer the wait, the greater the accumulation of fuel and the fiercer the holocaust when it finally comes. Core out the oldest trees in a stand, and you are likely to find thin bands of charcoal: these trees stood on the edge of an ancient burn. You can find the same sort of evidence by sampling the sediments in lakes and bogs: a paper-thin layer of ash appears like a colored leaf in a book. Using these methods, Heinselman and his team had compiled a history of fires reaching back more than three hundred years. Their findings revealed an overlapping mosaic of burns, at irregular intervals and of varying size. Generally, however, a given area can expect to burn about once a century under natural conditions.

This fire cycle is invisible to us because its period exceeds the span of a human life. But all species who live here must shape their lives to its curve. Heinselman took the jack pine as an example. The persistent cones are sealed by a heat-sensitive resin. When a fire comes through, the cone opens to release its seeds, whose internal chemistry has been activated by heat. (Foresters attempting to raise jack pines found they had to bake the seeds before they would sprout.) The seeds land on a mineral soil enriched with ash and open to the sun. They cannot get started if they land on shady duff. The species *needs* fire in order to reproduce. Every stand marks a place that was once burnt to the ground.

After hearing all this, the students and I had to see for ourselves. I stuck one of the stubby cones on my knife and held it over the stove. At first nothing happened. The cone blackened and started to smoke. Then suddenly it began to arch like a worm. It was alive! I yanked it away, but it continued to bend. The scales opened like spreading fingers, slowing as it cooled. I tapped it on the table, and several seeds fell out. They were shiny black and smaller than the head of a pin. Each bore a long translucent wing shaped like a feather. I tossed one into the air and watched it drift away, spinning like a fan. We opened several other cones, and even the oldest and grayest held glistening seeds, each one ready to catch the wind. I believe that my affection for jack pines dates from that moment, when I first beheld their seeds. Such frail tokens upon which to set all one's hope! Yet the numberless, scraggy stands showed the species knew how to survive, and not just survive, but prevail.

That fall I stood for tenure and was denied. Four days before Christmas the dean and the president called me in and told me that my time at the college was up. I had not, in their view, demonstrated "the qualities of mind necessary to sustain a permanent teaching position." They did not wish to discuss the decision; I had the right to request a written explanation from the dean.

It was early morning, the shortest day of the year. I walked blinking into the pale light. My lungs felt as if they were stuffed with wool. The campus buildings, so comfortable and familiar, were shimmering as if seen through a heat flicker. The air tasted of dust and ash. My body felt weightless and disoriented, as if I were falling through space.

To some, this may seem like an extreme reaction. It certainly was for me. I had never expected anything like this to happen. It was a disaster far worse than being plucked out of graduate school by the draft. I had lost not just my job, but my career. Incredible as it may seem, teaching experience counts for little in academia: professors, like fashion models, grow less attractive with age. But that was not all. I had thought I was paying close attention, both to my department and to the college administration. Yet now it appeared that I had grossly misread the signs.

For about two weeks I lived in shock. At night I would lie awake, heat rolling off my body in waves. My thoughts raced back and forth through my six years at the college, throwing old fears into sudden, lurid relief or magnifying the already monstrous silhouettes of my enemies. No place was safe. The air stung with betrayal. When I awoke at dawn, my sheets would be damp and clinging.

Word got out after New Year's Day when classes resumed. My students and colleagues were outraged. They urged me to appeal–what else was there to do? Gradually, my shock settled into a hard and glowing rage. I spent hours conferring with my supporters. I filed the appeal, and thereby obtained some of the documents from my review. I requested an explanation from the dean. His letter described a person I hardly recognized. So all my free time went into building a case. It was exacting, lawyerly work, comforting in a way, though I had little hope for success. The documents hinted at some reasons for the decision–suspicion of my teaching methods, my wilderness trips, and my practice of nature writing–but, since tenure reviews are confidential, I knew the real reasons would always be hidden.

Meanwhile, I forgot all about the Boundary Waters and the jack pine. Life went on, not the life I had known as a member and citizen of this idealized community, but a kind of internal, psychic exile. On the surface, everything looked the same: I taught my classes, dozed through department meetings, and ate my hamburger in the student union. But underneath, all my relationships had gone into suspense. Everything I had taken for granted was now called into question. To the college, I was both a nonperson and a cause célèbre. I belonged and did not belong. This was an anguishing condition, but it had the virtue of turning me into an observer.

Almost immediately, my enemies began to reveal themselves by their behavior. Certain members of my department greeted me with the same bland courtesy they had affected for six years, as if nothing extraordinary had happened. Others became effusive, suddenly interested in my research and my plans. One of these was a man who had come up to me after the departmental review, clasped my hand, and congratulated me on winning their endorsement for tenure: shortly thereafter, he had written a lethal report to the dean. Others, less subtle, expressed their regrets and then made a point of avoiding me. That winter was strewn with such brittle, inauthentic encounters, the scorched debris of an ideal professional life.

At the same time, however, I received all kinds of unlooked-for support. The students wrote angry editorials and launched a petition drive. My friends in the English department released the confidential letters they had submitted for my review. Other professors, some only distant acquaintances, called me to say they had protested the decision. Letters came in from faraway parts of the country. Even the janitor in my building who drove the bus for canoe trips stopped by the office every day, just to check in. One morning he told me about the time he and his wife had come home to find their farmhouse in flames. Nothing was insured; they lost all they had. But people came from all over with offers of food, clothing, a place to stay. It gave them hope, he said. And, two years later, they had jobs in town, a snug new house, and a baby girl.

Meanwhile, as I say, I had forgotten the jack pine, for my intellect was consumed with the legalities of my appeal. Yet, as the winter wore on, I became aware of a growing clarity in my emotional life. I began to realize that every relationship based on some calculus of power–anything from professional envy or ambition to campus politics to private social agendas–had begun to wither the moment I was fired. But those based on a free gift of love–straight talk, a favor, a moment of affirmation, a small forgiveness–bloomed and flourished more vigorously than before. Some, indeed, had sprung up from roots of which I was not even aware. And so, broken and poor in spirit, I began to feel spiritually enriched, as if a table were being spread for me in full view of my enemies.

The appeal process required a formal hearing that was finally scheduled for May. I have only the dimmest memories of the first weeks of my nature writers course, which had been planned in happier times. I did not really expect to win tenure from the appeal, since the hearing board could only ask the president to reconsider. But I did hope the faculty would condemn the decision and the process by which it had been reached as a violation of principles in which–supposedly–we all believed. I hoped, in short, for a moral victory.

Spring came late, and the board rejected my appeal–for lack, as the chairman said, of a "smoking gun." Thus the community declared itself. I no longer had a future here, nor anywhere in my chosen vocation.

A few days later, my class left for the Boundary Waters. Throughout the long drive I sat quietly on the bus, numb with the ache of impending exile. We followed winter as it retreated north. Five hours into the trip, we crossed the Laurentian Divide, beyond which all the streams flow toward Hudson Bay. Up here the woods were budding, open, and full of light. The aspen crowns were barely misted with green. As we approached our jumping-off place, I noticed jack pines clustering, dark and shaggy, among the smooth, chalky trunks of the aspen. I noticed them the next morning as we launched canoes onto the twisting muskeg stream that led to Horse Lake. We camped in our old places under the tall pines. While the students bustled about, exploring, gathering wood, savoring the excitement of adventure, I sat looking out on the water, as if fixing the place in my mind would somehow undo the decree of banishment. My throat was full of loss. I envied the students their youth, their freshness, their eagerness for the future.

Next afternoon, we dispersed to various parts of the lake for journal writing and meditation. (Most of our writers had encountered the land this way, and we wanted to simulate their experience.) Two students, who knew me from other courses, asked me to come along with them. I was grateful to be asked. No doubt they had sensed my mood.

We canoed to the northwest shore of the lake, where a high bluff plunged to the water. On top, a cluster of jack pines offered the only shade. We climbed up to them and sat down in the dry moss, lichen, and needle duff, looking out over the lake. The shores were quilted with aspens and evergreens: cedar, white spruce, and balsam fir. Here and there, a white pine spread its lone, oriental flag above them. I thought how pristine the country looked, and yet it was ripe for a conflagration. It was hard to imagine fire on such a fresh, clear day, with spring winds rippling the ice-cold water.

We sat making small talk for a while. Then one of the students asked, "What are you going to do?" It was not an unusual question. I had heard it often that spring, from my aging colleagues trapped in the English department, from students seeking letters of recommendation. I usually said something flippant, like "get another job." I did not want to own my grief. But here in the woods the question caught me off guard. I experienced a hot flash of anxiety, followed by one of those extraordinary moments when time slows down and everything seems brilliantly clear, as if seen through a microscope. "What are you going to do?" It was not just a question of what to do next, but of what to do now. What are you going to do now, right now, right here? It meant this moment. It meant every moment when someone else consents to listen. What are you going to do with the gift of their attention? It meant every moment of life. What are you going to do with it? Where will you take your stand?

I looked off to the far shore where aspens danced, glittering with hope. I felt the coarse, tindery duff beside me, laced with the nodding shadows of jack pine boughs. I saw the clenched, bulbous cones overhead, ready for lightning. They knew what to expect from that guileless sky.

And so I told those students everything, everything I have just told you. And as I did so, I felt myself stretching and cracking open, and from behind the charred crust of my anger I felt winged words falling into the wind, spinning away to take root God knows where. I realized that this was true teaching at last: the act of bearing witness, to own a truth you have lived beyond all pretense. I realized, too, that the tenure review had come as a gift, for it had clarified all my relationships. It had opened my eyes to the spiritual dimension of life, the network of love that sustains us through times of despair and empowers us to transmute suffering into wisdom. This world is unseen, like harmony in music or the complex ecology of the Boundary Waters, yet it determines the character of our life. It leaves a signature in each work of our nature writers, just as the fire cycle leaves its mark in the jack pine cone. With each winged seed, the jack pine speaks with its whole being the wisdom of centuries of evolutionary time. It has learned to ride into the future on the energy of its own destruction.

Across the lake a stiff wind had arisen, scuffing the aspen groves to white and darkening the water as it approached. Soon our canoe began bumping against the shore. Other canoes were already heading back toward camp. From this height, they looked like grains of rice.

We got up and brushed the lichens and twigs from our clothes. It was time to move on. As the students ran down to grab the canoe, I stayed a moment under the jack pines. I reached up and plucked a cone, savoring its gnarled surface, the thought of its winged and hidden life. In my hand it felt strangely warm. I heard the students calling and started down. I put the pine cone in my pocket. Here it is.

Animals as Brothers and Sisters

BRENDA PETERSON

As a child I played a game with my siblings: *What country are you? What body of water? What war? What animal?* My sister was Ireland, the South Seas, the War of Independence, and a white stallion. My brother was Timbuktu, the Amazon River, the Hundred Years' War, and a cobra. I was South America, the Gulf of Mexico, the Civil War, and a dolphin. Sometimes we called upon our animals–my sister galloping away from grown-ups with a powerful snort and a flick of her fine, silver mane; my brother summoning the fierce serpent hiss to ward off his older sisters; and I soaring through sea and air with my tribe of dolphins.

Our parents didn't think it odd then that their children metamorphosed into animals, oceans, or wars right there in the middle of the lliving room or backyard. My father always planted his family next to a forest, a river, or an ocean–all of which were expansive and natural enough to absorb our wildest play. One of the few times our transformation was curbed was at the dinner table–if, say, my brother as cobra poised above my hand as I cut the cake in exact equal pieces, or if my sister was pawing the tablecloth with her pale equine impatience. Then my father, whose own play was raising horses and hunting, might threaten my sister with a tight bit or suggest my brother uncoil himself and cool down until his blood was really reptilian, slow and grounded.

"The cobra can't uncoil until he strikes and eats," my brother would mutter as he sighed and right before us changed back into the youngest child. But his eyes remained hooded.

"The white stallion is never broken," my sister would warn my father, who did raise her with a freer hand as if she were one of his fine, high-strung thoroughbreds.

I was always underwater during these discussions, in the green, shady depths of my warm gulf, listening more intently to a language that creaked and chattered like high-speed hinges–dolphin gossip. Or sometimes I just tuned in to their other language: the pictures dolphins send one another in their minds. Because I had to come up for air, and my eyes were as good above water as below, I did keep a lookout on my family's dinner dramas. But if my mother was having one of her bad moods or my father was giving one of his lectures, back down I'd go to my other family, who welcomed me with wide-open fins. Even without hands, the dolphins embraced me more than most people did. It was body-to-body, full embrace, our eyes unblinking, utterly open as we swam, belly-to-belly, our skin twenty times more sensitive than that of humans.

The play my siblings and I chose as children is mirrored in the way we live as grown-ups. And I suspect it has much to do with our career choices, our relationships, even where we choose to live. My sister finds her South Seas body of water (and reunites with our family's Seminole blood) by living in Florida and marrying into an old Key West family. She is still fighting her War of Independence, a ripsnorting battle, which involves her husband and three daughters as high-spirited playmates. Every so often I see her snort and toss her full mane of hair; and when she really means business, she paws the ground with her delicate, high-heeled hooves. My brother, as a navy jet navigator, has traveled the world, is caught up in all sorts of military intrigue in faraway places–enough to last one hundred years easily. His serpentine ways have surrendered more to the feminine aspects of the snake, for at the births of his three daughters, my brother shed his toughened military skin and was reborn. And me, well I now live in a whole city under water: Seattle. And I'm still swimming with dolphins.

This is difficult to do in Puget Sound with its year-round temperature variation from forty-six to forty-eight degrees. So aside from sighting Dall's Porpoise schools from shore or ferry, I've had to go to warmer waters to make my psychic life match up with my actual life. How convenient then that my sister's Conch Republic connections carried me to the Florida Keys to find my animal allies.

Actually, it was a kind of coincidence. Five years ago I was sitting in my Seattle study listening to the splatter of rain on my roof, reading a *New York Times* article about a Florida Keys research program that reversed our society's usual prejudice against animals: the dolphins were not there for human amusement. Instead, we were their "toys," and the researchers studied the interaction between humans and dolphins while in the cetacean's own environment. Everything was geared toward what fascinated the dolphins, what made them choose a particular person as a swimming partner over another. Researchers don't know why, but dolphins prefer children first, then women, and then men. But why do they ignore some people completely and gather around others with absolute attention?

As I was reading this article, my sister Paula called. Seems she was stranded in a motel along the string of coral keys, en route to Key West. I could just hear her champing at the bit. "We're stuck here overnight. The girls are bored silly," she said. They weren't the only ones, I suggested, then I told her about the dolphin research that just happened to be only miles from their motel.

"All right, all right, we'll go swim with your dolphins," Paula said.

My sister was eight months pregnant with her third daughter, and none of her deliveries had been simple. Lowering herself and her swollen belly into the warm tropical water, my sister showed her true mettle–she was, as my father always recognized, fine, great-hearted horseflesh. My nieces needed no courage to dive into the lagoons where dolphins chattered about them. It was delight at first sight.

These dolphins are in elective captivity, which means the underwater fences that separate them from the saltwater canal leading to the ocean are opened twice a day to let the dolphins return to their home territory. They return to the research center of their own free will. No dolphin has ever chosen to escape; they seem as fascinated with humans as we are with them, though we've given them much reason to keep their distance. There is no record, since antiquity, of a dolphin harming humans; yet despite a recent U.S. ban on drift nets, some countries still routinely kill thousands of dolphins each year in a search for tuna. Caught in these "death nets," the dolphins die dreadfully; they drown.

Because dolphins breathe as we do, nurse their young, and are warm-blooded, there is a mammalian bond, which perhaps explains why dolphins have anything whatsoever to do with humans. The bond was evident as Paula lost her pregnant waddle and floated weightless, waiting for the dolphins. But first they played with her daughters. My five-year-old niece, Lauren, with the fierce grip of all newborns and single-minded children, grabbed hold of a dorsal fin and held on as she was sped around the lagoon at what seemed like the speed of light. She doesn't remember seeing anything but bright bubbles. Careful to keep Lauren's small head above water, her dolphin, who weighed about three hundred pounds and was itself a relative child (only six years old in a lifespan of approximately forty years), carried Lauren as it would a precious baby doll.

Another dolphin swam sister Lindsay, two and a half, round and round until she was dizzy. Then they let her bob about in her life jacket, singing at the top of her lungs. The dolphins showed their approval with some tail slaps, spins, and leaps, always careful about their motors, those great tails. With their phenomenal 360° overlapping vision, the dolphins always know exactly where you are. After playing with the children, the dolphins circled my sister, and when their echolocation heard the fetal heartbeat, they got very excited. The high-frequency whines and creaks increased as their sonar sounded my sister's belly, read the fetal blood pressure, and scanned the infant's stomach gasses for signs of stress.

"What are they doing?" Paula asked. Her whole body was buzzing.

"Offering to midwife you," the researcher replied. "They seem concerned about the baby. Is . . . is there anything wrong?"

"I don't think so," Paula answered, and for the first time in that lagoon, she felt fear. My sister is a nurse and knows all about ultrasound. But perhaps there was something the dolphins deciphered that our technology didn't.

Then the researcher told my nieces how the dolphins midwife one another, assisting the mother as she swirls and spins in labor by stroking her flanks, and at the moment of birth, when the newborn dolphin eases out of one watery womb into another, the midwives lift the calf with their long, sensitive beaks up to the surface. There the newborn dolphin takes its first breath. Every breath thereafter for the rest of the dolphin's life will be taken consciously. A cetacean's brain, somewhat larger than that of a human's, has had thirty million more years of evolutionary development than our species. Some scientists theorize that the dolphins exist in an alpha state–what we experience as meditation–and since they never really sleep, just switch sides of the brain being used, researchers wonder what kind of intelligence is here.

My sister certainly wondered when she gave birth three weeks later to a daughter with a rare blood disease. Had the dolphins diagnosed it? After much trauma and weeks of watching her newborn double as a tiny human pincushion, Paula brought her daughter, Lissy, home from the hospital.

On Lissy's second birthday, in gratitude and out of curiosity, we took her back to swim with dolphins. But the rules had changed: no pregnant women and only children who are excellent swimmers. So little Lissy jumped and leaped on the side of the lagoon, shouting, "I am a dolphin! I am a dolphin!" as her sisters and Paula and I all slipped back into the warm salt water.

This was my second swim with dolphins, and my first time at the Dolphins Plus Marine Mammal Research and Education Center in Key Largo. My dolphin companions, Niki, Dreamer, and Sara, were six-year-old females in elective captivity only two years. Exuberant, still quite wild, they are children themselves.

"Remember," our researcher reminded us as we eased into the water, "you'll have to be creative if you want them to play with you–don't just bob about gawking. They've already got enough float toys."

The dolphins are not rewarded with food for interaction with humans; that is the old model of performance. Food is given the dolphins at another time, separate from human-cetacean interaction. The real reward for all of us is the play itself.

As I swam, snorkel mask down, arms at my side to signal that I would wait for them to choose to play with me, I heard far below the familiar high-frequency dialogue. It sounded like the high-pitched whine of a jet engine right before takeoff, combined with rapid creaks and bleeps. The sounds encircled my body, and then, as the dolphins came closer, there was that astonishing physical sensation of being probed by their sonar. It's as subtle as an X ray, but exhilarating. My whole body tingled, stomach gurgled, head felt pleasurable pricking as if a high-speed ping-pong game played with light was bouncing around my brain.

I am reminded of my friend John Carlyle, who has researched, trained, and played with dolphins for twenty years, telling me of one of his experiments with dolphin echolocation. Trying to discern the limits of dolphin sonar, he placed eyecups on his dolphins and then asked them to recognize certain symbols by echolocation. In an experiment that had taken him months to design, the dolphins learned the symbols in five minutes. So John had to come up with more difficult ways of testing the depth of their sonar. After much research, his final experiment, which was the limit of human technology at the time, discovered dolphins could discern a symbol one one-thousandth of an inch square; they could also differentiate varying carbon densities in metal rods and could distinguish colors—all by echolocation. Knowing of their precision made the experience of having my body echo-scrutinized more than simply a physical sensation. I was scanned more profoundly than by anything our medical science has yet invented. But there is another element here, not at all scientific. It is what happens to my heart, not physiologically, but emotionally.

Every time I'm sounded by a cetacean, I feel as if my cells are penetrated, seen, and—what is the most remarkable—*accepted*. I've never felt judgment, even if the dolphin chooses to bypass me for another playmate. The Dolphins Plus researchers report that often, whether a dolphin spends five or forty-five minutes with a swimmer, everyone will say it was enough, all they needed, as much as they could receive. In fact, every time I've swum with dolphins, my human companions and I have admitted afterward that we each felt like the favorite. Could it be we have something to learn about parenting from dolphins?

As I swam on the surface, peering through my mask into the dense green depth, I wondered what I must look like to a dolphin. Humans are the most ungainly mammals dolphins see in the ocean. We are the only creatures in the sea who splash at both ends of our bodies. Our appendages don't move in sync with the sea as do the long arms of anemones. There is only one dance in the sea, one pulsing movement of all that lives, one law. Even if one of our bombs exploded here, its harm would be muted. And after it exploded, its metal innards would settle to the sea bottom as no more than an artificial reef adorned by pink brain coral, starfish, and barnacles. Swimming and hoping a dolphin might play with me, I wondered about those ancient dolphin ancestors who decided millions of years ago–while humans were still hanging from trees–to go back to the sea. Did those early cetaceans foresee the fate of our species' self-destruction? Is that why they left us to our weapon-and-tool-making hands (the use of which takes up so much of our brain's functions), while their skeletal hands slowly evolved into flippers to flow *with* rather than change their environment?

The dolphins always come when I'm most distracted, when my mind is not on them at all, but drifting, perhaps dreaming. In my underwater reverie, I was startled by the sensuous skin stroking my legs. I happily recognized the silken, clean, elegant feel of dolphin belly as Dreamer gently surfaced over me, running her whole body across my back like a bow glides across violin strings. And then she was gone. There were only the sounds fading, then coming closer as suddenly all three young dolphins swam toward me. I still see in my dreams those gray globelike domes with brown, unblinking eyes meeting mine as the dolphins greeted me underwater. "Intimate" is the only way I can describe their eye contact. Benevolent, familiar, and again that acceptance. Any fear one feels vanishes once those eyes hold yours.

"Choose one!" the researcher shouted above me. Having been underwater so long, I could barely hear his voice. But I remembered his instructions; the dolphins are possessive of their toys, and I needed to bond with only one or else they'd squabble among themselves. So I chose Niki, though Dreamer was my favorite, because if truth be told, Niki made the choice. She slipped her dorsal fin under my arm and raced off with me at such a speed I saw only bubbles and sky. Then she dove with me and we both held our breaths. As we surfaced, I saw in the opposite lagoon two dolphins leaping with my nieces like calves in tow. No time to see anything else–I inhaled and dove down again.

Thrilling, this underwater ballet, as I twirled with my dolphin, my hands along her flanks. Fluid, this liquid life below where all is weightless and waves of warmth enfolded my body as I breathed air in this watery element. And I was not alone. Everywhere was sound–my nieces' singing and the dolphins' dialogue. My mind suddenly filled with pictures. Then I realized that every time I imagined my dolphin doing something, a split second later she did it. It was not a performance at my request; it was an answer to my wondering. Call and response. It was also an anticipation of my delight, a *willingness* that is the purest form of play.

I pictured myself spinning round, one hand on Niki's heart–it happened. I saw both my arms outstretched, a dolphin's dorsal offered each hand–and suddenly I was flying between Niki and Dreamer. It was impossible to tell who was sending whom these pictures. But they all happened. It was like instant replay of everything imagined. And now I understood why the child in me chose dolphins. What more perfect playmates?

Ahead in the water swam my sister. Paula was galloping with her dolphin, and my niece Lauren had a dolphin gently resting its long beak on her legs like a paddle to push her through the water. Distracted, I broke one of the basic rules: I got too close to a dolphin and her favorite toy (Paula). Suddenly a wallop to my shoulder. My world turned upside down, and though I was face-up in the air, I breathed water. Sputtering, I broke another rule: my body tilted vertically, a sign to the dolphins of distress. Another whack of a pectoral in the lower back, then a beak thrust under my bottom to raise me above the water.

"Horizontal!" the researchers yelled. "They think you're drowning."

I would rather play with a dolphin than be rescued by one. Those whacks are painful reprimands, a lesson in life and death to a wayward human. Blowholes fiercely expelled their air everywhere around me. Surrounded by all three dolphins, I started to cry. I failed, I felt. I was a fool. And for the first time ever, I was afraid of them.

It was hard not to cower there in the water with them. All the pictures flooding my mind overwhelmed me, and I couldn't figure anything out. Except I remembered to float, though my body was rigid and what I would most have liked to do was curl up into a fetal ball and be safe on shore, the way long ago I'd surface from my own darker daydreams to find myself at the comfortingly ordinary dinner table I first sought to escape. But this was real; I couldn't imagine my way out of it. Or could I?

Again and again one picture appeared in my head. It was I, still shaken, but surrendering to all three dolphins at once. I breathed raggedly, the snorkel like an intruding fist into my mouth. But after closing my eyes, I allowed it. Yes, they could come back and find me again where I floated in fear. At first Niki and Sara were tentative, their beaks very gently stroking my legs. Now that I wasn't going to drown, would I play with them again?

I am small, I thought, and hoped they could hear. *I am just a human being—afraid and fragile in your element. Be careful with me?*

And they were. Together the three of them floated me so slowly my body barely rippled water. Then began the deepest healing. Dreamer gently eased me away from the others with a nudge of her dorsal fin. Her eyes steadily held mine as she swam gracefully in wide arcs of figure eights around the lagoon. In and out through warm water. My body surrendered to the massage, not of hands, but of water and sound. I thought of the others who come here who are not as healthy as I—the autistic and Down's syndrome children, the handicapped, the terminally ill, all of them nursed by the dolphins who embraced me. Deeper than the play, more moving than the sense of another mind in these waters, is the simple kindness of the creatures. I do not understand it. I want to.

When I closed my eyes, the pictures grew stronger, as did my senses. My hands slid down Dreamer's silken body, memorizing notches and scars as a blind woman does her loved one. I remembered that in China those born blind were believed to be the most gifted masseurs—because hands are another way of seeing. My hands still hold the exact feel of dolphin skin. Even now, across time and continent, my hands can still grow warmer, tingle with the memory of that cool, sleek skin that trembles when touched.

Dreamer's name comes from her eyes. Half-lidded, there is in her mild, dark eyes a different light. Sloe-eyed, they call it down South—and the sweet, fizzy drink made from those black sloe berries is a euphoric mix reminiscent of humid, fragrant southern nights. *Down home,* I thought, as we glided through dark green depths. I closed my eyes and felt that this underwater world, too, was down home.

As Dreamer circled with me, I was so relaxed I barely recognized the voices far above in the high, harsher air. "Come back," the researcher called. "It's time . . . but the dolphins are having so much fun with you, they're not going to let you get out easily."

There was a firmness to our researcher's voice, like a parent calling children in from play. We'd been swimming with the dolphins three times longer than the allotted half hour, and I suddenly realized I was utterly exhausted. I felt like I'd been moving heavy furniture for days. My snorkel mask fogged and the balmy wind felt abrupt. I remembered gravity and how it works against me.

"You'll all have to link arms to signal the dolphins that you're serious about getting out. They'll respect your tribe. But they'll protest!"

As my sister and my nieces and I moved toward the dock, the dolphins leapt over our heads, chided us for spoiling their sport, and swam figure eights between our legs. Even as we hoisted ourselves up onto the platform, Niki cajoled my niece by opening her long beak and running it up and down Lauren's small leg.

"She's tasting you," the researcher told Lauren and laughed. "They only do that when they *really* like you."

"It's a compliment," Lauren confirmed in her most matter-of-fact voice. "She likes me best."

Of course we all secretly felt that way. I still feel that way, after five years of swimming with these same dolphins. In my Seattle study I sit surrounded by my photos–Dreamer's eyes still hold mine as she glides by in a shining green background; Niki exuberantly leaps above the surface; Sara offers her abiding companionship. My niece Lauren, now ten, sends me drawings of dolphins and whales; her sister Lindsay has decided to speak nothing but dolphin dialect when I call long-distance. We cluck and click and make sounds deep in our throats like a Geiger counter. Anyone crossing wires on our conversations might think there was electronic equipment trouble on the line.

So the second generation of our family carries on the tradition of claiming our animals within. I often tell my nieces a story about the Northwest Coast Indian belief that before humans came on the scene, the world was made up of beings whose spirits could change into anything from salmon to rock, from raven to waterfall. Every form had its lessons. And the human form, being the most recent, was considered to have the most lessons. Long ago, when my own father taught me that animals were part of our larger family, he echoed this common wisdom. It is wisdom that still serves me well.

I'll often find myself in some situation thinking, "What would a dolphin do?" Animals do not change the world; they adapt. In my own life, the flexibility and adaptability of a dolphin mind, their sense of tribe and play, guides me. I can call upon the dolphin inside me for counsel as well as companionship. And the irony is that apprenticing myself to an animal like a cetacean somehow teaches me more about becoming a human being. As John Lilly, the respected dolphin researcher, wrote, "You see, what I found after twelve years of work with dolphins, is that the limits are not in them, the limits are in us. So I had to go away and find out, who am I? What's this all about?"

These days here in the Northwest, where the Puget Sound offers some of the world's most fertile habitat for marine animals, I realize that becoming a dolphin, like becoming a human, is a state of mind. Here, where the Native Americans remind us that everything shimmers with its own inner life, I walk by the water and send greetings in the form of mental pictures to all the mammals that swim in the Sound. Often I visit the belugas at Point Defiance Zoo, especially when I am sad or in need of inspiration. Those white, generous creatures gaze at me through glass and I put my hands up, hoping they'll feel my own little form of echolocation. Sometimes I sing to them and they give back with resonant mews and trills.

On a recent visit I was lucky enough to make physical contact with Maya and Inouk, the zoo's two older belugas. Each took my hand deep into its great mouth, by way of tasting and greeting me. Their soft pink tongues clasped my hand as their mellons (those dazzling white globe-like foreheads) subtly changed size and shape to scan me. It felt like they held the whole of me, their eyes on mine, as they gently took my hand. For days afterward, my hands tingled with warmth.

If I am to learn to live by water, what better teacher than a cetacean? If my brother and sisters are across a continent from me, what better siblings than marine mammal kin? And if I am to metamorphose and try to transform my life into what as a child I only dreamed about, what better myths to live by than the Northwest Indian stories that tell of mysterious beings who metamorphose back and forth between animal and human kingdoms?

In my study, next to my wall of Dreamer, Niki, and Sara photos, between my whale mobile and drawing of a purple Grandmother Whale drawn by my niece Lauren, is a small black-and-white sketch of a woman swimming upstream, her body half salmon. Entwined in a surging school of salmon, she leaps and insists herself toward her homeland. Drawn by Caroline Orr, a local Colville tribal member and native painter, this inspired storytelling-in-art reminds me of all the other worlds that co-exist alongside me: Salmon People's world, the sky world, this Sound's watery world. Maybe I can learn to swim between them. After all, Native Americans know that salmon are really people who live in underwater villages. It is these people who graciously change into fish each spring to give us our food.

Sometimes staring long enough at Orr's *Raven and Salmon Woman,* I feel silver scales glisten against my sides and am emboldened by the bravery of a being who seeks her birthplace while making the circle of death and renewal. Sometimes gazing into Dreamer's familiar eyes as she swims toward me, my room full of windows becomes an air-filled aquarium. And sometimes when Seattle is so low and gray, the misting rain so familiar, I know we human mammals here in the Northwest underwater villages are closely related to the Salmon People, the cetaceans, and all life in the sea.

Each of us has an animal totem, some are blessed with many. We can all summon our animals and they will come. They will be our brothers and sisters and live alongside us—even swim upstream to die with us so we will not be without a guide through that greatest change of worlds. Some myths say that our animals then enter other afterlife dimensions with us, and return to begin this Earth's journey all over again.

I know that claiming cetaceans as my kin is not just science, it's shrewd. Learning to be human and to know what I might become, I need all the help I can get.

The local storyteller Johnny Moses (Nuu Chah Nulth tribe) told this Salish tale at a gathering:

> Long ago the trees thought they were people.
> Long ago the mountains thought they were people.
> Long ago the animals thought they were people.
> Someday they will say . . .
> Long ago the human beings thought they were people.

Valley of the Crows

RICK BASS

Dave Blackburn lives with his wife and two young daughters and young son above the rocky bank of Montana's little-known Kootenai River. Dave's a logger but is studying to take an outfitter's exam this October so that he can take clients down the river to fish, rather than cut trees. Dave has remodeled a large turn-of-the-century cabin and barn on the north bank of the Kootenai, so close to the river that he can flip a stone in, side-armed, from his back porch. There is a small fence around the yard for his children to play in, and flowers of all colors grow around the borders.

Ospreys, goldeneye ducks, hummingbirds, mallards, mergansers, and an endangered species—the amazing Harlequin duck—are the birds I saw the day I floated the river with Dave. In the fall, Dave has bald eagles that perch in his cottonwoods to prey on the runs of spawning mountain whitefish as they head up the Kootenai for the confluence of the Fisher River, which lies a mile upstream of Dave's cabin.

The nearest town to Dave is Libby, population twenty-six hundred, and the mayor and city council and chamber of commerce of that town want to build a dam on the Kootenai, a dam that would put Dave's and his family's house beneath roughly fifty feet of water.

The town of Libby does not own the Kootenai River, of course–it's a beautiful wide and deep fast-flowing river that the Montana Department of Fish, Wildlife and Parks has ranked as the sixth-best trout-fishing river in the entire state, right behind well-known legends as the Yellowstone, Madison, and Gallatin–but the mayor of Libby thinks the energy produced from a dam could be sold to California.

It couldn't–not legally–and this fact has been explained to the mayor, but rather than acknowledging this fact and exiting gracefully after that fact was brought up (Libby has invested eighteen thousand dollars of city monies in this chase for good fortune, and public opinion feels that the mayor's simply too embarrassed at having been suckered by the Californians, that it's too late to back down or pull out)–the mayor of Libby–Fred Brown–instead falls back on his next argument, that if the city of Libby doesn't build the dam (ten miles downstream from the already existing Libby Dam)–then the U.S. Army Corps of Engineers will build the dam anyway.

And never mind that the dam would just be a dam, unable to sell power or *do* anything (there has been a surplus of electricity in the Northwest since 1937, when the first federal dam project was completed)–the mayor of Libby still has a point, however skewed the logic, because the Corps *does* want another dam, and the Corps has assured citizens of Libby and surrounding Lincoln County that it might take five years, ten years, or twenty, but that they (the Corps) intend to put another dam in.

The Corps tried once before, in 1981, but was beaten back by a court order due to cost-inefficiency (the General Accounting Office called it the most ineffective ratio of cost-benefit they'd ever seen on a hydro project). Despite the court's ruling, however, the Corps went ahead anyway and continued to let drilling contracts for the project, using taxpayer dollars–and there are old people living along the river, says Dave, an old couple named the Beltmores, old people living out the last years of their lives, who cannot decide whether to plant another fruit tree in their backyard, because it would be such a waste if the tree were buried by another reservoir similar to the one ten miles upstream.

Dave's a mild fellow, a sportsman, with a big wide grin, who tells flies to "shoo." He's not the kind of brawler you'd want on your side in a dam fight such as the one that is about to happen on the Kootenai; but Dave writes letters, talks to other landowners in the area, and takes anyone who wants to see the river down it in his beautiful little cream-

and-green fishing boat, and will show them how to catch the Kootenai's famous rainbow trout–the river has produced the world record–while they still exist.

Dave points out the Beltmores' backyard and shakes his head, forgetting, for the moment, that he's on the river, and what might almost be labeled a frown crosses his face.

"That just *gripes* me," he says, looking up at their well-kept lawn, and at the steep mountains above their home, winter range for deer, moose, and elk. Thirty-three years old, with a wife and three kids, car payments, two horses, a big barn, his built-by-his-own-sweat cabin about to be buried forever, and his favorite fishing river in the whole country about to disappear, and it *gripes* him.

"Look at that," he says, pausing at the oars and pointing down the river. An osprey is hovering over the center of the river like an archangel, holding, fluttering, and then it tucks and falls as if shot, and hits the water a hundred yards away from us with a crack! that sounds like cannonfire.

There's some splashing, and then quickly, wings flapping, the osprey's climbing back into the sky gripping a shining silver fish.

"They never miss," says Dave. "Never."

The reason the Kootenai produces so many rainbow trout, and such large ones, says Dave–he's got an eight-pounder on the wall of his cabin–is because it is so much deeper than any of Montana's better-known rivers. The center of the Kootenai, on the stretch by Dave's house, is about a quarter of a mile wide, and thirty feet deep in the center, at high water–twenty feet, at low water–and Montana fisheries biologists have measured 250 trout per thousand feet of river in the Kootenai, which is about double the usual number. The Kootenai's deep, cold waters are simply able to hold more trout.

It's a bright day in May, warm, and Dave guesses the water temperature to be around forty-four degrees. He pulls a thermometer out of a box and checks, and it is forty-six.

Tempers are rising in Montana these days, as the traditional export industries, such as mining, oil and gas, timber, and agriculture, hit hard by falling market prices, look for a scapegoat. In most instances it is the environmentalists whom the industries seek to blame for weak commodities markets.

A University of Montana professor says differently. Dr. Tom Power, chairman of the Department of Economics, notes that the primary component of Montana's income is now derived from "non-labor" sources–

retired people, and self-employed people moving into the state because of its natural beauty—and that Montana's natural beauty, small cities, and recreational opportunities draw independent sources of income totaling four billion dollars a year to the state—not tourists, but "non-labor" residents.

All of Montana's annual exports—timber, and the rest—combine for only two billion dollars.

Dave's an expert fly fisherman, and he casts his tiny flies at points distant with unbelievable accuracy, sometimes looking back over his shoulder and talking at the same time. He's got a sixty-pound anchor, a block of lead, with which he can anchor the boat in the middle of all but the swiftest currents, and cast to where he knows trout are—where he's seen them rising, or where a flow of current is broken up, a shelf of gravel, or behind a big boulder—and he points downstream to the small logging and mining town of Libby, towards which the river is running, carrying us in its drift.

"The Indians used to call it 'The Valley of Sickness,'" he says, still pointing to where the mayor and city council members live. "People were always getting sick in the winter—bad air would get trapped by all the mountains surrounding it, and it could never get out; it would just turn stagnant, until the end of winter chased it out."

There's a hatch of mayflies going on, a species of mayfly called the iron dun, and they're beautiful. Mayflies live in their larval stage on the stony underwater bottoms of cold-flowing rivers, and each day a new crop hatches, crawling out of their cocoons as nymphs and swimming for the surface. Trout get most of them before they ever make it to the top, and those that do make it to the top have to float along in their caddis-shell cocoons for a while, still struggling to get out—but what finally emerges from the trauma is, typically, beautiful.

The mayfly, once it is out of the shell and floating on the surface, has translucent, shimmering wings—hundreds of mayflies on the river's fast surface, floating like tiny sailboats, all lifting off as soon as their wings are dry—we timed them at about thirty seconds, for drying their wings after hatching—and if the mayflies can make it into the air, they've usually survived.

The trick to catching trout, says Dave, on the Kootenai or any other trout river, is simple—"match the hatch," he says, and puts his rod down and scoops one of the floating caddis-shells off of the top of the river as the current sweeps it past; he holds the little cocoon, built out of tiny pieces of twig and leaf—about half an inch long—in the palm of his hand.

The sun is bright, warm on our shoulders and faces, and the little cocoon is beginning to wiggle.

A pair of slender antennae poke out of the open end of the shell, and then a tiny pair of legs, and a tiny pair of beaded, suspicious eyes. Trout are feeding all around us, wild, savage trout making blip! blip! sounds as they swirl and suck in as many of the mayflies as they can, but all we can do is watch the struggle going on in the palm of Dave's hand.

The mayfly is pulling itself out like a person crawling out of the waves onto the beach. Its wings are wet and folded against its body, and it's not very attractive-looking; but there's a breeze, and suddenly it's able to lift its wings, and it pivots in Dave's hand, turns all around, gathering information, and it's suddenly beautiful, a deep sea-green color, almost iridescent, and the lacy wings are more intricate than anyone's grandmother's embroidery. It's got a forked tail, like some kind of god.

Dave reaches into his vest and pulls out an artificial fly that he tied this winter, some thread wrapped around the tiniest, sharpest hook, and places it in the palm of his hand next to the mayfly.

For a moment, it appears that there are two mayflies in Dave's hand, two iron duns, staring at each other, face-to-face; then, before we can see all of it that we want to, the real mayfly rises to the air with a whirring of wings, and is one of dozens, one of hundreds.

There are tall snow-capped mountains on either side of us, all around us, and we watch the mayfly until we can't see it. Dave is grinning, satisfied.

"That one made it," he says, rubbing his hands together, dusting off the old abandoned caddis-shell. "That one got away."

Dave's fishing with a dry fly—an artificial fly that floats on the surface—but because he wants me to catch a trout, my first trout on the Kootenai, he's got me drift-fishing a wet fly: a fly that does not float on the water's surface, like a hatched mayfly drying its wings, but instead floats beneath the surface, in a sort of suspended middle-state, imitating one of the mayflies rising from the bottom.

"Ninety percent of strikes occur below the surface," Dave says, watching my line, grinning. He's beside himself, laughing out loud sometimes, just glad to be on the river. "You're going to catch your first fish on the Kootenai." He's laughing again. "You'll see." He sits back down and pulls the anchor up and begins rowing, taking us along with the river, farther downstream, closer to Libby. Canadian geese, in pairs, are nesting in the tall river grass along the shore, in the Kootenai's backwaters. They're big birds, and they honk at us when we get too close.

Under the city council's plan, utility companies in Tacoma and Eugene would pay for and control the project–and would pay the town of Libby annual royalties based on energy sold. Since there is already (and always has been) a hydroelectric energy surplus in the Northwest, it's believed that most of this power would go to the more prodigious energy needs of California.

The water's so clear as we drift along that we can sometimes see the trout beneath us. Depending on what part of the story Dave's telling me, his casts are either fast or furious–like lashes, as he talks about the town's mayor–or soft and floating. When he talks about the Kootenai's natural values, and his family, he waves his fly rod back and forth like the tiniest, most subtle orchestrations of an overture, and his voice is soft; when he gets into the politics of earth-scraping and concrete-pouring his voice is still soft, but the rod goes mad, there's a whipping sound, all around my ears–though the fly still continues to land gently on the water.

Letting my wet fly drift along the bottom, the baby way, I catch the first trout, a flashing, leaping bolt of silver that amazes me with its strength. The fly is so tiny and the leader-line (tippet) is so light, and my rod's bending so much, that I'm afraid the whole outfit is going to break, and I'm hesitant to fight the fish; I feel as if I might do something wrong. But Dave's howling, he's laughing, moving around in the boat to see it and shouting every time it jumps, and then I'm shouting, and the fish dives, darts behind rocks, and there's that wonderful moment when I don't know if I'm going to get it or not–that brief moment when the fish, making full use of the river and its currents, is stronger–but then the fish grows tired, I'm bigger than it is, stronger of course, and it has to show me its beauty; it succumbs.

Dave slips the net under it, a two-pound rainbow–I take quick pictures–and then he wets his hands, takes the hook daintily out of the fish's fierce mouth, and lowers it back into the river, holds it there for a moment as it regains its bearings, and then he releases it. The fish darts away, but the river is changed, for me.

I like the river better, now.

Dave spots another, smaller trout rising to the hatch of iron duns, and whispers to me, "Watch this," and begins casting to a spot where he says he can see fish rising, though I can see nothing, and am still living in my memory, of how my fish leapt so high and so many times, of how a thing was–and then Dave's rod is bent, the line is stretched taut and cutting the water, and I'm beginning to panic, thinking of someone in California turning on a lamp at dusk, or a hair dryer; and of Dave's lovely old turn-of-the-century homestead, submerged, beneath fifty feet of water—and of the whole river disappearing, an entire stretch, and the geese that nest along it, and the wide gravel sandbars, the fast hurry of the current: all of these things being gone.

The infamous Libby Dam, ten miles upstream, was completed in 1975, at a cost of roughly three hundred million dollars, and a recent Price-Waterhouse (1981) accounting study revealed that the value of hydroelectricity sold from it is not even enough to make the annual *interest* payments on the cost of construction, which was built with money taken from U.S. taxpayers.

The Corps just loves to build dams, is the bottom line—it's what keeps them in business—and now that they've gotten Libby Dam, they want to move ten miles downstream to the next stretch of fast water. The Corps has stated that if the Tacoma-Eugene partnership is unable to get a dam built, it doesn't matter—that they'll do it, if someone else doesn't beat them to it—but what I'm thinking is, like hell they will.

Dave's not casting anymore, he's just seated in the middle of his boat at the oars, grinning, looking up at the mountains to see if he can spot any deer or elk. The fierce winters force them down out of the mountains into the riverbottom area, and he says he's seen as many as sixty at one time in the winter: but it's a warm day, and windy, and all we see are ospreys in the bright blue sky above us.

The real solution to the problem, says Dave, frowning a little and pulling on the oars, though the current's just fine, we're making good progress already—is to have this section of the Kootenai declared a National Wild and Scenic River: because even if the Tacoma-Eugene dam is defeated (as it appears it will be), the Corps represents a much greater threat, and a Wild and Scenic River would be the only thing that could prevent the Corps from even *considering* a dam there; and, according to the updated U.S. Forest Service Plan for the Kootenai National Forest, the river (along with three others) is eligible, based on a number of "outstandingly remarkable" features, not the least of which is its tremendous fishing, although we've put our poles away and are just drifting, listening to the water's rushings, and feeling the sun.

The Jennings Rapids Dam would bring only five hundred thousand dollars annually in royalties to the town of Libby, says Dave, but studies show that the recreational value of the Kootenai and its tributaries is in excess of three million dollars annually.

Dave knows these figures the way he knows the name of the trout flies and the hatches on this river–iron duns, March browns, gray-olive scuds. . . .

We drift past a charred stretch of gravel beach, a stump of land that the Corps bought when they were about to put the Jennings Rapids dam in the first time, back in 1981, even if against court order.

Dave's voice is still soft, and I'm not exactly sure how I can tell he's angry, as he points to the charred beach, but he is.

"Last week, that was the best perching spot for bald eagles on this whole stretch of river," he says. "They'd sit up in those cottonwoods. . . ." He pauses, for there are no cottonwoods on the Corp's strip of beach, not any more, only burned stumps–". . . they'd sit up there year after year, in the fall–the Corps knew how important those perches were–and the eagles would fish for the mountain whitefish that made their way upstream in October. The Corps says they were just burning some old brush, and that things got 'out of hand.'"

Marge Swanson of the National Audubon Society has photographs of the eagles in the cottonwoods from previous years, and she says that there were twenty-five cottonwoods on the beach. The fire got "out of hand" (though no call to the fire department was made, no request for help) on April 14–the day Dave and other pro-river advocates were away from their homes along the river, down in Missoula instead, two hundred miles away, testifying to the Northwest Power Planning Council why the Kootenai should be protected from hydropower development.

"I don't know why the Corps chose that day to burn brush," Dave says, and you can see the torment in his eyes, the guilt at actually thinking *badly* about someone.

Down the river we drift, looking at the clean stones beneath us, watching the mayflies skate past, and watching ospreys circle high above us; farther down the river we drift, closer to the Valley of Sickness. We pass between concrete pillars set in the river's wide middle, the beginnings of a haul bridge seven years ago that would have carried construction materials back and forth across the river for the first Jennings Rapids dam–that was how close the Corps got to building it, before the Ninth Circuit Court of Appeals stopped them.

"Somebody ought to take those things out of the river," says Dave.

"Wood chips" is what the mayor of Libby compares the river to–he says that the river upstream of him (and downstream) is a commodity, just like "wood chips," but it's not. Wood chips are renewable, and when you dam the sixth-best trout-fishing river in the state, it is not renewable. It's simply not the right of a town of twenty-six hundred to dam the second-largest tributary to the Columbia River (which is the fourth largest river in North America), and a National Wild and Scenic River designation would protect the Kootenai from both the town of Libby and the Corps. I like to picture Mayor Brown coming back in the next life as an iron dun, an iron dun on this stretch of the Kootenai, with 1,250 fish per mile, as punishment for making the wood chips statement. I tell the thought to Dave, and he laughs. I know he must think I am a hellion.

I think about what Dave's wife, Tammy, and their children are doing at that moment: if they are out in the sun, in the backyard, working in the garden. I wish the old people with the neat lawn above the river's banks would go ahead and plant their three fruit trees, win, lose, or draw.

There's a loud, shrill cawing going on over on the far side of the river, and dark, greasy objects—crows—are flying back into the dark woods, screaming and calling, perhaps a dozen of them, with more appearing from out of nowhere, and they're all flying back into the woods.

"They've found a nest, I'll bet you," Dave says, rising, trying to see back into the woods, but there's nothing he can do. His face is twisted, he wants to get out and save the eggs—geese, duck, osprey, eagle?—but the crows are too far back in the woods, and there are too many of them.

"They eat the eggs out of all those birds' nests," he says.

He watches the woods, listening to the raucous laughter as more crows beat their way up the river, cawing, and then Dave scowls and sits down, and shakes his head. He starts to say something bad, then thinks better of it. The crows call on in mad glee, destroying the nests back in the woods. They're coming from all over, rallying.

"Those crows," Dave says, still shaking his head. "I don't know about those crows."

Dust-blown Dreams and the Canadian River Gorge

DAN FLORES

The plains are almost wholly unfit for cultivation, and, of course, uninhabitable by a people depending upon agriculture for their subsistence.

—EXPLORER STEPHEN LONG, 1820

But dost Thou know that for the sake of that earthly bread the spirit of the earth will rise up against Thee and will strive with Thee and overcome Thee?

–FYODOR DOSTOYEVSKY
The Brothers Karamazov

So long, it's been good to know you.

–WOODY GUTHRIE, 1938

Disappearing into a thin red horizon line off to the west is a squashed, third-quarter moon, getting as broad and bloated as it sets as a countryboy beergut ballooning over sagging Wranglers. I am just north of Clovis, the Allsup's Convenience Store Capital of the World (with good reason–Lonnie and Barbara Allsup are native Clovisians), whooshing across the High Plains of New Mexico the way we late twentieth-century folk do. It is January in the Siberia of the Southwest, eighteen degrees at 5 A.M. Rocky Mountain time. I am running an errand, fetching a load of piñon for my woodstove, an excuse, really, to get out of West Texas for a day, to slip over into New Mexico and poke around the Canadian River Gorge for a few hours.

The Gorge. In New Mexico that is a name that conjures the Rio Grande, trout fishing, Wild and Scenic River float trips, white water, and The Box. Not many would connect it with the inches-deep Canadian slogging its way across the plains east of the Sangres. Once, at a highbrow backpacking store in Santa Fe, I looked through their topo map file for one of the Canadian Gorge. Zilch. The Land of Exploited Enchantment has too much else to offer to concern itself with a hard-to-get-to plains canyon. So the Canadian Gorge is one more of those out-of-the-way places in the West that one never hears about. But best you find your own. This one's taken already.

Like the plains canyonlands country over in Texas, the Canadian Gorge and its jangled maze of side canyons are lost beneath the horizon in a remote country with few roads. Most plains people know of the Canadian River, whose two forks drain across Texas and much of Oklahoma. But hardly anyone knows that the main (South) river cuts a deep canyon into the plains, or that the river itself, Rio del Cañada Colorado, was named that by the New Mexicans for this *gran cañada*. The first time I heard anything about it was in the summer of 1979, when I was doing a bicycle trip across the High Plains en route to Colorado. After wheezing up the thousand-foot Canadian Escarpment east of Mosquero, Ricardo's Bar in Roy seemed like a good idea. Friendly folks. If I was climbed out today, someone offered with a wide grin, best not ride west out of Roy. BIG canyon. I took the advice but remembered the characterization. A couple of years later, when I finally drove the Roy to Wagon Mound highway, I was impressed, too. The Canadian Gorge is, simply, the biggest and deepest canyon on the American Great Plains.

In pre-dawn light this frosty morning I drop off the Llano Estacado past Caprock Amphitheatre State Park, where cowboy musicals are performed in the summer. Past San Jon the basic physiography of the region sharpens. I am in the breaks between the two plateaus that make up the High Plains, their escarpments standing thirty miles apart and both visible, as is the familiar layercake of Tucumcari Mountain down on the southern horizon. (Tucumcari is possibly a Comanche term meaning "to lie in wait for someone to approach," although some sources believe the name comes from the Apache word for "breast"–just tilt your head to the horizontal.) To the west the white sandstone columns at the base of the Canadian Escarpment glow magenta in the winter sunrise. The truck breaks out of the blue light, its shadow rippling along the base of the scarp. Then comes the long pull up, a glowing vastness in the mirror and, all of a sudden, the mountains, snowcapped and one-dimensional as cardboard cutouts, sixty miles away.

And, astonishingly, there is the Gorge, too, hanging high in the air, its west wall clearly visible although the details are wavering as if seen through water. It's the winter mirage, phenomenon of the cold, still mornings on the plains, bending light downward so you can actually look into the canyons, and the best expression of it I've ever seen.

It's not an apparition; the Canadian Gorge is real. But apparitions from half a century ago yet loom atop the Mosquero Flat. Ramshackle farmhouses, crumbling to dust, hover in the distance. Yellow grasses carpet the plain, but beneath them the land corduroys, the unmistakable lines of what were once furrows throwing shadows in the low-angle sunlight. For this country was once part of the Llanos agricultural boom.

A raven flaps across the plain. With the windows up against the chill I can't hear what he has to say, but it's not hard to guess.

Four hours later I am bumping along a dirt road, climbing out of the mouth of the Gorge through bajada slopes of black lava blocks and lime-green prickly pear, past a spray-painted "Far Out" on a big boulder, leaving Sabinoso and Largo Canyon and the swift, turquoise-blue river behind.

It had been intended as a quick side trip to check out a theory. Although I have hiked the upper half of the Canadian Gorge, I'd not seen the mouth of the canyon where the main Gorge is joined by Mora and Largo canyons, a coiling junction twelve hundred feet below the rimrocks. For years I have been convincing myself that the Canadian Gorge can be floated through the greater part of its forty-five-mile length at some water level below outright flood; this trip was supposed to be float trip homework. But prowling around Sabinoso, a loose little Hispanic farming/ranching community strung out for three or four miles along the river, I had become intrigued instead by the images of people who had stuck, who had adapted to the harsh, isolated life of the Gorge. They had been here, had made this part of the West their living space, for a century and a half. Yet the farmers up top and those farther upcanyon hadn't lasted four decades. What was the explanation for that?

It is the West's grandest illusion, foisted on a population that wants to believe it by historians who made their names saying it, that the pockets of American culture that have sprouted like mushrooms across the American West over the last century have adapted to the environment of this country.

One of the best-known books about the American West is Walter Prescott Webb's *The Great Plains: A Study in Institutions and Environment,* which was first published in 1931. Three generations of plains people have now grown up reading it and accepting Webb's repeated premise that their culture has been shaped by the Great Plains environment in far-reaching ways, even to the point (as a recent president of the Southern Plains' major university, more recently a national political figure, would have it) that "like the plains themselves" the people are especially open, since there is "nothing to hide behind." Meanwhile, plains people practice precisely the same culture as people in the rest of the country, eat the same cereals for breakfast, work in the same service-related jobs, watch the same sitcoms and sports events on the same networks as everyone else, produce agricultural products for an international market economy in the same way that corn farmers in Iowa or cattle ranchers in Louisiana do. If, out the windows of farmhouses or their Fords and Chevies and Buicks and Cadillacs they see barbed wire and windmills and center-pivot irrigation systems, they remember Webb and conclude that if such symbols are still in place, then the adaptation must have been a success and must yet be going on. That is, if they think of such things at all. (Webb, naturally, did continue to think of such things. Twenty-five years after *The Great Plains* was published he wrote an essay, "The American West: Perpetual Mirage," in which he set forth revised thinking: that the heart of the West was desert, and that the regions and towns that ignored that were destined for abbreviated careers.)

The idea that we have adapted to the Western environment is a palpable fiction, of course, scarcely true anywhere in the West unless it be among some of the Southwestern Indians or the New Mexican Hispanic villagers. And it is a fiction nowhere more transparent than on the Southern Plains. Nowhere else in the West has nature served up a better example of how ill-adapted American culture is to fragile environments than in the Dust Bowls that periodically drive the Southern Plains to the brink of ecological and economic collapse. And if you want an example out of the historical record, one where history has accelerated enough to point the probable future for the rest of the High Plains, try Harding County, New Mexico, one of the counties (Mora is the other) lying athwart the Canadian Gorge.

This is Bell Ranch country, all these eroded mesas and breaks from the mouth of the Gorge down the Canadian River nearly to Tucumcari, almost fifty miles away. Founded by Wilson Waddingham in 1870, the Bell Ranch is still one of the largest working ranches on the Southern Plains.

At its northern periphery I bounce onto the highway and turn back toward Mosquero, past La Cinta Canyon with the pretty little Triassic red mesa standing in its portals like a sentinel. Once I prowled around in La Cinta Canyon and spent an hour talking to Ray Hartley, who owns a ranch there and who has spent his life, except for a few years getting a college degree up in Fort Collins, living in the canyon. I asked him about Sabinoso. "Those Mexicans have been in the deep canyons around the mouth of the Mora River forever," he said. "Floods and isolation and the Dust Bowl run everybody else out. But they won't never leave."

Atop the plain again I turn north towards Roy. Along with Bill, Wyoming, I think Roy, New Mexico, is one of my favorite towns on the Great Plains. Roy was named after two brothers from Canada, Frank and Eugene Roy, who arrived in 1901, just after the El Paso and Southwest Railroad, which was supposed to haul coal down from Colorado, was surveyed across the grasslands east of the Gorge. Sixty-five years before, all this country had been granted by the government in Mexico City to a consortium of individuals who were supposed to settle it. The Mora and Las Vegas grants (1835) and the giant (1.7 million acres) Beaubien & Miranda (or Maxwell) Grant did bring folks to the area. But the New Mexicans were practical settlers. They founded most of their communities, based on small irrigated farms and flocks of sheep, in the Gorge and the breaks east of the Canadian Escarpment. Sabinoso, Mosquero, Armento, Gallegos, and others were the result.

When the railroad arrived, the small New Mexican settlements were still alive but most of the grasslands surrounding the Gorge had meanwhile fallen into the hands of a Portsmouth, England, cattle company or had become public domain when the United States pried the Southwest loose from Mexico. But the Roy brothers had grandiose plans. While Eugene supervised their ranching operation, Frank became the first postmaster, the banker and city treasurer, store owner, saloon owner/bartender and mayor of the town they naturally named after themselves. After the railroad arrived in 1902, Mosquero (it means "swarm of mosquitos" if you wondered) was relocated from the canyon to the rail line south of Roy. Mills, a former frontier stagecoach way station named for the Mills family, whose irrigated ranch had been located in the Gorge in the 1870s, was likewise moved atop the plains north of Roy. These were typical frontier booster decisions: water was important, but hell, a railroad spelled bonanza, U.S. style.

I pull up to the postoffice on the southwest side of the little town square. Roy, of course, is dying. There are a couple of groceries, a pharmacy, a café, Ricardo's Bar. Most of the other buildings are empty now, in a town that sixty years ago was the hub of buzzing economic development. Bob Wills, of Western Swing fame, used to barber here between road trips with the Texas Playboys. But the halcyon days when Roy and Mosquero battled it out for the county seat of newly created Harding County (it was 1923: Mosquero won, but Roy got the high school) seem as long gone as the buffalo herds. Roy and Harding County have readjusted their visions considerably.

I turn over my couple of pieces of mail to the postperson and stroll over to the Roy City Market. The mounted heads of aoudads and African ibex, both nonnative big game animals that have been introduced into the Gorge, line the walls above rows and rows of Vienna sausages and every flavor and combination of sardines imaginable. It's a sardine Baskin Robbins. I settle for a Coke and walk out into the bright winter sunlight. Beyond the edge of town, beyond the edge of weeds and fences plastered with blown paper, brilliant yellow grasslands stretch away in every direction. The Gorge is visible to the west, a dark green slash running north and south through the yellow. Beyond another strip of yellow are the black-looking foothills and then the white tops of the Sangres, and north of them, up in Colorado, there are towering snowcapped peaks just now starting to gather clouds.

I start the truck and head north out of Roy and try to imagine the scene here half a century ago. It's not hard. It's still going on back in Texas, over on the Llano Estacado.

Moisture determines. And those mountains standing high on the western horizon determine the moisture on the plains sweeping away from them. They've decreed that the annual rainfall on the plains around Roy is only about fifteen inches, even less than the eighteen or so on the Llano Estacado, since the rainshadow effect is more pronounced here.

Initially it was commonplace—at least since Stephen Long came down the Canadian in 1820 and waffled not the slightest about his impression—to conceptualize the Southern Plains as a desert. By ecological definition it is not, at present, but it stands so close that in the years, or decades or centuries, when the bright summer clouds do not build rain-bearing thunderheads, the moisture lack tips the balance in a decidedly deserty direction.

This is something the New Mexicans evidently figured out for themselves. Aside from a few playa lakes, there was no water up on the High Plains. The water was in the Gorge, flowing as melted snow down the narrow canyon, leaking out of springs in the side gorges from what is now called the Canadian River Underground Water Basin, a narrow little strip of the Ogallala Aquifer that unfortunately doesn't store much water.

But the railroad was in place and boosters were doing what boosters in the West have always done, hoping to drown doubt in a din of chest-thumping. New Mexico Territory's Bureau of Immigration encouraged farmers from the East to come and participate in "breaking out" (plains terminology; its opposite is "hairing over") the grasslands in "this princely domain." The Enlarged Homestead Act of 1909 and the promise that wheat could easily be dryland farmed contributed to luring unsuspecting sodbusters to the New Mexico plains, just as the breakup of the giant ranches, the XIT in particular, did on the Texas side. On the Southern Plains the farming frontier did not end in 1890. It extended well into the 1920s, a twentieth-century frontier confronting a landscape that fifty years before had been regarded as one of the only uninhabitable parts of the West.

So they came, poor pioneers from Texas and the Midwest, following the American dream. Fabiola Cabeza de Baca, whose father was one of the New Mexicans the pioneers had come to supplant, described them in her memoir as arriving in wagons from the railheads, "kindly, simple folks," although one did mightily insult her father, a fair-haired, blue-eyed Spaniard of Galacian descent, with the comment, "I thought you were a white man when I saw you" ("I *am* a white man, Sir," he replied). All across the grasslands they settled on their rectangular squares of land, ripped away the grass cover so that gasoline-powered tractors and one-way disk plows could get at the soil below, built homes, raised children, and dedicated their lives to making the High Plains yield to agri-capitalism. The Big Breakout, forget the Romantic Jeffersonisms, made war on nature. Modern farming, particularly plains monoculture farming, with its ammonia phosphate fertilizers, its mined water, its poison chemical pest control, its genetically inbred crops, places the farmer in a nonreligious relationship with the land. His profession gets him about as close to the ancient Earth Goddess religious feeling of early agriculture as today's sport hunter is likely to get to the animal mythologies of the primal hunters. But who can blame the farmer? The lesson is held before him again and again: take advantage of technology, become a "businessman," or you don't get rich. You might not even survive.

Nature's lesson was simpler and, if anything, more cold-blooded.

The patterns of plains weather over geologic time demonstrate regular pulsations spanning long evolutionary cycles, products of the grand forces of the solar system like sunspot storms and oscillations in the earth's orbit, and of changes in the ocean currents and jet stream in response to the shifting of the continental plates. Cores taken from the seafloor indicate that over the last million years major warm/dry and wet/cold episodes have supplanted one another at roughly 550,000-year intervals. Within the larger swings are smaller pulses that still powerfully affect biological life, and within those yet others governing narrower and narrower slices of time. Pollen analysis and dendro-chronology have discovered significant oscillations on a pattern of 2,000–3,000 years, while our brief meteorological records show weak pulsations at intervals of 40 years (the droughts of the 1890s and 1930s) and 20 years (those of the 1950s and 1970s). Climatologists argue that we are presently in a slow drift in the warmer/dryer direction of one of the large swings. One prediction for the evolution of this stage is droughts spaced gradually closer in time and lingering longer until a 2,000-year peak is approached. What impact global warming might have towards accelerating this cycle is something no one knows, beyond the prediction that its effects will become increasingly noticeable over the next 30 years. But an annual temperature shift of only about three to four degrees would advance Chihuahuan Desert species two hundred miles into the Southern Plains. The increased evaporation and solar convection will likely turn much of the Southern High Plains into an American version of the Sahara.

Why then, in his prize-winning history, *Dust Bowl: The Southern Plains in the 1930s,* would Donald Worster call the Dust Bowl one of the three greatest man-induced ecological collapses in civilization's history? Because, while nature served up an ordinary forty-year drought like the kind that had been disrupting Native American cultures in the Southwest for thousands of years, American culture had made the plains ecologically vulnerable overnight. The drought started on the Northern Plains in 1932, reached the Southern Plains by 1934, and seemed to settle in around the point where Texas, New Mexico, Oklahoma, Kansas, and Colorado join. From 1935 until 1938, instead of getting fifteen to eighteen inches of rain a year, the Southern High Plains averaged less than eight.

Even where the vegetation is intact, such droughts burn up the plains. Botanical records from native mixed prairies during the Dust Bowl and the drought of the 1950s show far-reaching losses in diversity. Vegetation survived better in the canyons and breaks, but even here the tall grasses gave way to shorter ones that were then themselves burned up by the scorching sun. For vast stretches the only green was provided by Russian thistle (tumbleweeds), silverleaf horse nettle, sunflowers, and mesquite, which seemed to thrive and spread. Full recovery of mixed grass prairies on the Southern Plains takes between twenty and forty years and four succesion stages from annual weeds to a mature mix of grasses, forbs, and shrubs. The impact of regular droughts is a prime reason why "climax" is almost a meaningless botanical term on the Great Plains.

What made the drought of the 1930s into the Dust Bowl of American mythology was the presence of farmers in a country they shouldn't have been in, doing what was normal for farming but shouldn't have been done in that country. With the grass and herbs and their extensive root systems gone, the plains simply blew away. In several places all the topsoil blew off all the way down to the caliche rock. Rather than two or three dust storms a year, in the middle thirties there were sixty or seventy. The stories have become a genuine part of American mythology; in fact, the Dust Bowl is the great historical experience of the Southern Plains, producing tragedy and suffering, high literature and art, and a lasting folk music.

With the volcanic cone of Capulin Mountain against the northeast sky I turn west towards Springer, past one of the places I camped overnight when I was biking through in 1979, a camp I shared with a Florida lawyer hitchhiking to a tribal gathering of old sixties friends in Durango. Pronghorns glide across the short verdue, jackrabbits lope across the highway, and here is the Canadian River, shallow braids of water in a sandy channel. This is upstream from the beginning of the Gorge, very near the crossing of the Cimarron Cutoff of the Santa Fe Trail, which looped up this way to avoid having to cross the Gorge itself, but still sixty miles from the sources of the river up in Colorado. An amazing degree of geographic confusion prevailed about the Canadian as recently as fifty years ago. Settlers during the Big Breakout assumed that they were on the upper Red River of Texas. The Resettlement Administration disabused them of this notion in the late thirties, but for another decade this was known as the Canadian Red River.

I drive on through Springer and follow I-25 for a short distance before turning off for Cimarron, a tiny burg located where the Cimarron Fork of the Canadian leaves its mountain canyon, carved down from the high mountain park Texas developers have made over into a skiing and boating resort. Despite its farfetched nineteenth-century claims, Texas never managed to get possession of any of New Mexico except the Llano Estacado and the Trans-Pecos. Sagebrush rebels might take heed from the Texas lesson, for Texas offers an example of what would happen to the rest of the West if public lands were turned over to the states. With almost all of their own scenic lands privately owned, Texans have come to regard New Mexico as a Texas playground. The resulting "dollar imperialism" creates an almost Third World, love-hate attitude towards Texas on the part of the native New Mexicans. Introduce yourself as a Texan in Taos or Santa Fe and watch the corners of their mouths.

I make my firewood deal in Cimarron. Reeking of barely seasoned piñon, wallowing on flattened suspension like a drunk, the old Toyota and I go careening back through bright winter sunshine. At Springer I stop at the Stockman's Café, eat a trout covered with green chilis and piñon nuts, swill down cups of steaming coffee. Back on the highway to Roy, bald eagles perch like kingbirds on power poles along the highway. It is getting on in the afternoon.

A few miles from Roy I ease the pickup onto a dirt road and like a ship on an ocean sway along for ten miles into the approaching sunset. A few minutes before the sun hits the top of the Sangres I pull into a scattering of picturesque piñons and stop. A brown National Forest sign–this is the Kiowa National Grasslands–tells me that the next two miles are exceedingly steep and rough and aren't recommended for passenger vehicles unless the passengers are in search of that dwindling point of light at the end of consciousness. I've driven this road in all kinds of weather, and they're not kidding.

I walk down the road, out of the last gathering sunlight and into the shadow cast by the far wall of the Canadian Gorge. Behind me, through tall ponderosa pines, a waxing moon that is now two days from full hangs over the tawny National Grasslands, with a band of blue nightfall already rimming the horizon.

Drought and agriculture combined to turn enormous stretches of the Southern High Plains into sand dunes in the 1930s. Animals died of silicosis, whole counties simply blew away. Outmigration from the Southern Plains, much of it along famed Route 66, approached 20 percent; the plains lost nearly a million people between 1930 and 1940. Franklin Roosevelt's agencies did what they could. Shelterbelts were built along the 100th Meridian to contain the desertification. Most of the farmers on the plains were on relief. Roosevelt called for various ideas to resolve the crisis, got suggestions ranging from concreting over the plains to dumping used cars and junk across the region. Ecologists and land-use planners argued that far too much of the plains had lost its grass cover in the move to factory farming, an analysis seconded by the 1937 presidential report, *The Future of the Great Plains.* In that year the Bankhead-Jones Act provided funds for the reacquisition of homesteader lands on the Great Plains, and the Resettlement Administration was set up to relocate Dust Bowl families. Homesteading in the West was ended for all time; the remaining lands eventually were administered by the Bureau of Land Management. But two human developments—the massive spending of Hugh Bennet's Soil Conservation Service and the adaptation of ordinary auto engines to produce a reliable pump for plains irrigation—combined with a natural one to create a regional illusion that technology had conquered the Dust Bowl.

Nature's contribution was the swing towards wetter conditions. It was the forty-one inches of rain in 1940 that really broke the Dust Bowl.

The Gorge is a magnificent maze of remote canyonland country occupying an area of nearly seven hundred square miles. Scores of side canyons drain into it, almost all of them with names dating to the nineteenth-century period of New Mexican settlement: Mora and Largo canyons are the largest of them, but there are in addition Cañon Biscante, Arroyo Piedra Lumbre, Cañon Colorado, Cañon Vercere, Cañon Mesteñito and Cañon Mesteño, Cañon Emplazado, Cañon Blanco, Cañon Capulin, Cañon Armenta, Cañon Enciero, Cañon dos Nieves

Gachupin, Cañon Juan Maes, Cañon Osa and Cañon Osito, Cañon Hondo, Cañon Yegua, Cabra Cañon. And Mills, Beaver, Whitman, and Davis canyons. West and east along the Canadian Escarpment the mesas and canyons stand on the land as if stamped there by a giant cookie cutter, a landscape of juniper-speckled truncations like Mesa Herfana and Cerro Corazon, and rocky reentrant canyons like La Cinta. It's the Caprock escarpment on the grander scale of the farther west, with the Capulin and Turkey Mountain cones and the sheer gray block of Hermit's Peak to rest the eye on when you top the rimrock. These are the names that organize the erosion jumble that is the Canadian Gorge country.

Apparitions out of the past stand in plain view as you hike the Canadian River Gorge. The impression is of a great ghost canyon, an empty house where the echoes of human voices have barely fallen silent. Pottery shards and flint scatters lie beneath layers of dust in the overhang caves. Lines of piled rock mark ancient Hispanic sheep range boundaries. There are overgrown cemeteries and the crumbling plaza of the old abandoned town of Armenta. Bois d'arc trees scatter their pebbley fruit across ground once occupied by Southern pioneers. And there are rockhouse ruins everywhere, of the old Mills Hotel, which once served the stageline, of cowboy line camps; and, more sadly, of failed Resettlement Administration homesteads.

The late twentieth-century Gorge is part wilderness experience, part history lesson. Bill Brown and I hiked it in late September of 1986, the upper half that is now in the Kiowa National Grasslands. We left a pickup down at the Roy/Wagon Mound highway, the only road that bisects the 40-mile length of the Gorge. Katie Dowdy dropped us off up at Mills Canyon campground, near the head of the Gorge, on her way to doing a rockart reconnaissance of Eagletail Mesa. If things turned out right we planned to rendezvous with her at Ricardo's Bar in Roy the next evening.

Excerpts from my journal:

September 19, 1986

After almost a decade of promising myself this walk, Bill and I sit satisfied beside a popping juniper fire in the gorge of the Canadian River. We set out after lunch today on a 2-day excursion, about all it will take, even allowing for some side canyon exploration, to hike the 18–20 miles of the upper canyon. We did a leisurely 4 or 5 miles through "Mills Canyon" this afternoon. It is beautiful, a broad floor carpeted with buffalo grass and miles of smooth sandstone walls striped with the dripping paint stains of desert varnish, mineral residues left when moisture streaks evaporate. According to Katie, a method has recently been worked out for dating its layers, a boon to rockart research. Unfortunately, saltcedar thickets line the river here about as thickly as they do anywhere in the Southwest, a boon to the horrendous mosquito hordes that descended on us at dusk. *Tamarix chinensis* tends to thrive especially well upstream of reservoirs, where slowed water flow creates mudflats. And Conchas Reservoir is only about 75 miles down the Canadian.

We noticed as we walked this afternoon that autumn is touching the Gorge, more distinctly nearer the rimrocks, at an elevation of 6,000 ft., than on the warmer canyon floor, 800 ft. lower. But the scrubby wavy-leaf oaks that cover the upper slopes are already tinged with purple and red, big rabbitbush clumps are a dazzling fall yellow, and even the cottonwood galleries along the river are close to turning. The survivability of plains cottonwoods amazes me. They have evolved chemical defenses against grasshoppers, which will strip every other green thing in a country but pass up cottonwood leaves; they combat aphids by making certain of their leaf clumps so aphid-attractive that the insects ignore the rest of the tree. All this must be a product of cottonwoods' rapid generational turnover.

Present camp is on a grassy shelf on the E bank, 20 ft. above the river, which splashes along pleasantly as white noise. We're evidently about ½ mile below the mouth of Cañon Mesteño and near a cave overhang that we'll explore at first light. I write with the red punctuation point of Mars in the southern sky, Jupiter just over the canyon wall behind me, and a waning near-full moon about to slide into view. Planes, bound for L.A. or New York, sweep over but they're too high to hear above the sound of the river. No bawling stock, not even a coyote. This is an extraordinarily silent canyon. It got to the explorer James W. Abert, who somewhere in this very stretch in 1845 found the scenery lovely—"a smiling valley"—but was disturbed that the great vastness so utterly ignored him. He fired a shot into the Gorge just to break its composure. Now, just as I scribble this, a coyote babbles eerily off to the SW; another falsetto-voiced one joins in. It must be a moon seranade. They're up the canyon wall, in the chill blue glow of the moonrise.

It is all wildly beautiful, at times (when the fire dies and the mosquitos swarm) pretty uncomfortable. But Bill, curled in the fetal position in his bag, is happy. His graduate thesis is on sequential cultures along the Canadian River, and this is his second field trip along it; he's already hiked a long stretch of it in the Texas Panhandle.

I confess to some partiality to the wonderful but unsung places of the world: canyons like this, unknown, unvisited, with the bark still on, a place you can make your own by dint of experiential immersion. My place. If I write about it, it's not to sing it as a place for everyone to know. We all have to find our own places.

September 20:

Too conscious of the evolving night to sleep well, I crawl out of the bag 2 or 3 times to stoke the fire, sit sleepily beside it as the twigs catch. Once, adjusting my bedroll, I notice in the moonlight a big furry plains tarantula, near cereal bowl size, waltzing across my chest. Probably a male. We'd noticed big autumn tarantula migrations (usually all-male) crossing the roads yesterday, much like the kind, Scott Momaday recalls in *Way to Rainy Mountain,* that in September of 1874 had frightened the Kiowas into joining the Palo Duro village. This one pauses a few inches from my face, scrutinizes me with apparent horror in all 16 compound eyes before scurrying off. Tarantulas are actually pretty passive, with a bite not much more toxic than a wasp sting. Nothing like the poison in the mesquite thorn I jabbed into a finger joint yesterday. A quick application of tequila into the wound is the only antidote I've found to mesquite toxins, and we have no tequila. The joint is so stiff this A.M. I can barely move it.

Around 1 or 2 A.M. by the Dipper the wind came in high from downcanyon but by early dawn it has died down. When Sirius rises like a Christmas sparkler over the east rim I blow the fire to life and put on a pot of water. It's warm this morning and the irascible little mosquitos are delighted. They and the coffee smell finally wake Bill, about the time the west wall turns red-gold. In the dawn quiet the sound of rapids downriver fills the aural space. A little plains black-headed snake, no larger than a pencil, crawls across my foot in hot pursuit of a centipede. For two hours after sunup our camp stays in cool blue shadow. A good place to be, this.

While Bill works on his journal I explore the overhang cave in the wall behind us. It is a large cave, 12 ft. high, 25–30 ft. across at its mouth, maybe 15 ft. deep, and as I approach I see on its ceiling characteristic smoke smudges. The next thing I see is a discarded dig screen. The cave has already been seined by someone. Although the Comanches regarded the Gorge as the western boundary of their range, this was probably an Archaic site. The Canadian Gorge has always looked like prime Anasazi country to me, but I am unaware of any Anasazi sites here.

The sun lifts higher and soon the riverbed is bright with the reflections of wet rock. A mist rises from the river. The Gorge is already starting to trap solar radiation, is heating up, and we decide to move out now and dry the dew from our bags later in the day.

So it's down the canyon, indulging that simplest of lusts–to know what's there. What does it look like around that bend we've been gazing on since yesterday? Of course we know very well that around that bend it looks very much as it does right here. Nevertheless, there's no denying the impulse to see. So we shoulder the packs, pick up a deer or aoudad trail on the east side shelf, and go have a look.

It is more of the same, but somehow different, too. After half a mile along a ledge 30 ft. above the river we make a beautiful open meadow with scattered piñons and junipers. It is an extraordinary year for piñon nuts, and this spot is a scrub jay's paradise. Across from the meadow the river alternates between slow green pools and quick, rippling falls. At this stage the Canadian is not floatable, although it could be traversed by canyoneering, a sort of scrambling technique combining floating and hiking. Here a rock slide down the west wall has created a lane of ponderosa pines all the way down to the canyon floor. Ponderosas stick to the rims of the Canadian Gorge, but here's a big old lone pine, perhaps swept down as a seedling, looking a little wistful amongst the piñons and junipers. On the plain above, between here and Wagon Mound, the Canyon Colorado Equid Sanctuary, a 6,000-acre ranch owned by William Gruenerwald, is dedicated to saving true wild horses and asses, like the Asiatic Przhevalski's horse. We keep expecting to see zebras peering over the rim. But all we see up there are circling hawks.

We push through a saltcedar thicket, mosquitos rising from every limb, spot a grove of wild china trees. Bill says the Kiowas he knows in Oklahoma seek them out for tipi stakes. Under a piñon on the W. slope we munch on dried fruit, scribble in our journals, swig Canadian River water boiled this morning–drinkable, but with a definite calcium taste–and try to figure out where we are from the topo maps.

It is, perhaps, 11 A.M., and we step out into a Gorge that is beginning to glare. We cross the river, the snowmelt water almost shockingly cold, at the prettiest rapids we've seen on the river. Jurassic sandstone encircles the lower walls of a round basin. Against a sheer wall, on the far side of a deep pool, Rocky Mountain maples are starting to put on some color. The entire river is deep here, forces us by its turns against the walls into a neck-deep crossing, our packs and cameras held high overhead. And now, surprisingly, the Jurassic pitches downward as if it's crossbedded, forms staircase shelves over which the river pours.

We stop at the mouth of a large side canyon where a grove of boxelders provide a deep shade and look at the maps. A pair of rock pinnacles stands above the big rapids here, and they fix us. This, not the point where we had camped, is the mouth of Cañon Mesteño. It's a little unsettling. Here it is noon, already, and we have at least 14 miles left to do. What the hell. Bob Marshall used to do such stuff for prebreakfast warmups. Of course, as Bill points out, Bob Marshall died from exhaustion at 38.

It grows hot. We quicken our pace, passing isolated, mournfully lonely rock ruins. We slip through the last sandstone chute, one we thought we might have to climb around, at water level. A faint Jeep trail appears along the river now and we welcome it, the brisk, exhilarating walk of the morning turning a little wooden and mechanical in the hot glare of midday. Atop the blocky, Dakota rimrock, 800 ft. above us, pines groan and whip in the wind. But the deep Gorge is still. Black grasshoppers with red wings rise from the grass. More boxelders, and then a side canyon with a pinnacled mesa in it that we suppose must be Cañon Emplazado.

"Be damned. Look at this." Bill, purple bandanna stretched over his head, sweat dripping from that long, splendid nose, is inspecting a rusted sign. Faded white lettering warns us: "No Trepassing. Resettlement Administration." But stretching away in every direction is remote, wild country, low, collapsed rock ruins the only evidence that the fed tried to relocate Exodusters here.

The state archives over in Santa Fe tell the story. By 1925 or thereabouts almost 8,000 homesteaders had taken up plains land in Harding and Mora counties on either side of the Gorge. Within a decade the Dust Bowl hit. By 1935 one of the Resettlement Administration's projects was to relocate some 24,000 Texas and 9,600 New Mexico settlers. Someone had the idea of emulating the Hispanic settlement pattern and a Mills Land Use Adjustment Project was hatched to move ranchers from the Gorge to the plain, and farmers into the Gorge. The land exchanges were made. Homesteads were started, irrigation ditches dug. Then the Canadian River, whose normal flow through the Gorge is about 5–10,000 acre feet a day, sent 50,000 acre feet surging through the sandstone chutes, and not just once. The homesteaders abandoned their tracts; even the old New Mexican town of Armenta, between here and Sabinoso, was abandoned. By the early 1940s the fed's Dust Bowl land reacquisition program took back the upper Gorge and most of the plain on the east side of it. In 1960, when the National Grassland system was established, this became one of the core units of the Kiowa National

Grasslands. The rail line was ripped up, the plain reseeded in native grasses. It took 20 years, but the wild finally reclaimed this country. Except for the rusted signs, and the ruins of dust-blown, flood-washed dreams.

We're now into the last haul—about 3 miles—and it is late afternoon, the wind up, temperature over 80, our metabolisms down and dying. Some trudging; long silences. We've reached the stage where the telling will be more fun than the doing, as Bill says. Again and again we wade the shallows of the river, lop off an occasional bend where the streambed folds back upon itself. The canyon's geology continues the same as before, although those car-sized Cretaceous blocks at the rim are becoming house-sized. Here is a rock slab grave, and more ruins on either side of the Jeep trail. Desensitized by now, we are able to manage only marginal incredulity at how lonely and isolated from the world these homesteads would have been.

Last swing in the Gorge before the Roy/Wagon Mound highway. A big, thickly-forested canyon—Cañon Blanco—comes in from the NE, carrying a strong flow of water from numerous seep springs far up it. To the SE is another large stream flowing out of Beaver Canyon. Below where it comes in we climb down to the river, strip down and where the Canadian has cut a sleeve into the sandstone we perform the old trapper ritual of rinsing off in the crick before hitting the settlements.

The folks in Ricardo's Bar that evening were satisfyingly daunted at the ambitiousness of our hike, maybe because by the time we got there many of them lacked the ambition to change barstools. Katie arrived soon after we did, and between ingestions of tequila and various other uncontrolled substances the locals regaled us with local stories of dust and floods and population busts, down to fewer than 1,000 people in all of Harding County today. (I later checked the census figures. Interesting. Neighboring Mora County lost 3,000 people during the twenties, but held on during the thirties. Harding County had 4,421 people in 1930 and still had 4,374 in 1940. They survived the Dust Bowl. But dry ice-field discoveries failed to bring in an influx of people, and the underground aquifer that made other regions on the Southern Plains boom after 1940 was thin here; less than fifteen thousand acres were ever irrigated from it. Then came the floods of the 1940s and another drought in the 1950s. It was too much. Small towns like Mills disappeared. As the country haired over again, ranching replaced farming. By 1970 Harding County had just three towns and 1,348 people. And dropping.)

Watching the world slowly recede from their borders doesn't seem to affect the residents of Harding County overmuch. Bill was lured into an escalating world championship eight-ball tournament, whose stakes went even higher when a pair of attractive young Mexican girls challenged the table. Lewis, a quiet cowboy, kept buying drinks and asking Katie, "What's anthropophagy mean, anyhow?" Texas Tech and the University of New Mexico were thick into their interstate football rivalry in Albuquerque that night, and there was a radio on. No one seemed to be listening. When Mike, the bartender, mentioned that Tech had won, someone belched. There were shouts from the poolroom, but it turned out they were for the eight-ball challengers.

Next morning Katie and I drove into Roy to look for Bill, who had taken his chances in town. There was a small crowd gathered in a residential yard across from the city park where we were to rendezvous. Not spotting Bill in the park, we stopped to ask if anyone had seen him. The gathering–a Sunday morning outdoor mass?–parted as we walked up, and there was Bill, sound asleep, the contents of his pack strewn around him. The gathering sharpened. It included the mayor of Roy, the local constable, the overwrought citizen who had awakened to find this strange personage asleep on his lawn. While we reluctantly acknowledged our connection in this disturbance of the local peace, Bill opened an eye, staggered to his feet, almost succeeded in shaking hands with the mayor. It was a clear case of mistaken identity. In the dark of night he had taken the citizen's rather weedy yard for the park, and no harm intended. The mayor, an understanding fellow and up for reelection, was all for smoothing things over, and allowed the possibility that Bill could have hiked the Canadian Gorge but gotten lost in downtown Roy.

From the edge of the darkening Gorge I watch sunlight perform its last theatrics atop the Sangre de Cristo Range. The temperature is dropping fast now. It's time to haul this firewood back to my little ranch in Yellow House Canyon, five hours over those extending-into-infinity plains highways. I start the truck, fumble around for a tape to stick in the player. Townes Van Zandt is singing about a woman who fits just like his guitar when I pull onto the highway, but the imagery strikes me as uncomfortable and I turn the volume way down.

The farmers who had settled the High Plains in the teens and twenties were dryland farmers. But the existence of the Ogallala Aquifer had been known since the 1850s, when Capt. John Pope had experimented with water wells in eastern New Mexico under government aegis. Pope's experiences initiated a maddening three-quarters of a century of mechanical failure in getting at the vast freshwater lake saturating the High Plains subsurface. But the Dust Bowl, with millions in loans available from the government's farm programs, acted as catalyst to a resolution of the problem. In 1930 there were just 170 wells on the Llano Estacado; by 1940 there were 2,180, by 1957 42,225, by now more than 70,000. In the half century between 1930 and 1980, irrigated acreage on the Southern High Plains went from less than thirty-five thousand to well over six million acres. This mining of the aquifer did nothing to stop massive dust erosion when the droughts of the 1950s and 1970s struck the Southern Plains, but in combination with the techniques of scientific agronomy as taught by the Soil Conservation Service and the state ag extension services, it did create a booming irrigation empire out of land Randolph Marcy had once called the "Zahara of North America." Who can blame plainspeople if they assumed their situation was a long-term adaptation, like that of the Archaic cultures, rather than a too-narrow specialization with a meteoric but brief lifespan, like that of the Clovis hunters?

Because, of course, the Ogallala Aquifer is fossil water, a lake whose original Rocky Mountain sources have for the last hundred thousand years been cut off by the Pecos and Canadian rivers, whose only source of replenishment now is through seepage from playa lakes. And seventy thousand commercial waterwells pumping from five hundred to a thousand gallons a day each can suck the life out of even such a vast lake as the Ogallala at an astonishing rate. After five decades and a drop of 250 to 300 feet in the aquifer level, farmers whose American roots have taught them not to accept limits, whose Texas culture balks at any kind of government controls to enforce conservation, and who often haven't believed in geology anyway, are having to face the cruel truth.

It is bitter medicine to swallow, and not surprisingly it has produced a lot of denial. Some of the local underground water conservation districts have made some headway in stabilizing aquifer drawdown on the Southern Plains, and Wayne Wyatt, the director of District 1 in Lubbock, has fashioned a career preaching against the doom-and-gloom predictions.

Yet it is rationally impossible to ignore the fact of limits, and it would seem that the trend is already underway. A measure of the desperation lies in the farmers' insistence that Southern Plains agriculture is too important to be allowed to die. Someone ought to outdo California, construct an immense diversion project that will correct nature's error by pumping in water from somewhere else. Folks downstate in Texas and in the rest of the country either ignore the situation, however, or almost seem to take a perverse delight in watching Webb's prediction about the desert come true. Meantime, faced with near prohibitive pumping costs as the aquifer level has declined, Southern Plains farmers have returned more than a million acres to dryland during the past decade. A 1985 study indicated that most of the remaining irrigating farmers would rather quit than return to dryland farming, and evidently this is what they're doing. Between 1980 and 1986 five of the nine counties in the heavily irrigated area around Lubbock suffered Dust Bowl–size population losses (up to 11.5 percent in half a decade) as farmers finally gave up.

Most modern American farmers cannot think in terms of a reduction in scale. The subsistence approach that keeps those New Mexican villages alive on the land after more than a century and a half would be unthinkable for the twentieth-century Texas farmer. And it is, of course, the sacrifice of the opulent American life-style in favor of simplicity and continued ties with the land that is the secret of places like Sabinoso.

In effect, it seems that the present culture's life expectancy may be even less than that of the Clovis hunters – perhaps not much more than a century. Like that of the Comanches, whose cultural adaptation was never allowed to play out, the natural evolution of the present farming culture is not completed. Except, maybe, along the Canadian Gorge in New Mexico.

A Year As It Turns

EDWARD HOAGLAND

These seasonal editorials for the New York Times *quite wrote themselves. I wanted them to, not being prepared to put as much regular effort into the job as Hal Borland had done during his thirty-seven-year stint on this newsman's beat – which ended with his death in 1978 Nor did the new* Times, *though personally hospitable and ready for stylistic innovation, wish for as much "nature" from me. I'd loved Borland's stuff; used to clip out of the Sunday paper his unsigned pieces that said spring slipped north 16 miles and wound up a mountainside one hundred vertical feet in a day. Summer soul that I was, I'd sit in my New York apartment in April, impatiently calculating what I must be missing at my house in Vermont, which is eighteen hundred feet higher and 384 miles (by road) away. Perhaps unfortunately, I've been less informative, more contrapuntal than he.*

I soon came to enjoy thinking up my own offerings and phoning them in from a booth on the highway. Since I was two miles from the nearest electricity, most were written in the evening by kerosene. Nevertheless, the voice here is institutional as well as individual, "moderate" and anonymous as well as idiosyncratic. Though it is a voice too cheerful, I've not tried to change these editorial statements into something more personal or polemical than the Times *wanted to print under its own name, because I think that the attempt would wind up as a halfway measure, less satisfactory than these obvious hybrids, which already have a tradition in their original form.*

Walking the Dog

We are in favor of cleaning up after them, but we are also in favor of dogs. Manhattan was once the home of whistling swans and seals and mountain lions, and, walking the dog, we remember this in our bones. Walking a dog, we feel occasionally that we are with a living ancestor, as children seem to do also. Children are born with a liking for dogs; and when we are out with the family dog, we seem to remember aptitudes of nose and leg that we no longer have.

For the dog, one purpose of our walks is checking out the gutter—the chicken knuckles and Reuben sandwiches there. As a student of fermentation (wine and cheese buffs have nothing on him), he is immensely cheerful as we go around the block. Also, he marks his territory. You might say it's like the trappings of wolf territoriality without the territory, just as for us it is a walk in the woods without the woods. He looks particularly for irregularities to mark: a shovelful of dirt next to a Con Ed excavation, a clump of grass, houseplants or Christmas trees that have been thrown out but still smell of earth. Males found females by the process, but the other social function—when dogs were wolves—was to reinforce the order of rank and rule within the pack, increasing the pack's efficiency on a hunt.

We are animals too. We confront a cold wind with our backs, and turn grumpy if somebody unexpectedly grabs hold of us while we are bent over a steak. But the spirit of both man and dog is sociable, and most people will never be too old to get a kick out of whistling to a dog and seeing him wag his tail. The point of having a descendant of the Lost Wolf for company is not to crush his spirit but rather to direct it so that he can live in, even delight in, the city. The eagles and wild swans are gone, and we have an idea that dogs and the saving irregularities they look for add life to New York City.

Love Story

People in the country celebrate spring by picking wild leeks in the woods for salad and soup. In Greenwich Village a man with a conch shell walks out on the Bank Street Pier and blows his greetings to the *QE2* as she slides down the Hudson, hoping she'll answer with an ocean-deep toot. On a warm windy day everybody outside wears a bit of a grin. Riding the ferry to Staten Island, a boy scrutinizes his girlfriend's back teeth, while combing her hair with his hand, in a trance of love.

Not just gulls are riding the garbage barges; a few cattle egrets are back from the South to pick up what they can. In the wholesale meat market around Gansevoort Street there are gulls on the sidewalk and gulls on the pretty blue roof of the fireboat pier at the Battery.

But pigeons are busier, romancing. With their croony croak, their street minuet performed on red, lizard legs, pigeons are the birds of spring in the city. They fly like cliff-nesters adept at dodging a merlin, and are feeders of opportunity. Another adaptation that long predates cities but fits them for life in the metropolis is that they don't feed their squabs litter straight out of the gutter. Rather, both parents predigest the litter and manufacture "pigeon's milk," which is a curdlike, white, almost mammalian substance, triggered by the hormone prolactin and chemically resembling rabbit's milk, but formed of rapidly growing cells on the walls of the crop that are sloughed off and regurgitated into the infant's mouth. Though pigeons, which lay only a couple of eggs at a stint, run out of milk in about ten days, they've given their young a head start.

So when we see pigeons puff up their chests as they circle and strut, perhaps, besides courting, they are expanding their crops. And that whimsical man who goes out on the pier with his conch shell, instead of into the woods after leeks, is making his own happy adjustment to spring in the city.

Mountain House

The startling, looming barns, the intricate profusion of trees along the highway, then a dirt road winding up through woods, past melting banks of snow, to the notch of a mountain, where fields open out, all is so newly marvelous to city eyes that it seems almost too good to be true that the house itself is still standing, ready for another summer's use.

A week after Easter, snow is waist-high under the roof, but the fields are nearly bare. Two crows are eating thawing apple pulp under a tree just in back. A red-tailed hawk is cruising overhead, swimming upward in the thermals. The regular deer, which winter in a cedar swamp a couple of miles downhill, have not yet shown up, but a bear, incautious as always in the early spring, has made straight for the pond below the fields on the same path that fishermen will soon be using. There is also an otter's track; and a white snowshoe rabbit that the foxes didn't catch during the winter is already speckled with summer brown. The bear himself is a survivor. Hunters working through with a pack of hounds in the fall killed three other bears on the mountain.

A freight train derailed in town, and the usual scattering of winter bankruptcies disrupted people's peace of mind. Nowadays it happens mostly to newcomers from New Jersey whom the native Vermonters have conned into buying defunct general stores. But everybody has stopped to take stock, looking around to see who else has lasted out the snowbound months without turning into a drunk.

It has been an uncertain maple-sugaring season—March's weather like April, and April's like March. But people are buying seed potatoes to plant, and digging last year's parsnips out of the ground. Parsnips, with a white, knotty-looking, carrotlike taproot, were a favorite vegetable among the pioneers. They winter in the garden as well as a bear does in his cave, and aren't just hardy—they actually sweeten there; they make better eating in the spring for the experience of overwintering.

Swamp Ensemble

Peepers hibernate among roots and under moss; wood frogs, in the punk of stumps or under logs; toads, in burrows under rocks and boards. But the spring releases all of them, as everywhere the water flows. Spring *is* water, and the streams turn brown, with duck tracks in the mud, old leaves shining like turtle shells. Leopard and pickerel frogs have hibernated under stones in brooks where the water ran too fast to freeze, but they, too, head for the pond.

The peepers sing in a ringing, monotonous, fitfully exhilarating call. Inch-sized, with x's on their backs, they seem to be in residence in every country neighborhood for a few weeks. The wood frogs congregate in woodside pools, where they cluck quite clamorously, like chickens falling on top of one another. The spotted leopard frogs converse with a snoring croak or rattle, and pickerel frogs with a sound like cloth ripping, before laying their eggs and heading for the meadowlands again.

Native to the pond are the green frogs—which have wintered on the bottom wedged between stones so that they wouldn't float up—as well as their large, less adventurous look-alikes, the bullfrogs, which merely dig down in the mud. Green frogs croak explosively, but bullfrogs calmly announce, "Be drowned. Better go 'round," as we stand on the bank looking at them.

A bullfrog takes a year to emerge from the tadpole stage, and, ever after, an extra month to arouse in the spring. But toads—quicker to metamorphose, wider-ranging—are kings of the Batrachians, one might say. With their proverbial sparkling eyes—which, like a magician's, are employed also in spooning down a hefty mouthful when suddenly retracted into the head—and with their changes of color several times a day, their habit of bursting out of and swallowing their skins, their passionate long breeding trill, toads are a triumph of mystery and versatility. Like a magician, a toad fights off its enemies with secretions of the skin. Turn-of-the-century violinists, indeed, are said to have rubbed their hands on an obliging toad before a performance because these poisons prevented their fingers from slipping.

Songs and Snakeskins

Spring makes nearly every creature exuberant, it seems. A friend, canoeing in Vermont, noticed a grandaddy snapping turtle, as big as a washtub, swimming alongside his craft for possibly a mile, with a curiosity the turtle is no doubt going to lose after a few more canoeists go by. And a bear emerges to graze the tender meadow grass in his back field as early as 5:00 P.M., and the cow moose that likes to eat pond weeds in the marsh downhill from him can hardly be scared away before 8:00 A.M.—these being the daylight feeding hours that moose and bear preferred before they had so many human neighbors to contend with.

Spring is the time when beasts stoke up after the hardships of the winter, and when birds court a mate and stake a territory. Some of the most beautiful birdsongs are contentious in intent. The flicker's speedy, bouncing flight as it crosses a clearing to pound its bill on a dead limb, the woodcock's yo-yo courtship display, spiraling high and plummeting—these are part of the inimitable panache of spring. Yet how can one explain the search great crested fly-catchers make for a snakeskin to weave into the lining of their nests? Where snakeskins have become hard to obtain, they substitute a scrap of cellophane. The bird is only robin-sized, but surely a seasonal and talismanic exuberance is involved here.

Our friend must scratch his blackfly bites, which also go with spring, and sometimes will wake up at 3:00 A.M. to a dead, wintry chill. He loads wood into the stove and reassures himself that he is on the younger side of middle age and, furthermore, that this is May. With dawn, the vireos and song sparrows strike up and say indeed it's so.

Complex Justice

Chipping sparrows like to line their nests with horsehair. If a farmer has no horses, they will sometimes pull hair for the purpose out of his cow dog as it sleeps in the yard.

The spring rains make a lovely din on his tin roof after the snowy silence of the winter. Rain brings up his hay and pasture grasses quickly, but torrents of rain may rot his seed corn and potatoes and make it difficult for him to maneuver his tractor and corn planter. (Sometimes he thinks the sparrows are right to wish he still kept horses.)

Rain also brings out the horseflies and deerflies. Yet with the flies come the swallows that nest in the farmer's barn and swirl outside, clocking as much as six hundred miles a day in sweeps and zigzags, as if the sky were an ocean to sport in. At corn-planting time a flock of crows arrives to raid his fields for seed, but the swallows–with nests to defend–take out after the crows and drive them away.

The farmer, who has "buried his money for the summer," as he likes to say when he has plowed in store-bought fertilizer, appreciates the complicated justice of all this. If the flies weren't biting him he wouldn't have swallows, and if he didn't have swallows the crows would grab more of his corn. However, he only grows corn to feed his cows next winter, when there will be no flies around and the swallows will be in South America. So if he didn't keep cows he wouldn't need the corn, and wouldn't have either the problem of the crows that raid his fields or the clouds of flies drawn to his barn. The swallows then could stay in South America, and he'd just have a few sparrows picking nest hairs off his sleeping collie, and maybe a few pretty tiger swallowtail butterflies clustered around the mud puddles in front of his empty barn.

But *that* would be no way to try to raise a family.

Tug of Sweet Trout

Juneberries are among the earliest wild fruits. In pioneer times they were also named serviceberries, because their white blossoms bloomed almost as soon as the ground thawed, and a family that had been saving a body through icy weather to bury when the ground turned soft could cover the grave with these first flowers. Woods blossoms like trout lilies come nearly as early, in order to crowd the best of life into the few brief weeks between the time when the soil thaws and the growth of a full canopy of trees blocks out the sun. And trout–and fishermen–are active too, now that the confining cap of ice is off the ponds and a skyful of food is falling on the water.

Of course, the fish don't stop eating with the end of spring. Nor do our fishing friends quit angling for them with a whole miniature circus procession of gaudy flies that, week by week, approximate the cycles of insect life until midsummer. Where fishing pressure is heavy, the smarter anglers have listened carefully during the spring for frog songs originating in unexpected directions. Beavers may have constructed a new pond, which the frogs and trout discover. The fisherman who follows may find a spring peeper in the stomach of the first fat trout he catches. In a sense, therefore, with his game fish, he's eating flies and frogs.

But frogs' legs are an expensive delicacy; and little wild woods flies taste sweet, as any fair-minded person knows who has had one fly into his mouth and has stopped to analyze, after spitting it out, what he is tasting. In any case, most people fish not for the sweetness of the trout so much as for the tug–a tug that comes from the netherworld of mayflies, trout lilies, juneberries, and spring frogs.

The Prime of Life

Cotton fluff is blowing from the poplar trees on the mountainside. Chokecherries and wild strawberries are in blossom, and a flock of goldfinches has gathered to pick apart the dandelions. The porcupines are on the move, from the ledgy spruce forest where they wintered to juicy fields and toothsome orchards. At night an owl yaps at the dog and at dawn the wrens, redstarts, and warblers make the woods ring. A grouse is drumming, sounding like someone unsuccessfully cranking an outboard motor.

It is the time of year when one's best possession is one's legs. A wanderer can fish the culverts or nibble sorrel in the woods. Around an old cellar hole there are purple lilacs and moss phlox, apple trees covered with flowers, and a row of maples swelling as big as goons in silhouette against the sky. A pair of nesting ravens somewhere up along the cliffs croaks incessantly. They feel so inaccessible they don't mind betraying their position. Even two Vermont coyotes, intent on not giving away the location of their pups, can't help gabbling at each other for a second in the excitement of the season.

At the pond a dozen salamanders are feeding on an ice-killed fish. The trees, fighting for sun, jam their boughs together. They used to meet in an arcade above the road, but there are fewer tall ones now. With the pinch in fuel-oil prices, a tradition of New England democracy has been revived: trees along backcountry roads belong to whoever has a cold house. The climate is tough, and yet the ringing, rapid-fire birdsongs prove that here in the North is where all these hosts of migrators prefer to breed. They want the blackflies and the seeds pulled from the poplar fluff. They fly here for the prime of life.

In the Woods

A friend in the country with a woodlot at his disposal points out that even in the summer all this stored-up sunshine does him good. His woodpile helps to keep him fed because the rich soil underneath is the best place to dig fishing worms; and every June he sets up a small tent in the woods at the edge of a field, where, surrounded by goosefoot, bull thistle, and fir trees, he can spend the full-moon nights and other moments when the spirit moves.

The tent seems to breathe in the wind. It's always ready for him, with a sleeping bag and an air mattress full of his own hot breath on the ground. He goes out after any storm to guy the ropes snugly again, as if for the comfort of his alter ego, and will dawdle there an hour among the timber-doodles and the teacher-birds. A tree swallow darts high with a feather, drops it deliberately, then swoops to catch it again. A woodchuck is raising a family in her summer den–not the same den that she hibernated in; that's back in the woods, headquarters for a skunk family now. Once when the woodchuck sat up close to his tent, as brindled-brown and husky-torsoed as a grizzly bear, he thought he might be camping in Alaska–except that, at the same time, a catbird overhead was mimicking the song of some Southern bird that the catbird may have heard in Georgia last winter.

Many nights an owl flies to a tree overlooking the field and, after a watchful moment, hoots for an answer from another owl–although for want of a better interlocutor, it sometimes converses with him. His knowledge of the language of barred owls is rudimentary, but the eight-beat calls end with a sort of doggish bark. So for a few minutes he and the owl say back and forth something like, "Whooo cooks for you? Whooo cooks for you-ALL?"

Stars to Eat

Two country axioms are, that the last run of maple sap comes at the same time that the first spring frogs start to peep, and that wild strawberries are ripe to pick when the summer's fireflies flash their lights. Suddenly this last has become the case, and there are sweets to gather in the fields. The fireflies themselves are sweets to frogs–a firmament of stars to eat. Once the frogs have laid their eggs, they have no further duties except to fatten up.

The deer are fat as clams. The foxes have begun to teach their pups to hunt. Chanticleer, strutting around in the dooryard, must watch his step–although it sometimes seems as if the reason roosters have been endowed with such splendid necks is not to see over the grass to spot a fox but only so they can look around at their tall tails. In fuss and feathers, as they hunt for a grasshopper, they resemble many human beings.

We have friends who spend all summer oiling themselves at the beach, and friends who garden busily behind the house–they've already eaten their rhubarb and are starting in on their Bibb lettuce. Peerless salad makers, these are people who in the spring will line the kitchen windowsill with pots of cauliflower and broccoli instead of flowering plants. In September they will set a dozen ripening tomatoes there.

It's been said that in the summer we all fall into one of two groups: beach people or mountain people. We hope to receive invitations for the weekend from both kinds. And in fairness to the rooster and to all who resemble him, we should add that it is not just he who crows so proudly each summer dawn; it is the whole world of birds.

Summer Pond

Swimming in a summer pond, we notice how natural it is to use all four limbs to travel along. We're a quadruped again; even the stroke we do is called "the crawl." Opening our eyes underwater, we look down instead of straight ahead or up. A log sunk on the bottom looms like a snapping turtle. The stems of the pond lilies, rising five feet, tangle one's arms a little frighteningly–people have sometimes drowned that way–and leeches live among them, eating bullfrogs' eggs. But a porcupine will happily swim out to chew the lily pads, just as a beaver may climb the bank to eat raspberries for a change of fare.

Out deeper, in cooler water, where trout live, floating on one's back is a kind of free ride, like being fifteen again, like being afloat upon another sky. We turn and lapse into a dead man's float. Perhaps there is a bit of Tom Sawyer's pleasure at watching his own bogus funeral in this, but before we get overly morbid, a fish begins nibbling our toes. Floating on one's back is like riding between two skies. And then we do the crawl in a predatory manner again, watching for trout below—moving like a tiger in our mind's eye, forepaws padding up and down. We lose our poise, however, as soon as we remember the big snapping turtle that might be drifting underneath us in the muddy gloom.

Of course the snapping turtle has her nemesis too—the skunks that every year dig her eggs out of the sand. There is a complex citizenship to the natural world that we are a part of when we swim. We have no special human powers, no superior dispensation, then. In its mystery, its profound and changeable reverberations in both the memory and the mind, swimming is a decathlon all by itself. We love it as we love to walk and run—and in the summer, maybe more.

In the Paws of the Surf

Tossing in the paws of the surf under a buttery sunset at the end of the summer, it is pleasant to suppose that one really is at that moment a plaything of the sea. The few dangers, like jellyfish or an undertow, are not hard to deal with if one has chosen one's beach and one's day. On such an occasion nature seems luscious indeed, or tamed.

Even seamen now speak of crossing the Atlantic as "crossing the pond," and weathermen, interpreting satellite photographs on TV, wear feathery hairdos, as if they had never stepped out-of-doors and felt any rain. Farming, too, has been mechanized, and our other conquests over nature have accelerated to such a degree that we forget that a nuclear catastrophe, more than an old-fashioned war fought with gunpowder, could simply become nature functioning in the biggest way. We forget that hyperactive sexuality and big-league sporting events represent only a rearrangement of aboriginal energies that otherwise remain dormant in us until such time as primeval conditions may call them forth in an undisguised state.

Peregrine falcons are hunting pigeons over Central Park once again; and anybody who keeps chickens knows that although it is seldom possible for hens to brood their own eggs nowadays, if given a chance some of them will enter a fuguelike state and do so happily. The pigs that are being raised on factory farms without enough space to turn around, if let loose, would still be the smartest animals in the barnyard.

Under hard conditions nature endures. No matter where you store a potato—under the dankest sink—its eyes will sprout. Most of the saucing and seasoning of food that we do only parallels the piquancy that fermentation lends to the "kills" other predators eat; and it behooves us to remember that we are still a part of nature and that its strength vastly surpasses our own. Especially in a nuclear age, we bob in the paws of the surf in January as well as in the balmy summertime.

Barking Geese and Butternuts

Last spring's pigs have grown so big they're already having trouble peering out from underneath their ears. Maples are turning carmine and coral, beech trees bronze, and blackberry leaves wine-dark. Poplars are slower to change because they try to squeeze every last growing day out of the year, but oaks are slow from being rather stately anyway; they're slow both in the fall and spring.

Birds have good mating or territorial reasons for flaunting a spectrum of colors (and tropical species, in their density, achieve the widest variety). But nobody quite knows why our Northern trees should turn such marvelous colors. As fall begins, the leaves have died to a singed green, obviously finished for the year. Then, unnecessarily, it would seem, they blazon into clarion reds and yellows that will appear in tiers on a steep hill, the maples lower, the birches higher—all looking best when set off by a sensible stand of firs that have remained dark green. It is a spectacle most lovely during a rare, premature snowfall.

Dairy farmers are chopping fields of feed corn for their cattle, now that the first frost has caught the sugar in the leaves and dried the leaves so that the juice won't sink into the roots or drain onto the silo floor. You can pick up butternuts in the woods, staining your fingers with the dye Confederate uniforms were tinted with, and see the laddering of fresh claw prints on large beech trees where the impatient bears have scrambled up to shake the beechnuts off the limbs.

Open a milkweed pod and look at the brown seeds, as neatly overlaid as feathers on a pheasant's back. The butterflies that ate the leaves are on their way to Mexico, but birds and beasts that have remained must face the hunting season at the same time as they're fattening for winter. Baying beagles and coonhounds hit the woods, sounding like the first flight of Canada geese that very shortly will speed overhead in an arrowy V, barking vigorously to each other.

So, it's flying season for the geese, fattening season for raccoons, hunting season for the hounds, and rutting season for the moose. Moose have such long legs that, at least in our Eastern woods, they can winter wherever they like in the snow–halfway up a mountain as easily as down on a river bottom with the frailer deer. Wild dogs can't kill them–nothing but a poacher can–and when they want to nibble the buds on a small tree, they simply straddle it and ride down it.

City Pebbles

Just back from a country summer, we got all slicked up in a suit and tie to walk the avenues, and very soon encountered a movie being filmed, a handsome pocket park with crashing fountain, Saint Patrick's Cathedral getting a facewash, and Central Park's noble landscaping, with larger trees of more species than most woodsmen are used to. We saw so many people, and *liked* so many people, it was exhilarating.

Like pebbles in a river, people in a great metropolis come in more colors, shapes, and sizes than people elsewhere. And yet, for all the talk of abrasive eccentricity rife in New York City, we find people here, taken as a whole, more rounded–probably from rubbing against each other–than people in the country. "Sophistication" is another word for that inventive mix of tolerance, resilience, and resourcefulness city people develop. They aren't necessarily subtler, but they are more supple, which is why, against great odds sometimes, they stay so sane.

We wouldn't for a moment deny the stamina and good humor of country folk, who are the glue of the ages. But our heart leaped up when we set foot on pavement again, just as it had when we first plunged into the woods last spring. The steel-drum combos, the walking stereos, the businessman boasting sotto voce to his svelte companion, "I have a national hookup from here to California," the nut wearing gloves but no shoes–we liked it. City people think life is short and is what you make of it. They believe that you can alter life. Even more than stamina, they believe in drama.

Heel and Toe

A friend of ours looks out on the West Side Highway, downtown where it has been abandoned for vehicular use. Only joggers, strolling lovers, heel-and-toe walkers, boxers working out, and people running with their dogs are up there now. A model gets her exercise while holding an umbrella over her head to avoid a burn, and several men who might be Wall Street brokers run by with watches in hand, much as they time themselves by the ticker tape the rest of the day. Particularly curious is the slender, diminutive figure who runs quite hard, like a professional (say, a circus professional), juggling three red balls.

Our friend remembers the morning of the New York City marathon last fall. There were fewer runners past his window; most were either entered in the race or cheering from the sidelines. But that foggy October morning was the occasion when the first Canada geese came through on their thousand-mile flight south. Honking, hollering to each other, barking like foxhounds, they sped down the Hudson just as their ancestors did when the Dutch first settled here and the Hudson River was full of salmon, porpoises, and otters. The astonished gulls who live along the piers took to the air in whirling white lariats and great alarm.

On the waterfront there are eel fishermen, prostitutes, and pushcart peddlers selling hot dogs. Perhaps the democracy of the sea affects them, they get along so well. The other day two actors were rehearsing Tybalt's duel with Romeo. And people come to where the land meets the water for special conversations. They can propose marriage; they can simply relax. Even when our friend is gloomy, the neighborhood cheers him up. He trapped a mouse the other day, a depressing event. But when he flushed it down the toilet, a speck of life leaped free and out. Say that it represented what you like. It was a flea.

Rattlesnake Steaks

One man's meat is another man's poison. But we suspect one reason why some of the he-man power brokers who dine at Dominique D'Ermo's gourmet restaurant in Washington, D.C., like to eat rattlesnakes is that in life the snakes were poisonous. A formerly dangerous creature sautéed in wine and safely tucked into the stomach makes them feel stronger and is something to boast about. Cannibals felt the same way about consuming an enemy. So do cowboys after a meal of "prairie oysters"–bull-calf testicles. Cecil Andrus, who, as secretary of the interior, is in charge of the endangered-species program, eats at Dominique's and says he hates rattlesnakes. He fired a scientist in his department who wrote the restaurateur to protest the menu listing of an Eastern rattler that is fast dwindling in numbers.

Secretary Andrus comes from Idaho, and it has not been long since some of that state's mountain men were frying steaks cut out of cougars and grizzlies. Who's to say that, in their day, they shouldn't have? The trouble is that formerly dangerous creatures have a way of vanishing, just like creatures that are not dangerous. Rhinoceroses are endangered in Africa because rich Asians believe that powdered rhino horn prolongs male potency. Tigers in wildlife preserves in India have been cut down partly for their whiskers, which are reputed to possess comparable powers. On the other hand, several species of dolphin are in danger of disappearing because for years fishing boats have followed them to locate yellowfin tuna, which the dolphins eat, and have drowned thousands of dolphins as the tuna were netted. Great whales have been minced into margarine oil, cosmetics, and car lubricants to the point where many species have nearly perished.

Secretary Andrus is in favor of protecting dolphins, whales, even tigers, but he is quoted as finding it humorous that rare rattlesnakes might be worth protecting. Such a personal whim should not determine the fauna of the future. Snake venom is useful in cancer, antibiotic, and other medical research, and even if there were no practical considerations, a question would remain. Does Mr. Andrus or anyone else believe that it is more dangerous to allow small numbers of rattlesnakes to survive in remote areas than to trifle with the diversity of life itself on earth?

Cold Males, Neo-females

Audubon magazine reports that nesting temperatures on the beach help to determine the sex of hatchling sea turtles. Warmer nests produce females; cooler nests, baby males. We were reminded that jack-in-the-pulpit plants tend to become male in years when undernourishment has left them weak, but female when local conditions have infused the same flower with renewed strength.

There are fish and shellfish that start life as males and later change into females, as if being female were indicative of maturity. The common toad, however, possesses a special, curious device called the Bidder's organ, which is present in both sexes close to the original genitalia. Though ordinarily it has no role, in case of a castrating injury it will promptly develop into a functioning ovary, even in adults that have previously fathered tadpoles. Such males become "neo-females," mating with normal males and laying eggs.

The transsexual potential of a Bidder's organ represents a fallback position for the toad. If he can't be a male, he re-creates himself as a female to continue a productive life. It's testimony of a slightly different sort from that of the sex-change fish, or of the jack-in-the-pulpit and sea turtle.

Should we assume, therefore, that femaleness stands for maturity in the history of an individual; or perhaps a life of particular warmth and vigor—or a kind of magic fallback permanence that may perpetuate a species? On the other hand, one might argue from these examples that males face more hardship.

Luckily, people's psyches seem to include a "Bidder's organ" for both sexes that adds complexity and flexibility and fallback possibilities for human beings.

Banking for Winter

Apple men prune their trees "so that a crow can fly between any two branches," as the adage goes. And now is the time when they want some apples of the winter varieties, "keepers" for the storage bin. Brussels sprouts, beets, and carrots can still be got from the garden and stored down in the cellar too.

But before there were beets and apples, there were beavers—and trappers before farmers. A good trapper hardly needed a rifle to feed himself. His wolf traps would as conveniently catch a deer; his bear traps were just right for moose or buffalo. Mainly, he lived on beavers, and mostly on the tails of the beavers, which were a frontier luxury on a par with buffalo tongues and moose noses.

Beavers rudder or scull themselves, as they swim, with their footlong, tongue-shaped, broad, scaly tails. They also use the tail to brace themselves as they stand up to gnaw a tree, and as an extra leg for balancing as they clasp mud in their arms and walk upright when dambuilding. Warning each other of danger, they whack their tails on the water. The tail provides a means of regulating body temperature in the summer and a place to store fat for the winter.

It was this combination of fat and muscle that made for delicious eating. And now is the time when beavers are stacking poplar branches underwater for winter feeding—ramming them into the mud or piling stones on them to keep them from floating up and freezing in the ice that forms.

For the trapper, all this busy preparation before the ponds closed over added to his own larder as well. The more poplar and birch he saw them haul into the water for winter meals of bark, the fatter he knew the beavers' tails were going to grow, to sizzle in his campfire, and the more money John Jacob Astor would pay him for his catch of furs, when he came out of the woods next April.

December Song

As an example of our divorce from nature, the word "creepy" has come to mean behavior most unnatural. Yet if house cats walked as upright as we do–if they didn't creep so magnificently that they remind us of almost the entire world of nature by themselves–we wouldn't have them living with us in every city apartment building. People who do not like cats or dogs keep bowls of Celebes rainbow fish, red snakeskin guppies, calico angelfish, upside-down catfish, and Yucatan mollies. And animals in cages would be astounded if one could ever possibly explain to them that the reason they are being held captive is only so that we can *watch* them. (How creepy it would seem!) Though parrots don't talk nearly as sensibly as many of the feeble-minded human beings we choose to institutionalize, other people are willing to pay thousands of dollars for the pleasure of a parrot's company. Some marvelous indefinable Amazonian wildness enhances its camaraderie, to the point that many species have been endangered by the pet trade.

Particularly as the winter gathers, we hang Malaysian tree ferns in the window, above a tableful of Sonoran cactus, potted spider grass, and zebra and impatiens plants–impatient ourselves to crowd the narrowest dwelling with green life. Some people buy cut flowers, wreaths, and terrariums in an expansive mood; others fill the house with plants in a bit of panic, as if in December they already feel the walls close in. With houseplants, we reassure ourselves that we, too, will stay green all winter, as in many other ways we are gearing up for the hard months to come.

December in the woods is an undistinguished time, however. The weather hasn't yet turned bitter or hungry. The deer are through their rutting season, but are still fat from eating apples and beechnuts. Bears and weasels bred early last summer in order to give birth in February and April. Coyotes, coons, and foxes won't mate until about February to meet the same April schedule as the weasels.

Only for the humble porcupine is December a festive month. Porcupines have left the summer greenery of the fields for a winter woodland diet of bark, sheltering under rocks and evergreens. But squalling to each other across the snow, the males and females home in. The male eventually enacts a three-legged nuptial dance before the female while gripping his testicles with one forepaw. For both of them, winter begins on a note of celebration.

About the Contributors

RICK BASS is the author of a collection of short stories, *The Watch,* and four collections of essays: *The Deer Pasture, Oil Notes, Wild to the Heart,* and *Winter: Notes from Montana.* His latest book is *The Ninemile Wolves.*

MARCIA BONTA has written four books: *Escape to the Mountain, Appalachian Spring, Outbound Journeys in Pennsylvania,* and *Women in the Field.* She has also published more than 125 nature-related magazine articles in state and national publications and is the editor of the University of Pittsburgh Press's Pitt Nature Series.

CHARLES BOWDEN scrounges for a living in Tucson, Arizona. He has written six books, most recently *Desierto,* and is currently working on *The Blue Flowers,* an inquiry into the carnage of botany in the Sonoran desert.

DAN FLORES is a professor of history at Texas Tech University; his academic interest in environmental history finds an alternative expression in his nature essays. A member of the Texas Institute of Letters, his four books and numerous articles have won six literary prizes. He lives with a horse, two wolf-hybrids, and three cats on twelve acres of canyon country in the Southern High Plains.

JEAN CRAIGHEAD GEORGE has just completed her fifty-ninth book, a sequel to her award-winning *My Side of the Mountain,* entitled *On the Far Side of the Mountain.* A trip to Venezuela with her son and friends was the inspiration for *One Day in the Tropical Rain Forest.* A second ecological mystery, *The Missing 'Gator of Gumbo Limbo* was published in early 1992.

JOHN HAY is a naturalist who has taught in the Environmental Studies Program at Dartmouth College and was president of the Cape Cod Museum of Natural History for twenty-five years. He is the author of many books, including *The Bird of Light, The Run, The Great Beach, In Defense of Nature,* and *The Immortal Wilderness.*

EDWARD HOAGLAND is the author of thirteen books of fiction and nonfiction, and he is the editor of the Penguin Nature Library. Since the death of Hal Borland, he has written many seasonal editorials for the *New York Times.*

WILLIAM KITTREDGE teaches at the University of Montana. He is the author of *Owning It All* and *We Are Not in This Together.* His essays have appeared in *Harper's, The Paris Review,* and elsewhere. His forthcoming memoir is *Hole in the Sky.*

BARRY LOPEZ is the author most recently of *The Rediscovery of North America* and *Crow and Weasel,* a fable with illustrations by Tom Pohrt.

THOMAS J. LYON teaches at Utah State University and edits the journal *Western American Literature.* He was the editor of *This Incomperable Lande: A Book of American Nature Writing.*

GARY NABHAN, who currently lives in Stinking Hot Desert National Monument, is an ethnobotanist and nature essayist. His book with artist Paul Mirocha, *Gathering the Desert,* won the John Burroughs medal.

SHERMAN PAUL, Carver Professor Emeritus of English at the University of Iowa, now lives on Wolf Lake in northern Minnesota. He has recently published *Hewing to Experience: Essays and Reviews on Recent American Poetry and Poetics, Nature and Culture,* coedited a special issue of *North Dakota Quarterly* (Spring, 1991) on nature and ecological writers, and completed *For Love of the World,* essays on Henry David Thoreau, John Muir, Aldo Leopold, Henry Beston, Loren Eiseley, Barry Lopez, and Richard Nelson.

BRENDA PETERSON is the author of three novels and a collection, *Living By Water: Essays on Life, Land, and Spirit.* Her latest novel is *Duck and Cover.* She lives on Puget Sound in Seattle, Washington.

GARY SNYDER lives in the northern Sierra Nevada and teaches part of every year at the University of California, Davis. "The Woman Who Married a Bear" is from *The Practice of the Wild.*

JOHN TALLMADGE is dean of the graduate school at the Union Institute. His essays on wilderness travel have appeared in *Orion Nature Quarterly.*

SCOTT THYBONY frequently contributes to National Geographic Society publications and writes for such magazines as *Smithsonian, Outside,* and *National Wildlife.* He is currently at work on a book of travels that finds itself off the map more often than on it.

STEPHEN TRIMBLE is a writer and photographer living in Salt Lake City. His books focus on western landscape and native peoples, most recently *The Sagebrush Ocean: A Natural History of the Great Basin* (winner of the Ansel Adams Award) and *The People: Indians of the American Southwest.* "Sing Me down the Mountain" comes from a book of essays about children and wilderness Trimble is writing in collaboration with Gary Nabhan.

JACK TURNER is a mountain-climbing instructor in the Tetons. He has traveled extensively in India, China, Peru, Nepal, Tibet, and Pakistan. He is at work on a collection of essays.

TERRY TEMPEST WILLIAMS is a naturalist-in-residence at the Utah Museum of Natural History in Salt Lake City. Her book *Pieces of White Shell: A Journey to Navajoland* received a Southwest Book Award. She is also the author of *Coyote's Canyon* and of two children's books. Her most recent book is *Refuge: An Unnatural History of Family and Place.*

On Nature's Terms was composed into type on a Compugraphic digital phototypesetter in eleven point Galliard with two points of spacing between the lines. Galliard italic was selected for display. The book was designed by Jim Billingsley, typeset by Metricomp, Inc., printed offset by Thomson-Shore, Inc., and bound by John H. Dekker & Sons, Inc. The paper on which this book is printed carries acid-free characteristics for an effective life of at least three hundred years.

TEXAS A&M UNIVERSITY PRESS : COLLEGE STATION